P9-AQT-952

SLAVES, FREE MEN, CITIZENS

LAMBROS COMITAS is Professor of Anthropology and Education, Director of both the Center for Education in Latin America and the Center for Urban Studies and Programs, and Associate Director of the Division of Philosophy and Social Sciences at Teachers College, Columbia University. He is also Associate Director of the Research Institute for the Study of Man, an institution for research and scholarship of the Caribbean. Mr. Comitas was awarded a Fulbright Graduate Study Grant (1957–58) and a Guggenheim Fellowship (1971–72) and has done field research in Barbados, Jamaica, Bolivia, and the Dominican Republic. He has written numerous articles, was editor of *Caribeana 1900–1965: A Topical Bibliography,* and serves as consultant or editor for several publishing projects.

DAVID LOWENTHAL, a geographer and historian, has devoted twenty years to research on the West Indies. He has taught at Vassar College and has been visiting professor at a number of universities in the United States and at the University of the West Indies, where he was Fulbright Research Fellow at the Institute of Social and Economic Research (1956–57). During 1961–62 he worked in the Lesser Antilles with the assistance of a Rockefeller Foundation research grant and later received a Guggenheim Fellowship. Until 1972 he was Secretary and Research Associate at the American Geographical Society, and he is currently Professor of Geography at University College, London. His most recent book is *West Indian Societies,* a comprehensive study of the non-Hispanic Caribbean.

Four books, edited and introduced by Lambros Comitas and David Lowenthal, provide a broad variety of material on the West Indies; each has the subtitle *West Indian Perspectives*:

SLAVES, FREE MEN, CITIZENS
WORK AND FAMILY LIFE
CONSEQUENCES OF CLASS AND COLOR
THE AFTERMATH OF SOVEREIGNTY

SLAVES, FREE MEN, CITIZENS

West Indian Perspectives

Edited and Introduced by
Lambros Comitas and David Lowenthal

Anchor Books
Anchor Press/Doubleday
Garden City, New York, 1973

The Anchor Books edition is the first
publication of *SLAVES, FREE MEN, CITIZENS:*
West Indian Perspectives.

Anchor Books edition: 1973

ISBN: 0-385-04289-2
Library of Congress Catalog Card Number 72–84929
Copyright © 1973 by Lambros Comitas and David Lowenthal
All Rights Reserved
Printed in the United States of America

CONTENTS

EDITORS' NOTE

The West Indies, the earliest and one of the most important prizes of Europe's New World and the first to experience the full impact of the black diaspora from Africa, were also the most enduringly colonized territories in the history of the Western Hemisphere. Here more than anywhere else masters and slaves constituted the basic ingredients of the social order; here more than anywhere else class and status were based on distinctions of color and race. Yet out of that past, here more than anywhere else societies with black majorities have emerged as self-governing, multiracial states.

This collection of four volumes—*Slaves, Free Men, Citizens; Work and Family Life; Consequences of Class and Color;* and *The Aftermath of Sovereignty*—chronicles the remarkable story, played out on the doorstep of the North American continent, of transitions from slavery to freedom, from colonialism to self-government, and from self-rejection to prideful identity.

The West Indies face a host of continuing problems—foreign economic domination and population pressure, ethnic stress and black-power revolts, the petty tyranny of local rulers and an agonizing dependence on expatriate culture. For these very reasons, the West Indies constitute an exceptional setting for the study of complex social relations. The archipelago is a set of mirrors in which the lives of black, brown, and white, of American Indian and East Indian, and of a score of other minorities continually

interact. Constrained by local circumstance, these interactions also contain a wealth of possibilities for a kind of
creative harmony of which North Americans and Europeans are scarcely yet aware. Consequently, while these
volumes deal specifically with the Caribbean in all its aspects, many dimensions of life and many problems West
Indians confront have analogues in other regions of the
world: most clearly in race relations, economic development, colonial and post-colonial politics and government,
and the need to find and express group identity.

It can be argued that the West Indies is a distinctive and
unique culture area in that the societies within it display
profound similarities: their inhabitants, notwithstanding
linguistic barriers and local or parochial loyalties, see themselves as closely linked. These resemblances and recogni-
tions, originally the product of similar economic and social
forces based on North European settlement, plantation
agriculture, and African slavery, have subsequently been
reinforced by a widespread community of interest, along
with interregional migration for commerce, employment,
marriage, and education. These volumes focus mainly on
these underlying uniformities. Within the Caribbean itself,
however, one is more conscious of differences than of
resemblances. While each Caribbean land is in part a mi-
crocosm of the entire archipelago, local conditions—size,
resources, social structure, political status—also make it in
some significant fashion unique.

The range of these essays is the entire non-Hispanic
Caribbean, but most of the material that is not general in
character deals with the Commonwealth Caribbean, a pre-
ponderant share of this specifically with Jamaica and Trinidad. This reflects neither a bias in favor of these territories
nor a belief that they are typical, but rather the fact that
most recent scholarly attention has concentrated on, and
literary expression has emanated from, the Commonwealth
Caribbean. Closer understanding of, and expression in, the
smaller French and Netherlands Caribbean and larger but
less well-known Haiti lie in the future.

In the Caribbean, a real understanding of any problem

requires a broad familiarity with all aspects of culture and society. Thus the study of economic development relates intimately to that of family organization, and both of these interlink with aspects of political thought, systems of education, and patterns of speech. Consequently, the subject matter of this collection lies in the domains of history, geography, anthropology, sociology, economics, politics, polemics, and the arts. For example, essays on work and family life by economists and anthropologists are complemented by other studies tracing the historical background and sociological interplay of these with other themes. Throughout these volumes economists and geographers indicate how social structure bears on and is influenced by economy and land use; and linguists, *littérateurs,* lawyers, and local journalists provide insights on the impact of these patterns in everyday life.

The reader will find here not a complete delineation of the Caribbean realm but rather a sketch in breadth, with fuller discussion of significant themes, given depth and personality by picaresque flavor. He may gain a sense of what West Indians were and are like, how they live, and what problems they confront; he can see how their own view of themselves differs from that of outsiders; he will know where to look for general studies and for more detailed information. And if there is such a thing as a regional personality, this collection may enable him to acquire a sense of it.

What is currently available to most students of Caribbean affairs is woefully inadequate by comparison with many other regions of the world. A few general histories, technical analyses of particular aspects of Caribbean society or culture, and detailed studies of one or two individual territories comprise the holdings of all but the best-equipped libraries. Moreover, no book has yet been published that includes a broad variety of material for the area as a whole, and few studies transcend national or linguistic boundaries. We therefore aim to make available a wide range of literature on the Caribbean that is not readily accessible anywhere else.

Most of this collection is the work of West Indians them-selves, for they contribute forty-five of the seventy-two selections. Seventeen of these are by Trinidadians, fifteen by Jamaicans, four by Guyanese, three each by Vincen-tians and St. Lucians, two by Martiniquans, and one by a Barbadian. Non-West Indian writers contribute twenty-seven selections: fourteen by Americans, ten by British, two by Canadians, and one by a French author. Many of the North American and European contributors either have been permanent residents in the West Indies or have worked there for long periods of time.

Editorial comment has been held to a minimum, but readers will find three levels of guidance. An introduction to each of the four volumes summarizes the general im-plications of the issues therein surveyed. A paragraph of topical commentary together with a few lines identifying the author introduces each selection. Finally, a selected West Indian reading list appears at the end of each vol-ume, and a general comprehensive bibliography is ap-pended to *The Aftermath of Sovereignty*.

The papers and documents included here have been altered only for minimal editorial consistency and ease of reference. All original titles of articles have been retained, but where none appear or where book chapter headings do not identify the contents of excerpted material, we have added descriptive titles, identified by single asterisks in the text. Series of asterisks also indicate the few instances where material is omitted. When required in such cases, we have completed some footnote references. Otherwise, only obvious typographical and other errors have been corrected. Our own two translations from French sources adhere to the originals as closely as possible, within the limits of comprehensibility.

The editors are grateful to those who have assisted them in this enterprise, both in and out of the Caribbean. We owe special thanks to Marquita Riel and Claire Angela Hendricks, who helped with the original selections and styled the references. Miss Riel also made the original translations from the French. We are indebted to the Research Institute for the Study of Man, and its Director, Dr. Vera Rubin, to the American Geographical Society, and to Teachers College of Columbia University, and notably to their library staffs, for many facilities.

Our main gratitude goes to the contributors represented in these pages and to their original publishers, who have in most cases freely and uncomplainingly made available their work and have helped to correct errors. We are particularly obliged for cooperation from the Institute of Social and Economic Studies and its Director, Alister McIntyre, and to the Department of Extra-Mural Studies, both at the University of the West Indies, under whose auspices a large number of these studies were originally done. We are also obligated to M. G. Smith for encouragement throughout the course of selection and composition.

Lambros Comitas
David Lowenthal
March 1972

INTRODUCTION:
The Shaping of Multiracial Societies

In the minds of most West Indians, history is a living reality. They see themselves as largely determined by, if not living in, a past which has shaped their present circumstances and future hopes. Many contemporary Caribbean problems can, in fact, easily be traced back several centuries. To come to terms with the constraints of their own history is a formidable task for a people long taught that, as insignificant colonials, they did not make history but only endured it.

The complete dominance of plantation agriculture and all its social concomitants early differentiated the West Indies from the rest of the New World. Spanish discovery and conquest emptied the Caribbean of most of its aboriginal Indians, and European nations displaced one another in the scramble for Antillean wealth: England, France, Holland, and Spain were joined by Denmark, Sweden, and such minor sovereignties as the Order of St. John in a competition that endured for centuries.

After a brief period of small family farming with indentured servants, seventeenth-century North European entrepreneurs in the West Indies, inspired and financed in part by Dutch merchants, turned to great sugar plantations requiring large supplies of labor. To meet this demand, slave traders brought in millions of West African slaves, followed after emancipation in the nineteenth century by a million more indentured workers, in semislavery, from Asia and elsewhere. Neither the ruling European elites nor the sub-

jugated African and Asian majorities regarded themselves
as West Indians, even though most of them were eventually
Caribbean-born, and many had lost all contact with their
ancestral homelands. For many West Indians, "home" was
a European country they may never have seen. The resi-
dues of an absentee mentality still linger in these societies,
where it is widely believed that the way to get ahead is
to get away, and where the prizes to be won and the ex-
emplars to be followed beckon from London, Paris, and
New York.

Slavery and indenture created and sustained highly stratified social orders, in which distinctions of race and ethnicity
reinforced class differences. The melange of European and
African in a plantation environment set the basic structure
of West Indian societies, each then modified by its unique
historical circumstances and by an exclusive relationship
with its imperial center. But racial inequality, segregation,
prejudice, and self-denigration are threads that run throughout West Indian history everywhere from the beginning to
the present day.

In each territory a different balance of slave and free,
of black and colored and white, and of various economic
enterprises made for a different social order; and distinctions of religion, nationality, and imperial relationship mag-
nified these differences. The nineteenth century added new
sociocultural complications, for economic adjustments after
emancipation brought East Indians, Chinese, Portuguese,
and Syrians into the West Indian economic and social order. Given such racial and ethnic diversity, it is no wonder
that contemporary West Indian societies exhibit so wide a
range of cultures and languages, social and political systems, and relationships to their European metropoles.

Yet the general outline of West Indian history is similar
throughout the whole area. Mercantilism, the economic
counterpart of nationalism, was from the outset the guiding
doctrine of the competing European powers in the West
Indies. Colonies were sought and developed for the sole
purpose of producing goods and markets useful to the
mother country. For England and France, in particular, the

chief value of the West Indies was the intensive cultivation of sugarcane. In all these plantation colonies, regardless of imperial and sociocultural differences, overriding economic forces imprinted similar organizational patterns. The imprint has been of lasting importance for West Indian social structure. Colonizing policies, relations between master and slave, the intermediate role played by their free-colored offspring, the struggle for emancipation and its general failure to alter the social structure, the "creolization" of custom and attitude in all segments of society, including the feeling of not being at home in the Caribbean—these themes are repeated in almost every territory.

Three salient moods stand out in West Indian history. The first is the enduring sense of racial and ethnic difference felt by people whose disparate ways of life were largely determined by enforced occupational and social roles. A second is the pervasive influence of the past and a lack of faith in future prospects; the appearance of change is assumed to be illusory, the trappings alter but not the substance. The slow pace of popular participation and of self-rule over the past century, the inability of local governments to make much of a dent on inherited inequalities, the relative smallness and weakness of Caribbean states are all conducive to a sense of futility, of being determined by the past.

A third mood stems from relatively recent attempts to read meaning and even virtue into local history, a history of a past burdened with the degradation of slavery, the denial of belonging, and the difficulties of local self-definition. But if the search for identity has not yet led West Indians to manufacture a new history for themselves, it has begun to persuade them to view their old history in new ways.

The consequences of that history are to be seen in the extraordinary heterogeneity of contemporary West Indian culture and social institutions. The typical West Indian "Creole" society is distinguished by a tripartite division into white, colored, and black, rather than merely white and black as in the United States. Class and color still closely converge despite legal sanctions against discrimination; most whites are well to do, most colored people are middle class, the mass of the peasantry and proletariat is black. Only in the political arena are blacks now in principle dominant; in social and economic affairs they remain subordinate and relatively powerless. Yet an essential feature of the West Indian Creole hierarchy is its general acceptance by all but a militant few; class and color together play defining roles in occupation, life style, and social interaction.

In several territories, this color-based hierarchy is compounded by the existence of sizable minorities, if not majorities, of East Indians, whose culture and language are in large measure now West Indian but whose inherited sense of separate identity is reinforced by patterns of endogamy and by religious and occupational differences. Simultaneously denigrated and feared by Creole West Indians, East Indians resist assimilation on terms that would deny them their distinctive culture.

Along with East Indians, other smaller ethnic minorities —Chinese, Jews, Portuguese, and Syrians—have contributed significantly to West Indian societies in commerce, civil service, and the professions. The relatively small number of Chinese, for example, includes a recent Governor-General of Trinidad and Tobago and the President of the Co-operative Republic of Guyana. However, while the conspicuous success of the minorities earns them a place among the new West Indian elites, it also brings them the envious hostility of less fortunate black West Indians.

The interplay of relationships within the general West Indian class-color hierarchy, those between blacks and East Indians, and those between the different majorities and the small ethnic minorities makes for a social fabric that varies with the proportions of each element in a territory and with differing perceptions of their ethnic roles. What emerges ultimately is less a unified canvas than a collage in which fragments of extraordinarily diverse antecedents dynamically interact.

This volume surveys that collage from the broad perspectives of past and present. The first section, "Slaves, Masters, and Freedmen," deals with the day-by-day experiences and interactions of the three main elements of colonial plantation society, each seen through the eyes of a contemporary eye-witness and of a modern scholar. The emergence during slavery of a large free-colored population, intermediate between whites and blacks, was critical in the development of West Indian society. Following these vignettes come discussions of some persisting themes in West Indian history: the extent and impact of absentee ownership and office-holding; the consequences of emancipation for plantation and peasant agriculture; and the prospects of black rule in the West Indies, as viewed by a white supremacist and then by a black West Indian advocate of multiracialism.

The second section, "The Nature of the Social Order," opens with a consideration of the sociocultural distinctiveness of class-color segments in Jamaica today, followed next by a comparative analysis of racial, ethnic, and class interactions in West Indian social orders. The value orientations stemming from class-color stratification are then seen in a specifically Trinidadian context, focusing on the metropolitan and white bias of all social segments. The endurance of an economically potent white minority in Martinique is next explained in terms of group interactions and sanctions against intimacy with outsiders. The East Indian–Creole situation in Trinidad is described by one scholar who finds extensive cultural assimilation and a minimum of ethnic separateness, and by another who sees sociocultural and ethnic differentiation reinforced by segregation and mutually hostile stereotypes. Finally, East Indian–Creole institutions in Guyana are analyzed at local and national levels to comprehend conflicting currents of ethnic stress and of national integration.

I SLAVES, MASTERS,
AND FREEDMEN

1.

This selection is taken from a classic description of slavery in Saint-Domingue, the oldest, wealthiest, and, in its treatment of slaves, the most notorious Caribbean colony. Since its initial settlement by Columbus in 1494, Saint-Domingue (the western part of Hispaniola) has had a checkered history. Columbus inaugurated the practice, later extended throughout the West Indies, of enslaving the native Indians for work in gold mines and elsewhere. As a consequence of Spanish conquest, enslavement, and disease, the Indian population was virtually exterminated within a couple of generations. Thereafter European settlers in the West Indies turned to Africa for agricultural slave labor. Slavery became especially significant in the West Indies with the advent of large-scale sugar plantations. In the eighteenth century, the system of production and coercion described here had reached its apogee. Elsewhere in the Caribbean, slavery endured until the middle of the nineteenth century; but in Saint-Domingue, under the guiding genius of Toussaint L'Ouverture, slaves mounted a major and uniquely successful rebellion in the 1790s, out of which emerged the Republic of Haiti, the New World's first independent black nation. The extreme harshness of slave treatment that James describes helped to reap the revolutionary whirlwind.

C. L. R. JAMES, born in Trinidad in 1901, has been teacher, journalist, novelist, revolutionary, Socialist, pan-Africanist, and cricket devotee. He played a major role in anti-imperialist activities in England during the 1930s and 1940s and returned to Trinidad in the late 1950s to serve as editor of *The Nation,* the organ of the People's National Movement, only to break with that party's leader a few years later. He currently teaches in New York and Washington, D.C.

The Slaves*
C. L. R. James

The slavers scoured the coasts of Guinea. As they devastated an area they moved westward and then south, decade after decade, past the Niger, down the Congo coast, past Loango and Angola, round the Cape of Good Hope, and, by 1789, even as far as Mozambique on the eastern side of Africa. Guinea remained their chief hunting ground. From the coast they organised expeditions far into the interior. They set the simple tribesmen fighting against each other with modern weapons over thousands of square miles. The propagandists of the time claimed that however cruel was the slave traffic, the African slave in America was happier than in his own African civilisation. Ours, too, is an age of propaganda. We excel our ancestors only in system and organisation: they lied as fluently and as brazenly. In the sixteenth century, Central Africa was a territory of peace and happy civilisation.[1] Traders travelled thousands of miles from one side of the continent to another without molestation. The tribal wars from which the European pirates claimed to deliver the people were mere sham-fights; it was a great battle when half-a-dozen men were killed.

The Black Jacobins, New York, Random House (second edition, revised from the 1938 edition), 1963, pp. 6–22. Used by permission of the author.

*[Editors' title]

[1] See the works of Professor Emil Torday, one of the greatest African scholars of his time, particularly a lecture delivered at Geneva in 1931 to a society for the Protection of Children in Africa.

It was on a peasantry in many respects superior to the serfs in large areas of Europe, that the slave-trade fell. Tribal life was broken up and millions of detribalised Africans were let loose upon each other. The unceasing destruction of crops led to cannibalism; the captive women became concubines and degraded the status of the wife. Tribes had to supply slaves or be sold as slaves themselves. Violence and ferocity became the necessities for survival, and violence and ferocity survived.[2] The stockades of grinning skulls, the human sacrifices, the selling of their own children as slaves, these horrors were the product of an intolerable pressure on the African peoples, which became fiercer through the centuries as the demands of industry increased and the methods of coercion were perfected.

The slaves were collected in the interior, fastened one to the other in columns, loaded with heavy stones of 40 or 50 pounds in weight to prevent attempts at escape, and then marched the long journey to the sea, sometimes hundreds of miles, the weakly and sick dropping to die in the African jungle. Some were brought to the coast by canoe, lying in the bottom of boats for days on end, their hands bound, their faces exposed to the tropical sun and the tropical rain, their backs in the water which was never bailed out. At the slave ports they were penned into "trunks" for the inspection of the buyers. Night and day thousands of human beings were packed in these "dens of putrefaction" so that no European could stay in them for longer than a quarter of an hour without fainting. The Africans fainted and recovered or fainted and died, the mortality in the "trunks" being over 20 per cent. Outside in the harbour, waiting to empty the "trunks" as they filled, was the captain of the slave-ship, with so clear a conscience that one of them, in the intervals of waiting to enrich British capitalism with the profits of another valuable cargo, enriched British religion by composing the hymn "How Sweet the Name of Jesus sounds!"

On the ships the slaves were packed in the hold on gal-

[2] *Ibid.*

leries one above the other. Each was given only four or five feet in length and two or three feet in height, so that they could neither lie at full length nor sit upright. Contrary to the lies that have been spread so pertinaciously about Negro docility, the revolts at the port of embarkation and on board were incessant, so that the slaves had to be chained, right hand to right leg, left hand to left leg, and attached in rows to long iron bars. In this position they lived for the voyage, coming up once a day for exercise and to allow the sailors to "clean the pails." But when the cargo was rebellious or the weather bad, then they stayed below for weeks at a time. The close proximity of so many naked human beings, their bruised and festering flesh, the foetid air, the prevailing dysentery, the accumulation of filth, turned these holds into a hell. During the storms the hatches were battened down, and in the close and loathsome darkness they were hurled from one side to another by the heaving vessel, held in position by the chains on their bleeding flesh. No place on earth, observed one writer of the time, concentrated so much misery as the hold of a slave-ship.

Twice a day, at nine and at four, they received their food. To the slave-traders they were articles of trade and no more. A captain held up by calms or adverse winds was known to have poisoned his cargo.[3] Another killed some of his slaves to feed the others with the flesh. They died not only from the régime but from grief and rage and despair. They undertook vast hunger strikes; undid their chains and hurled themselves on the crew in futile attempts at insurrection. What could these inland tribesmen do on the open sea, in a complicated sailing vessel? To brighten their spirits it became the custom to have them up on the deck once a day and force them to dance. Some took the opportunity to jump overboard, uttering cries of triumph as they cleared the vessel and disappeared below the surface.

Fear of their cargo bred a savage cruelty in the crew. One captain, to strike terror into the rest, killed a slave and

[3] See Pierre de Vaissière, *Saint-Domingue, 1629–1789* (Paris, 1909). This contains an admirable summary.

dividing heart, liver and entrails into 300 pieces made each
of the slaves eat one, threatening those who refused with
the same torture.[4] Such incidents were not rare. Given the
circumstances such things were (and are) inevitable. Nor
did the system spare the slavers. Every year one-fifth of
all who took part in the African trade died.

All America and the West Indies took slaves. When the
ship reached the harbour, the cargo came up on deck to
be bought. The purchasers examined them for defects,
looked at the teeth, pinched the skin, sometimes tasted the
perspiration to see if the slave's blood was pure and his
health as good as his appearance. Some of the women affected a curiosity, the indulgence of which, with a horse,
would have caused them to be kicked 20 yards across the
deck. But the slave had to stand it. Then in order to restore
the dignity which might have been lost by too intimate an
examination, the purchaser spat in the face of the slave.
Having become the property of his owner, he was branded
on both sides of the breast with a hot iron. His duties were
explained to him by an interpreter, and a priest instructed
him in the first principles of Christianity.[5]

The stranger in San Domingo was awakened by the
cracks of the whip, the stifled cries, and the heavy groans
of the Negroes who saw the sun rise only to curse it for
its renewal of their labours and their pains. Their work began at day-break: at eight they stopped for a short breakfast and worked again till midday. They began again at two
o'clock and worked until evening, sometimes till ten or
eleven. A Swiss traveller[6] has left a famous description of
a gang of slaves at work. "They were about a hundred men
and women of different ages, all occupied in digging ditches
in a cane-field, the majority of them naked or covered with
rags. The sun shone down with full force on their heads.
Sweat rolled from all parts of their bodies. Their limbs,

[4] *Ibid.,* p. 162.
[5] This was the beginning and end of his education.
[6] Girod-Chantrans, *Voyage d'un Suisse en différentes colonies*
(Neufchâtel, 1785), p. 137.

weighed down by the heat, fatigued with the weight of their
picks and by the resistance of the clayey soil baked hard
enough to break their implements, strained themselves to
overcome every obstacle. A mournful silence reigned. Exhaustion was stamped on every face, but the hour of rest
had not yet come. The pitiless eye of the Manager patrolled
the gang and several foremen armed with long whips moved
periodically between them, giving stinging blows to all who,
worn out by fatigue, were compelled to take a rest—men
or women, young or old." This was no isolated picture. The
sugar plantations demanded an exacting and ceaseless labour. The tropical earth is baked hard by the sun. Round
every "carry" of land intended for cane it was necessary
to dig a large ditch to ensure circulation of air. Young canes
required attention for the first three or four months and
grew to maturity in 14 or 18 months. Cane could be planted
and would grow at any time of the year, and the reaping
of one crop was the signal for the immediate digging of
ditches and the planting of another. Once cut they had to
be rushed to the mill lest the juice became acid by fermenta-
tion. The extraction of the juice and manufacture of the
raw sugar went on for three weeks a month, 16 or 18 hours
a day, for seven or eight months in the year.

Worked like animals, the slaves were housed like animals, in huts built around a square planted with provisions
and fruits. These huts were about 20 to 25 feet long, 12
feet wide and about 15 feet in height, divided by partitions
into two or three rooms. They were windowless and light
entered only by the door. The floor was beaten earth; the
bed was of straw, hides or a rude contrivance of cords
tied on posts. On these slept indiscriminately mother, father
and children. Defenceless against their masters, they strug-
gled with overwork and its usual complement—underfeed-
ing. The Negro Code, Louis XIV's attempt to ensure them
humane treatment, ordered that they should be given, every
week, two pots and a half of manioc, three cassavas, two
pounds of salt beef or three pounds of salted fish—about
food enough to last a healthy man for three days. Instead
their masters gave them half-a-dozen pints of coarse flour,

rice, or pease, and half-a-dozen herrings. Worn out by their labours all through the day and far into the night, many neglected to cook and ate the food raw. The ration was so small and given to them so irregularly that often the last half of the week found them with nothing.

Even the two hours they were given in the middle of the day, and the holidays on Sundays and feast-days, were not for rest, but in order that they might cultivate a small piece of land to supplement their regular rations. Hard-working slaves cultivated vegetables and raised chickens to sell in the towns to make a little in order to buy rum and tobacco; and here and there a Napoleon of finance, by luck and industry, could make enough to purchase his freedom. Their masters encouraged them in this practice of cultivation, for in years of scarcity the Negroes died in thousands, epidemics broke out, the slaves fled into the woods and plantations were ruined.

The difficulty was that though one could trap them like animals, transport them in pens, work them alongside an ass or a horse and beat both with the same stick, stable them and starve them, they remained, despite their black skins and curly hair, quite invincibly human beings; with the intelligence and resentments of human beings. To cow them into the necessary docility and acceptance necessitated a régime of calculated brutality and terrorism, and it is this that explains the unusual spectacle of property-owners apparently careless of preserving their property: they had first to ensure their own safety.

For the least fault the slaves received the harshest punishment. In 1685 the Negro Code authorised whipping, and in 1702 one colonist, a Marquis, thought any punishment which demanded more than 100 blows of the whip was serious enough to be handed over to the authorities. Later the number was fixed at 39, then raised to 50. But the colonists paid no attention to these regulations and slaves were not unfrequently whipped to death. The whip was not always an ordinary cane or woven cord, as the Code demanded. Sometimes it was replaced by the *rigoise* or thick thong of cow-hide, or by the *lianes*—local growths of reeds, supple and pliant like whalebone. The slaves received the whip with more certainty and regularity than they received their food. It was the incentive to work and the guardian of discipline. But there was no ingenuity that fear or a depraved imagination could devise which was not employed to break their spirit and satisfy the lusts and resentment of their owners and guardians—irons on the hands and feet, blocks of wood that the slaves had to drag behind them wherever they went, the tin-plate mask designed to prevent the slaves eating the sugar-cane, the iron collar. Whipping was interrupted in order to pass a piece of hot wood on the buttocks of the victim; salt, pepper, citron, cinders, aloes, and hot ashes were poured on the bleeding wounds. Mutilations were common, limbs, ears, and sometimes the private parts, to deprive them of the pleasures which they could indulge in without expense. Their masters poured burning wax on their arms and hands and shoulders, emptied the boiling cane sugar over their heads, burned them alive, roasted them on slow fires, filled them with gunpowder and blew them up with a match; buried them up to the neck and smeared their heads with sugar that the flies might devour them; fastened them near to nests of ants or wasps; made them eat their excrement, drink their urine, and lick the saliva of other slaves. One colonist was known in moments of anger to throw himself on his slaves and stick his teeth into their flesh.[7]

Were these tortures, so well authenticated, habitual or were they merely isolated incidents, the extravagances of a few half-crazed colonists? Impossible as it is to substantiate hundreds of cases, yet all the evidence shows that these bestial practices were normal features of slave life. The torture of the whip, for instance, had "a thousand refinements," but there were regular varieties that had special names, so common were they. When the hands and arms were tied to four posts on the ground, the slave was said

[7] De Vaissière, *op. cit.*, pp. 153–94. The author uses chiefly official reports in the French Colonial archives, and other documents of the period, giving specific references in each case.

to undergo "the four post." If the slave was tied to a ladder it was "the torture of the ladder"; if he was suspended by four limbs it was "the hammock," etc. The pregnant woman was not spared her "four-post." A hole was dug in the earth to accommodate the unborn child. The torture of the collar was specially reserved for women who were suspected of abortion, and the collar never left their necks until they had produced a child. The blowing up of a slave had its own name—"to burn a little powder in the arse of a nigger": obviously this was no freak but a recognised practice.

After an exhaustive examination, the best that de Vaissière can say is that there were good masters and there were bad, and his impression, "but only an impression," is that the former were more numerous than the latter.

There are and always will be some who, ashamed of the behaviour of their ancestors, try to prove that slavery was not so bad after all, that its evils and its cruelty were the exaggerations of propagandists and not the habitual lot of the slaves. Men will say (and accept) anything in order to foster national pride or soothe a troubled conscience. Undoubtedly there were kind masters who did not indulge in these refinements of cruelty and whose slaves merely suffered over-work, under-nourishment and the whip. But the slaves in San Domingo could not replenish their number by reproduction. After that dreaded journey across the ocean a woman was usually sterile for two years. The life in San Domingo killed them off fast. The planters deliberately worked them to death rather than wait for children to grow up. But the professional white-washers are assisted by the writings of a few contemporary observers who described scenes of idyllic beauty. One of these is Vaublanc, whom we shall meet again, and whose testimony we will understand better when we know more of him. In his memoirs[8] he shows us a plantation on which there were no prisons, no dungeons, no punishments to speak of. If the slaves were naked the climate was such as not to render this an evil, and those who complained forgot the perfectly disgusting

[8] Quoted extensively in de Vaissière, *op. cit.,* pp. 198–202.

rags that were so often seen in France. The slaves were
exempt from unhealthy, fatiguing, dangerous work such as
was performed by the workers in Europe. They did not
have to descend into the bowels of the earth nor dig deep
pits; they did not construct subterranean galleries; they did
not work in the factories where French workers breathed a
deadly and infected air; they did not mount elevated roofs;
they did not carry enormous burdens. The slaves, he con-
cluded, had light work to do and were happy to do it.
Vaublanc, in San Domingo so sympathetic to the sorrows
of labour in France, had to fly from Paris in August, 1792,
to escape the wrath of the French workers.

Malouet, who was an official in the colonies and fellow-
reactionary of Vaublanc against all change in the colonies,
also sought to give some ideas of the privileges of slavery.
The first he notes is that the slave, on attaining his majority,
begins to enjoy "the pleasures of love," and his master has
no interest in preventing the indulgence of his tastes.[9] To
such impertinent follies can the defence of property drive
even an intelligent man, supposed in his time to be sympathetic towards the blacks.

The majority of the slaves accommodated themselves to
this unceasing brutality by a profound fatalism and a
wooden stupidity before their masters. "Why do you ill-
treat your mule in that way?" asked a colonist of a carter.
"But when I do not work, I am beaten, when he does not
work, I beat him—he is my Negro." One old Negro, having lost one of his ears and condemned to lose another,
begged the Governor to spare it, for if that too was cut
off he would have nowhere to put his stump of cigarette.
A slave sent by his master into his neighbour's garden to
steal, is caught and brought back to the man who had only
a few minutes before despatched him on the errand. The
master orders him a punishment of 100 lashes to which
the slave submits without a murmur. When caught in error
they persisted in denial with the same fatalistic stupidity.

9 *Ibid.*, p. 196.

A slave is accused of stealing a pigeon. He denies it. The pigeon is discovered hidden in his shirt. "Well, well, look at that pigeon. It take my shirt for a nest." Through the shirt of another, a master can feel the potatoes which he denies he has stolen. They are not potatoes, he says, they are stones. He is undressed and the potatoes fall to the ground. "Eh! master. The devil is wicked. Put stones, and look, you find potatoes."

On holidays when not working on their private plots, or dancing, they sat for hours in front of their huts giving no sign of life. Wives and husbands, children and parents, were separated at the will of the master, and a father and son would meet after many years and give no greeting or any sign of emotion. Many slaves could never be got to stir at all unless they were whipped.[10] Suicide was a common habit, and such was their disregard for life that they often killed themselves, not for personal reasons, but in order to spite their owner. Life was hard and death, they believed, meant not only release but a return to Africa. Those who wished to believe and to convince the world that the slaves were half-human brutes, fit for nothing else but slavery, could find ample evidence for their faith, and in nothing so much as in this homicidal mania of the slaves.

Poison was their method. A mistress would poison a rival to retain the valuable affections of her inconstant owner. A discarded mistress would poison master, wife, children and slaves. A slave robbed of his wife by one of his masters would poison him, and this was one of the most frequent causes of poisoning.[11] If a planter conceived a passion for a young slave, her mother would poison his wife with the idea of placing her daughter at the head of the house-

---

[10] Incredible as this may sound Baron de Wimpffen gives it as the evidence of his own eyes. His record of his visit to San Domingo in 1790 is a standard work. A good selection, with very full notes, is published, under the title *Saint-Domingue à la veille de la Révolution*, Albert Savine, ed. (Paris, 1911).

[11] See Dr. Norman Leys, *Kenya* (London, 1926), p. 184. "Some rivalry for a native woman is probably the explanation of most crimes of violence committed by Africans against Europeans in Kenya."

hold. The slaves would poison the younger children of a master in order to ensure the plantation succeeding to one son. By this means they prevented the plantation being broken up and the gang dispersed. On certain plantations the slaves decimated their number by poison so as to keep the number of slaves small and prevent their masters embarking on larger schemes which would increase the work. For this reason a slave would poison his wife, another would poison his children, and a Negro nurse declared in court that for years she had poisoned every child that she brought into the world. Nurses employed in hospitals poisoned sick soldiers to rid themselves of unpleasant work. The slaves would even poison the property of a master whom they loved. He was going away; they poisoned cows, horses and mules, the plantation was thrown into disorder, and the beloved master was compelled to remain. The most dreadful of all this cold-blooded murder was, however, the jaw-sickness—a disease which attacked children only, in the first few days of their existence. Their jaws were closed to such an extent that it was impossible to open them and to get anything down, with the result that they died of hunger. It was not a natural disease and never attacked children delivered by white women. The Negro midwives alone could cause it, and it is believed that they performed some simple operation on the newly-born child which resulted in the jaw-sickness. Whatever the method this disease caused the death of nearly one-third of the children born on the plantations.

What was the intellectual level of these slaves? The planters, hating them, called them by every opprobious name. "The Negroes," says a memoir published in 1789, "are unjust, cruel, barbarous, half-human, treacherous, deceitful, thieves, drunkards, proud, lazy, unclean, shameless, jealous to fury, and cowards." It was by sentiments such as these that they strove to justify the abominable cruelties they practised. And they took great pains that the Negro should remain the brute beast they wanted him to be. "The safety of the whites demands that we keep the Negroes in the most profound ignorance. I have reached the stage of believing firmly that one must treat the Negroes as one treats beasts." Such is the opinion of the Governor of Martinique in a letter addressed to the Minister and such was the opinion of all colonists. Except for the Jews, who spared no energy in making Israelites of their slaves, the majority of the colonists religiously kept all instruction, religious or otherwise, away from the slaves.

Naturally there were all types of men among them, ranging from native chieftains, as was the father of Toussaint L'Ouverture, to men who had been slaves in their own country. The creole Negro was more docile than the slave who had been born in Africa. Some said he was more intelligent. Others doubted that there was much difference though the creole slave knew the language and was more familiar with his surroundings and his work. Yet those who took the trouble to observe them away from their masters and in their intercourse with each other did not fail to see that remarkable liveliness of intellect and vivacity of spirit which so distinguish their descendants in the West Indies to-day. Father du Tertre, who knew them well, noted their secret pride and feeling of superiority to their masters, the difference between their behaviour before their masters and when they were by themselves. De Wimpffen, an exceptionally observant and able traveller, was also astonished at this dual personality of the slaves. "One has to hear with what warmth and what volubility, and at the same time with what precision of ideas and accuracy of judgment, this creature, heavy and taciturn all day, now squatting before his fire, tells stories, talks, gesticulates, argues, passes opinions, approves or condemns both his master and everyone who surrounds him." It was this intelligence which refused to be crushed, these latent possibilities, that frightened the colonists, as it frightens the whites in Africa to-day. "No species of men has more intelligence," wrote Hilliard d'Auberteuil, a colonist, in 1784, and had his book banned.

But one does not need education or encouragement to cherish a dream of freedom. At their midnight celebrations of Voodoo, their African cult, they danced and sang, usually this favourite song:

> Eh! Eh! Bomba! Heu! Heu!
>   Canga, bafio té!
>   Canga, mouné de lé!
>   Canga, do ki la!
>   Canga, li!

"We swear to destroy the whites and all that they possess; let us die rather than fail to keep this vow."

The colonists knew this song and tried to stamp it out, and the Voodoo cult with which it was linked. In vain. For over two hundred years the slaves sang it at their meetings, as the Jews in Babylon sang of Zion, and the Bantu today sing in secret the national anthem of Africa.[12]

All the slaves, however, did not undergo this régime. There was a small privileged caste, the foremen of the gangs, coachmen, cooks, butlers, maids, nurses, female companions, and other house-servants. These repaid their kind treatment and comparatively easy life with a strong attachment to their masters, and have thus enabled Tory historians, regius professors and sentimentalists to represent plantation slavery as a patriarchal relation between master and slave. Permeated with the vices of their masters and mistresses, these upper servants gave themselves airs and despised the slaves in the fields. Dressed in cast-off silks and brocades, they gave balls in which, like trained monkeys, they danced minuets and quadrilles, and bowed and curtseyed in the fashion of Versailles. But a few of these used their position to cultivate themselves, to gain a little education, to learn all they could. The leaders of a revolution are usually those who have been able to profit by the cultural advantages of the system they are attacking, and the San Domingo revolution was no exception to this rule.

Christophe, afterwards Emperor of Haiti, was a slave—a

---

[12] Such observations, written in 1938, were intended to use the San Domingo revolution as a forecast of the future of colonial Africa.

waiter in a public hotel at Cap François, where he made
use of his opportunities to gain a knowledge of men and
of the world. Toussaint L'Ouverture[13] also belonged to
this small and privileged caste. His father, son of a petty
chieftain in Africa, was captured in war, sold as a slave
and made the journey in a slave-ship. He was bought by a
colonist of some sensibility, who, recognising that this
Negro was an unusual person, allowed him a certain liberty
on the plantation and the use of five slaves to cultivate a
plot of land. He became a Catholic, married a woman who
was both beautiful and good, and Toussaint was the eldest
of his eight children. Near to the household lived an old
Negro, Pierre Baptiste, remarkable for his integrity of
character and a smattering of knowledge. The Negroes
spoke a debased French known as creole. But Pierre knew
French, also a little Latin and a little geometry, which he
had learned from a missionary. Pierre Baptiste became
Toussaint's godfather and taught his godson the rudiments
of French; using the services of the Catholic Church he
instructed him also in the rudiments of Latin; Toussaint
learned also to draw. The young slaves had the care of the
flocks and herds, and this was Toussaint's early occupation.
But his father, like many other Africans, had some knowledge of medicinal plants and taught Toussaint what he
knew. The elements of an education, his knowledge of
herbs, his unusual intelligence, singled him out, and he
was made coachman to his master. This brought him further means of comfort and self-education. Ultimately he
was made steward of all the live-stock on the estate—a
responsible post which was usually held by a white man.
If Toussaint's genius came from where genius comes, yet
circumstances conspired to give him exceptional parents
and friends and a kind master.

But the number of slaves who occupied positions with
such opportunities was infinitely small in comparison with
the hundreds of thousands who bore on their bent backs

[13] As a slave he was called Toussaint Bréda.

the whole structure of San Domingo society. All of them
did not submit to it. Those whose boldness of spirit found
slavery intolerable and refused to evade it by committing
suicide, would fly to the woods and mountains and form
bands of free men—maroons. They fortified their fastnesses
with palisades and ditches. Women followed them. They
reproduced themselves. And for a hundred years before
1789 the maroons were a source of danger to the colony.
In 1720, 1,000 slaves fled to the mountains. In 1751 there
were at least 3,000 of them. Usually they formed separate
bands, but periodically they found a chief who was strong
enough to unite the different sections. Many of these rebel
leaders struck terror into the hearts of the colonists by
their raids on the plantations and the strength and deter-
mination of the resistance they organised against attempts
to exterminate them. The greatest of these chiefs was
Mackandal.

He conceived the bold design of uniting all the Negroes
and driving the whites out of the colony. He was a Negro
from Guinea who had been a slave in the district of Limbé,
later to become one of the great centres of the revolution.
Mackandal was an orator, in the opinion of a white contemporary equal in eloquence to the European orators of
the day, and different only in his superior strength and
vigour. He was fearless and, though one-handed from an
accident, had a fortitude of spirit which he knew how to
preserve in the midst of the most cruel tortures. He claimed
to predict the future; like Mahomet he had revelations;
he persuaded his followers that he was immortal and exercised such a hold over them that they considered it an
honour to serve him on their knees; the handsomest women
fought for the privilege of being admitted to his bed. Not
only did his band raid and pillage plantations far and wide,
but he himself ranged from plantation to plantation to
make converts, stimulate his followers, and perfect his
great plan for the destruction of white civilisation in San
Domingo. An uninstructed mass, feeling its way to revolution, usually begins by terrorism, and Mackandal aimed at
delivering his people by means of poison. For six years he

built up his organisation, he and his followers poisoning not only whites but disobedient members of their own band. Then he arranged that on a particular day the water of every house in the capital of the province was to be poisoned, and the general attack made on the whites while they were in the convulsions and anguish of death. He had lists of all members of his party in each slave gang; appointed captains, lieutenants and other officers; arranged for bands of Negroes to leave the town and spread over the plains to massacre the whites. His temerity was the cause of his downfall. He went one day to a plantation, got drunk and was betrayed, and being captured was burnt alive.

The Mackandal rebellion never reached fruition and it was the only hint of an organised attempt at revolt during the hundred years preceding the French Revolution. The slaves seemed eternally resigned, though here and there a slave was manumitted or purchased his freedom from his owner. From their masters came no talk of future emancipation. The San Domingo colonists said that slavery was necessary, and for them that finished the argument. Legislation passed for the protection of the slaves remained on paper in face of the dictum that a man could do as he liked with his own. "All laws, however just and humane they may be, in favour of Negroes will always be a violation of the rights of property if they are not sponsored by the colonists. . . . All laws on property are just only if they are supported by the opinion of those who are interested in them as proprietors." This was still white opinion at the beginning of the French Revolution. Not only planters but officials made it quite clear that whatever the penalties for the illtreatment of slaves, these could never be enforced. The slaves might understand that they had rights, which would be fatal to the peace and well-being of the colony. That was why a colonist never hesitated at the mutilation, the torture or the murder of a slave who had cost him thousands of francs. "The Ivory Coast is a good mother" was a colonial proverb. Slaves could always be bought, and profits were always high.

2.

This segment of a Jamaican sociologist's work on slavery in Jamaica approaches the topic from a perspective different from the previous essay. Here the daily life of the slave is viewed as structured by his cumulative experience in Africa, during the Middle Passage, and in the West Indies. Slave behavior is explored also in terms of relationship with whites. Stereotypes of slave personality, the subject of much scholarly and polemical discussion today, are analyzed here in terms of slaveowner coercion and slave response.

A sociologist of Jamaican origin, ORLANDO PATTERSON took his undergraduate degree at the University of the West Indies and a graduate degree at the London School of Economics. He returned home to become a lecturer at the University of the West Indies before moving to Harvard, where he taught in the Black Studies program and is now Professor of Sociology. Novelist as well as social scientist, Patterson is the author of *The Children of Sisyphus* and *An Absence of Ruins,* which graphically describe contemporary Jamaican society from shanty town to suburb.

The Socialization and Personality Structure of the Slave
Orlando Patterson

There were two types of adjustments to slavery. First, there was that of the African slave whose introduction to the system was sudden and traumatic; and there was that of the creole slave whose socialization was gradual and less painful. This chapter examines these two types of socialization into slavery and the subsequent personality traits that the system appears to have produced.

Both types of adjustments were closely related to each other. The basis of the creole slave society was originally laid down by the first group of Africans enslaved in the island. On the other hand, once the creole slave society was established it formed the main host society for the newly arrived African slaves. However, if we were to examine the slave society at any given time we would find a basic division between the community of the African and creole slaves. The extent to which one group dominated the other varied from one period to the next. Before examining the processes of socialization, therefore, we shall trace briefly the development of the relationship between the two groups.

CREOLE AND AFRICAN SLAVES

Until near the end of the seventeenth century about a quarter of the slaves [entering Jamaica] came from other

The Sociology of Slavery, London, McGibbon & Kee, 1967, pp. 145–54, 170–81. Reprinted by permission of publisher and author.

West Indian islands, mainly Barbados, while the rest were
brought directly from Africa. We cannot say what proportion of the slaves from the other islands was creole, but
since Barbados succeeded more than any other island in
breeding her own slaves and, since the planters who
brought over their slaves with them were the very ones
who were more likely to breed their own slaves, it is likely
that a substantial minority of them were Barbadian creole.
One may speculate that these slaves may have contributed
to the speedy development of a creole slave community
in Jamaica.

After 1800 the small creole minority in the island was
swamped by the greatly increased inflow of African Negroes. The records relating to the late seventeenth and
early eighteenth centuries make little reference to the
creole minority.[1] By the 1760s, which is about the time
Edward Long began writing his *History of Jamaica*,[2] we
are informed that the African slaves 'are chiefly awed
into subjection by the superior multitude of Creole
Blacks . . .'[3] In 1789 it was estimated that the Africans
constituted 25 per cent of the total population[4] but the
more accurate figures of 1817 showed them to be 37 per
cent of the total,[5] an increase which may be partly accounted for by the large influx of Africans during the last
decade of the slave trade. As early as the 1760s Long found

[1] Leslie, speaking of the fear of the Africans for the military
'muster and exercise' of the Whites, adds, 'Tis true, the Creolian
Negroes are not of this number; they all speak English and are
so far from fearing a Muster, that they are very familiar with
it, and can exercise extremely well' (Charles Leslie, *A New History of Jamaica* [London, 1740], p. 311).

[2] Long went to Jamaica in 1757 at the age of 23 and published his *History* in 1774; see Vol. I of the history of his family by R. M. Howard, *The Longs of Longville, Jamaica, and
Hampton Lodge, Surrey* (2 vols.; London, 1925).

[3] Edward Long, *The History of Jamaica* (3 vols.; London:
T. Lowndes, 1774), Vol. 2, Bk. 3, p. 444.

[4] Report of the Select Committee of the Jamaican House of
Assembly, 1789.

[5] Great Britain, Select Committee on Slavery (1721) *British
Parliamentary Papers*, Vol. 20 (1831–32), Q7937.

that the creoles differed from the Africans 'not only in manners, but in beauty of shape, feature and complexion',[6] and to a friend of Edwards they 'exceed the Africans in intellect, strength and comeliness';[7] but these views are likely to be biased. More important was the fact that the creoles held the Africans 'in the utmost contempt styling them "salt-water Negroes" and "Guineybirds" '.[8]

On Lewis' estate, where the Africans, mainly Ibos, formed a substantial minority, there was strong rivalry and dislike on the part of each group for the other. The Ibos exhibited marked tribal solidarity and were organized around elected leaders and after an incident in which the Africans were mortified by the mistaken zeal of one of the leaders, the creole head cook appealed to Lewis that 'Massa ought to sell all the Eboes, and buy Creoles instead'.[9]

At holidays and festivals both groups tended to have separate recreations. Differences may be discerned too, in their funeral practices, eating habits, dress[10] and the like. Yet, one should be careful not to over-emphasize this distinction for there were many areas of life in which both groups participated. The most important was their work situation where bodily strength and fitness mattered far more than place of birth. Again, the most feared and respected Negro on every estate (though not necessarily the most liked) was the obeahman who in the great majority of cases was African. Finally, it must be remembered that the African born slaves, even when they were in the minority, had considerable influence over the first and second

[6] Long, *op. cit.*, Vol. 2, Bk. 3, p. 410.

[7] Bryan Edwards, *The History, Civil and Commercial, of the British Colonies in the West Indies*, 5th ed. (5 vols.; London: Whittaker, 1819), Vol. 2, p. 185.

[8] Long, *op. cit.*, Vol. 2, Bk. 3, p. 410.

[9] M. G. Lewis, *Journal of a West Indian Proprietor* (London: John Murray, 1834), p. 190.

[10] Lewis tells us that creole and African slaves competed with each other in their funeral festivities (*ibid.*, p. 335); Long and Lewis stated that Africans were very fond of cane field rats while the creoles had nothing to do with them, or so they said; Africans tended to be more scantily dressed.

generation creole slaves. Lewis wrote of the strong influence
of an African negress over her mulatto daughter who
having 'imbibed strong African prejudices from her
mother' refused to become a Christian.[11] Martin also informs us that 'the Negro population is . . . formed into
classes, according to the country they came from, or that
which their progenitors belonged to'.[12]

THE ADJUSTMENT OF THE AFRICAN SLAVE

Elkins has described the transformation of the African
tribesman into a New World slave in terms of a series of
shock experiences, namely—capture, journey to the coast,
sale to the white captains, the middle passage and enslavement on the plantation.[13] Such categorization, while of
some use, is too schematic, and neglects certain important
factors. First, many slaves were captured in genuine war-
fare, and as soldiers, one would hardly expect them to be
shocked at being taken prisoners of war. Secondly, many
of the slaves came from the coast itself and were thus
spared the horrors of the journey from the interior. And
thirdly, it must be admitted that many of the slaves sold
into slavery were guilty of genuine crimes for which they
would otherwise have been executed. But these reservations aside, there can be little doubt that most African
slaves had a terrifying experience, both in the nature of
their capture, transportation and sale on the coast and in
the West Indies. The Ibo slave, Equiano, has left us a vivid
account of his capture and later experiences.[14]

He was captured when alone with his sister in his family
compound; gagged, tied up and carried to the woods. When

[11] Lewis, op. cit., p. 335.
[12] R. M. Martin, The English Colonies (6 vols.; London,
1851–57), Vol. 4, pp. 95–96.
[13] Stanley Elkins, Slavery: A Problem in American Institutional and Intellectual Life (Chicago: University of Chicago Press, 1963), pp. 98–103.
[14] Olaudah Equiano, The Interesting Narrative of the Life
of Olaudah Equiano or Gustavus Vassa, the African, Written
by Himself (2 vols.; London: 1789).

he cried out he was placed in a sack.[15] After many days
of travel, he was sold. For the next three months he was
resold several times. But he was generally well treated and
understood the language and customs of his twelve masters.
Finally he was sold by a widow to some traders from the
coast. This turned out to be his first real and lasting shock
experience. 'The change I now experienced', he wrote, 'was
as painful as it was sudden and unexpected', involving 'such
instances of hardship and fatigue as I can never reflect on
but with horror'.[16]

As he passed through strange countries on his way to
the coast he was forcibly struck by the differing customs,
but more, by the new, awe-inspiring natural sights. The
sight of a large river for the first time filled him with astonishment as he had 'never before seen any water than a
pond or a rivulet'. It was not until the end of seven months
after he was first kidnapped that Equiano finally reached
the coast. The physical confrontation with the sea immediately filled him with sheer terror. No less terrifying was his
experience of being forced aboard ship; and the strange
sight of the white men who came to inspect him, juxtaposed
with that of a large copper boiling on the ship, convinced

[15] There are a few other slave autobiographies, but none as
vivid as Equiano's. A Fanti slave published an autobiography
entitled *The Narrative of the Enslavement of Ottobah Cugoano,
a Native of Africa,* in 1787. Like Equiano, Cugoano was kidnapped when still a youth. The technique used in his case was
slightly different, he being duped into going to the coast rather
than being brutally pulled along. A short autobiography of a
Jamaican slave is appended in R. R. Madden's *Twelve Months'
Residence in the West Indies* (2 vols., Philadelphia, 1835) and
is entitled, "The History of Abon Becr Sadika, known in Jamaica
by the name of Edward Donlan." Donlan claimed that he was
from 'Timbuctoo' and could read and write Arabic. Describing
the first stage of his enslavement, he wrote: 'As soon as I was
made prisoner, they stripped me, and tied me with a cord, and
gave me a heavy load to carry' (Vol. 2, p. 129). In 1834 a
Senegambian ex-slave published an autobiography entitled *Some
Memoirs of the Life of Job, the Son of Solomon, the High Priest
of Boonda in Africa.* It includes interesting material on capture
and transportation to the coast.

[16] Equiano, *op. cit.,* Vol. I, pp. 65–66.

him that the whites intended to eat him,[17] whereupon he fainted on the deck.[18] Taken to the hold of the ship, together with the rest of the black cargo, the atmosphere became 'absolutely pestilential':

> The closeness of the place, and the heat of the climate added to the number in the ship, which was so crowded that each had scarcely room to turn himself, almost suffocated us. This produced copious perspiration, a variety of loathsome smells, and brought on a sickness amongst the slaves, of which many died, thus falling victims to the improvident avarice, as I may call it, of their purchasers. This wretched situation was again aggravated by the galling of the chains, now become insupportable, and the filth of the necessary tubs[19] into which the children often fell and were almost suffocated. The shrieks of the women and the groans of the dying, reduced the whole to a scene of horror almost inconceivable.[20]

Like most of the other slaves, Equiano was overcome with extreme dejection and would have committed suicide had he the opportunity. Isaac Wilson, a surgeon on one of the slave ships, said that melancholy and dejection were 'one great cause' of death. Both Wilson and Falconbridge reported cases of outright insanity caused directly by the impact of the slave ship.[21]

Then followed the indescribable horrors of the middle passage. There is no need to repeat here the well known barbarities of this journey. One experience did take place on the middle passage which was of lasting importance,

---

[17] Cugoano, op. cit., wrote, '. . . in the evening (we) came to a town, where I saw several white people, which made me afraid that they would eat me, according to our notion as children, in the inland parts of the country.'

[18] Equiano, op. cit., pp. 70–71.

[19] These 'tubs' were the lavatory of the holds.

[20] Ibid., pp. 78–79.

[21] Great Britain, Minutes of the Evidence Taken before a Committee of the House of Commons . . . respecting the African Slave Trade, 1790–91, House of Common Sessional Papers, Vol. 34. The findings of this Committee support Equiano's descriptions in every detail.

and paradoxically, of great subsequent comfort to the slave. It was the formation of the strong bonds of friendship between all the slaves on the slave ship. These friends became known in the West Indies as 'shipmates' and their love and affection for each other was proverbial. Stewart tells us that the term shipmate 'seems synonymous in their view with brother or sister',[22] and according to Kelly, 'Shipmate is the dearest word and bond of affectionate sympathy amongst the Africans . . . they look upon each other's children mutually as their own'.[23] It was customary for children to call their parents' shipmates 'uncle' or 'aunt'.[24] So strong were the bonds between shipmates that sexual intercourse between them, in the view of one observer, was considered incestuous.

After the horrors of the middle passage came the sale at the West Indian ports. The pernicious practice of sale by scramble continued in Jamaica until well into the 1780s. On one such scramble the ship was darkened beforehand by covering it over with sails; male slaves were exhibited on the main deck, females on the quarter deck. At the shot of a gun a large horde of waiting planters scrambled aboard and dashed madly for the slaves of their choice 'with the ferocity of brutes'. This created terror among the slaves, many of whom flung themselves overboard.[25]

Equiano wrote that during this time fears of being eaten were again revived among the slaves. When bought by means other than scramble, the experience of being bought in the island, coming after the horrors of the middle passage, was not particularly harsh. Indeed on such occasions most of the slaves 'express great eagerness to be sold',[26] no doubt so as to get the whole thing over with.

[22] John Stewart, *A View of the Past and Present State of the Island of Jamaica* (Edinburgh, 1823), p. 250.

[23] J. Kelly, *Voyage to Jamaica and Narrative of 17 Years Residence in that Island* (1838), p. 45.

[24] Lewis, *op. cit.*, p. 350.

[25] Alexander Falconbridge, *An Account of the Slave Trade on the Coast of Africa* (London, 1788).

[26] Edwards, *op. cit.*, Bk. 4, p. 153.

Finally came the long period of seasoning. The slave was taken to the estate, branded with a silver brand heated in spirits, and given a name.[27] What took place after this varied from one estate to the next. On most estates the official period of seasoning was three years but in actual practice the period was usually restricted to a year. Beckford wrote that there were two basic forms of seasoning, that in which new Negroes were put under the supervision of elderly seasoned slaves from their own country; and that in which the master assumed primary responsibility for their safeguard, keeping a provision ground 'ready planted, full of provisions, and apportioned to them upon their arrival'.[28] The first type of seasoning often led to tyranny on the part of the supervising slaves, the latter forcing his ward to work his ground for him at the expense of the ward's ground, and this neglect was often responsible for leading the new Negro to steal in order to prevent himself from starving.[29] Edwards, however, paints a brighter picture of the relationship between the new Negroes and their wardens, claiming that old seasoned Africans usually avidly sought after newcomers from their homeland with whom they could revive memories of their youth and whom they sometimes adopted.[30] But this is quite likely a gross overstatement.

[27] African slaves were often given names taken from popular literature or the Greek classics. On Rose Hall estate there were: Hannibal, Ulysses, Scipio, Hercules, Othello, Antony, Mark, etc.
[28] W. Beckford, *Remarks upon the Situation of the Negroes in Jamaica* (London, 1788), p. 27.
[29] H. Coor, in Minutes of the Evidence Taken before a Committee of the House of Commons . . . respecting the African Slave Trade, 1790–91, *House of Commons Sessional Papers,* Vol. 34.
[30] Edwards, *op. cit.,* Bk. 4, pp. 155–56. This passage reads unconvincingly, like so many of Edwards' remarks concerning the slaves. Slave fathers had little control over their sons, and, as a rule, cared even less about them. They certainly would not have gone out of their way to seek suitable wives among the new Negroes for them. But there may have been some truth in the other remarks relating to the relationship between newly arrived slaves and their supervisors.

The disadvantage of the second type of seasoning, according to Beckford, was that it led to discontent and feelings of injustice among the new Negroes since they were forced to work on Sundays on the grounds prepared for them, not of their own free will, but under the supervision of a driver. Some masters got around this problem by simply allowing the new Negroes one year's provisions from the stores.

What of the personality of the Africans in these first few months on the island? Beckford has left us a penetrating account of them which strongly suggests all the symptoms of a broken trauma-ridden personality. They were cold, unfeeling and completely unpredictable, their general attitude being one of total indifference:

> It is amazing to see how little they interest themselves in the common occurrences of life; they do not foresee the want of means, are careless of what may happen and thoughtless of what they have; in short, their characters for many years after their arrival can hardly be defined by the most perspicacious eye of those by whom they are governed, so that for what we know they may be happy when silent or dangerous when sullen.[31]

The Seasoned African Slave. By the time the African's period of seasoning was over he was sure to find himself defined in a certain social position and drawn towards certain groups. During the early period, when the Africans formed the majority of the slaves, divisions between the different African tribes were as great as that between the Africans as a whole and the creoles. Leslie wrote that:

> The slaves are brought from several Places of Guiney, which are different from one another in Language, and consequently they cannot converse freely; or, if they could, they hate one another so mortally, that some of them would rather die by the Hands of the English, than

[31] Beckford, *op. cit.,* p. 88.

join with other Africans in an attempt to shake off their yoke.[32]

These differences continued until the end of slavery, a nineteenth century observer noting that at the Christmas festivities the different tribal stocks 'formed into exclusive groups competing against each other in performing their national music'.[33] But the differences were now only expressed in amusements. The different African groups from a much earlier date had far more in common with each other, by virtue of being African, in their confrontation with the creole group. Later on in the celebrations Kelly informs us:

> These Africans took the sides and corners of the hall, whilst the Creoles occupied the centre and piazzas, and evidently considered themselves entitled to the best places, which the Africans cheerfully conceded to them, evincing the greatest deference to the superior civilization of the upstarts! The one class, forced into slavery, humbled and degraded had lost everything and found no solace but the miserable one of retrospection. The other, born in slavery, never had freedom to loose; yet did the Creole proudly assume a superiority over the African . . .[34]

It is the common view that Gold Coast Negroes dominated the rest of the Africans, and indeed the entire slave community. There are, however, no grounds for this assertion. Certainly, it cannot be denied that a significant number of Gold Coast cultural elements have survived in Jamaica. According to Cassidy, Twi words make up a half of the two-hundred and fifty loan-words found in the Jamaican dialect.[35] The spider hero of the Akan-speaking peoples, Anansesem, survives in the Jamaican spider hero, Anancy;

[32] Leslie, *op. cit.*, pp. 310–11.
[33] Kelly, *op. cit.*, pp. 20–21.
[34] *Ibid.*
[35] Frederic G. Cassidy, *Jamaica Talk* (London: Macmillan, 1961), pp. 21, 397.

and so on. We shall discuss these cultural problems in more detail as we come to them. For the moment, only a few salient points need to be made. Firstly, it is not justifiable to draw conclusions about the historical dominance of a group solely on the basis of the survival of its cultural elements; and secondly, the survival of cultural elements from the Gold Coast is in no way out of proportion to the number of slaves brought from that region. . . . Unlike the viewpoint of the modern scholars, it would appear that large numbers of cultural survivals indicate social isolation rather than social dominance. The data suggest that Gold Coast Negroes managed to preserve more of their culture partly because they kept to themselves and were generally disliked by the other slaves. 'On many estates', Long wrote, 'they do not mix at all with the other slaves, but build their houses distinct from the rest; and, herding together, are left more at liberty to hold their dangerous cabals without interruption'.[36] The passage quoted above from Leslie is also of relevance here. He tells us that the different tribal groups hated one another. What is more significant is his statement that they would rather die than 'join with other Africans in an attempt to shake off their yoke'. Now until the time that Leslie wrote, every rebellion in the island was carried out by the Coromantee slaves and there seems little doubt that Leslie was here obviously referring to the hatred of the other African groups for the Coromantees.

Finally, it should have been obvious that slavery was no place for one enslaved group to dominate another. It was common for the weaker party in a dispute to declare: 'This no for we country; this for Buckra (whites) country; Buckra country everybody have right'.[37]

In any case, the whole problem of cultural domination of one African group by another is largely an overplayed

[36] Long, *op. cit.*, Vol. 2, p. 475.
[37] John Wedderburn, in Minutes of the Evidence Taken before a Committee of the House of Commons . . . respecting the African Slave Trade, 1780–91, *House of Commons Sessional Papers*, Vol. 34.

issue when it is considered that almost all the Africans imported to Jamaica came from the same culture area,[38] where, as Daryll Forde observes, 'underlying the great regional or tribal differences . . . there is a very widespread substratum of basic ideas that persists in the rituals, myths and folk-tales of West African peoples'.[39]

* * * *

THE SOCIALIZATION OF THE CREOLE SLAVE

The Influence of the White Group. Despite the strong bond between mother and child, in the long run other agents were of more importance in the slaves' upbringing than she was. This was due to the fact . . . that the amount of time she could devote to her children was very limited. Usually less than two years after they were weaned, children were placed under the command of a driveress in the grass gang and later moved to other gangs which were always separate from their parent. The driver became, then, the direct authority figure for the child. But it was not long before the child became aware of the fact that the driver's authority was derived from a higher source and that this higher source was the white group. He would have been told this by his mother. More important, he would constantly see the authority of the whites demonstrated in the frequent orders given by the white book-keepers or overseers to the drivers.

In the case of the children of domestic slaves—who always formed a significant minority of the slave children—the social superiority of the whites was demonstrated from an early age through their relationship with their white peer group. In our [Patterson's] chapter on the creole whites we have seen that white children were allowed to

[38] See M. J. Herskovits, 'The Culture Areas of Africa', *Africa*, Vol. 3 (1930), where nine cultural areas are demarcated.

[39] Daryll Forde, 'The Culture Map of West Africa', in Simon and Phoebe Ottenberg, eds., *Cultures and Societies of Africa* (New York: Random House, 1960), p. 123.

mix freely with their black peers. M'Mahon has left us an account of what happened in these early peer group associations:

> The inbred arrogance of a white child brought up among black children is painfully pressed upon the observation of a person unaccustomed to such a land of tyranny as a slave colony always is. At even two years of age the black child cowers and shrinks before the white child, who at all times slaps and beats it at pleasure and takes away its toys without the smallest manifestation of opposition on the part of the piccaninni. I have frequently seen a white child crying, when the little slave, so utterly a slave from his birth, would say to the crying child,—'Massa, knock me, don't cry; you my massa; me you nega'.[40]

In later life, the slave discriminated between the different orders of whites. Generally, if the owner was absentee, the attorney (who paid periodic visits to the estate) was seen as their owner and true master. Should the absentee owner visit the island, his authority was immediately recognized and all the apparent adoration due to him was given. Note for example, the tumultuous welcome given M. G. Lewis when he visited his estate for the first time. Of course, if the owner actually lived on the estate, the matter was made that much simpler.[41]

On one level, Long's assertion that 'they eye and respect their master as a father and are extremely vain in reflecting on the connexion between them'[42] may have been generally true. Thus their own estimation *vis-à-vis* the slaves of other estates was largely a reflection of their master's status in the community. The slaves also appeared to emulate their masters and copied 'not only their dress but imitate

[40] B. M'Mahon, *Jamaica Plantership* (London, 1839), p. 293.

[41] It should be remembered that while the majority of owners lived on the island, because of the unequal distribution of slaves among whites, the majority of slaves were owned by masters who were absentee.

[42] Long, *op. cit.*, Vol. 2, p. 410.

their every action and expression'.[43] The status of the
master was so important in the slaves' assessment of themselves and of each other that they considered it the greatest
disgrace if their ownership was in doubt. Lewis mentions
the case of the mulatto Mary Wiggins who threw herself
at his feet with joy when it was finally established that she
belonged to him, adding that 'to be told by the Negroes of
another estate that they belong to no massa is one of the
most contemptuous reproaches that can be cast upon
them'.[44] One aspect of this veneration for the master was
the almost childlike habit of the slaves of making quite
fatuous complaints to him simply to be able to be near him
and to address a few words to him.[45] Lewis also wrote
that many of his slaves regarded him as their kin and addressed him as such:

> In particular, the women called me by every endearing
> name they could think of. 'My son! my love! my hus-
> band! my father! You no me massa, you my tata!' said
> one old woman . . . and when I came down the steps
> to depart, they crowded about me, kissing my feet and
> clasping my knees, so that it was with difficulty that I
> could get into the carriage.[46]

The word 'tata' meant father and was a common mode of
expression for the master, especially among the slave children. Barclay wrote of masters who, on returning to their
estates were greeted by 'the little Negro children . . .
vociferating the endearing expression, "Tata come, Tata
come" '.[47]

Not only was the master overtly loved and venerated,

[43] T. Jelly, *Remarks on the Condition of the Whites and Free
Coloured Inhabitants of Jamaica* (Montego Bay, Jamaica,
1826), p. 42.

[44] Lewis, *op. cit.*, pp. 68–69.

[45] Both Lewis and De La Beche noted this habit. Lewis, *op.
cit.*; Henry Thomas de la Beche, *Notes on the Present Condition of the Negroes of Jamaica* (London, 1825).

[46] Lewis, *op. cit.*, p. 240.

[47] Alexander Barclay, *A Practical View of the Present State
of Slavery in the West Indies* (London, 1826), p. 212.

but his decree was considered infallible. Lewis was amazed at the manner in which the slaves accepted his judgment on disputes among them:

> I must acknowledge, however, that the Negro principle that 'massa can do no wrong' was of some little assistance to me on this occasion. 'Oh! quite just, me good massa! what massa say quite just! me no say nothing more; me good massa!' Then they thanked me 'for Massa's goodness in giving them so long talk!' and went away to tell all the others how just massa had been in taking away what they wanted to keep, or not giving them what they asked for.[48]

While the overt attitudes of the slaves to their masters were clearly those of respect and adoration one must remain doubtful about the sincerity of their feelings. The masters themselves were not always fooled by their slaves. Lewis wrote of his jubilant welcome: '. . . whether the pleasure of the Negroes was sincere may be doubted; but certainly it was the loudest I ever witnessed'. Later he wrote that they were excellent flatterers 'and lay it on with a trowell'. Long also pointed out that they were great 'dissemblers', and McNeill warned his readers that 'he (the slave) has great art and may deceive you'.[49]

The relationship with the overseer was quite different from that with the master. He may have stimulated fear and terror, but never respect or co-operation. To the slaves he was an enemy never to be trusted, and to be foiled at every opportunity. We have shown in another chapter [of Patterson's book] the barbarity of these whites and it is not surprising that there was constant conflict between them and the slaves they supervised. There was some flexibility in the overseer-slave relationship in that, while he was always covertly despised, the slaves were often prepared to be tractable if the overseer treated them with moderation,

[48] Lewis, *op. cit.*, pp. 404–05.
[49] Hector McNeill, *Observations on the Treatment of the Negroes in the Island of Jamaica* (London, 1788), p. 29.

one of their favourite expressions being 'Good massa, good Negro'.[50]

This basic distinction in the attitude of the slaves to their masters and their overseers is to be noted in a slave song recorded by Moreton, one verse of which expresses the longing for the master as against the restrictions imposed on them by their overseer:

> If me want for go in a Kingston,
> Me cant go there!
> Since massa go in a England,
> Me cant go there![51]

Unfortunately, it was under the overseer that the slave spent most of his working life. Thus all the psychological techniques which had to be employed in outwitting him and thwarting his every action, were constantly in use and eventually became 'a kind of second nature'.[52] It was primarily within the context of the overseer-slave relationship, then, that the peculiar personality traits of the slaves, noted by almost every one of the multitude of chroniclers, came about and functioned. To the nature of these personality traits we shall now turn our attention.

AN ANALYSIS OF 'QUASHEE'

The various traits of the personality of the Negro slave fell into a general pattern that has been recognized all over the New World. Stanley Elkins has recently analysed what he termed the 'Sambo' personality.[53] His descriptions bear a remarkable resemblance to those which existed in Jamaica. The term used in Jamaica to designate this personality pattern was Quashee. This term came originally

[50] Kelly, op. cit., p. 36.
[51] J. B. Moreton, Manners and Customs in the West Indies (London, 1790), p. 153.
[52] B. Lucock, Jamaica, Enslaved and Free (London, 1846), pp. 91–92.
[53] Elkins, op. cit., Ch. 3, passim.

from the Twi day-name meaning 'Sunday'.[54] In addition to being a popular name for slaves, Long's own use of the term demonstrates that by the beginning of the second half of the eighteenth century at the latest it came to designate peculiarly Negro character traits. Writing at the beginning of the nineteenth century, Stewart, speaking of the illiteracy of the creole white women, remarked that many of them exhibit much of the 'Quasheba' (the feminine of Quashee). Cassidy has pointed out that today 'Quashie simply means a peasant, but one also finds it glossed as "fool" '.[55] From my own experience as a Jamaican I have often heard the word used in the hyphenated manner 'quashie-fool'. It is clear, however, that during slavery the term related specifically to Negro personality traits.

Perhaps the best comment on quashee was made by Stewart, who wrote that: It is not an easy matter to trace with an unerring pencil the true character and disposition of the Negro, they are often so ambiguous and disguised.[56]

This evasive, indefinable, somewhat disguised and ambiguous quality was the most essential element of Quashee. Stewart also remarked: 'The Negroes are crafty, artful, plausible; not often grateful for small services; but, frequently deceitful and over-reaching.'[57]

The evasiveness of quashee manifested itself in various ways. It was evident, first, in what appeared to have been

[54] Long gives these day-names, commonly used among the slaves, as follows:

Male	Female	Day
Cudjoe	Juba	Monday
Cubbenah	Beneba	Tuesday
Quaco	Cuba	Wednesday
Quao	Abba	Thursday
Cuffee	Phibba	Friday
Quamin	Mimba	Saturday
Quashee	Quasheba	Sunday

(Long, *op. cit.*, Bk. 3, p. 427)

[55] Cassidy, *op. cit.*, p. 157.
[56] John Stewart, *An Account of Jamaica and Its Inhabitants* (London, 1808), p. 234.
[57] *Ibid.*

a compulsion to lie. Cooper speaks of his 'low cunning and contempt of truth'.[58] The editors of the *Jamaica Journal* who, though pro-slavery, were liberal minded within the context of Jamaican slave society, wrote:

There is in the Negro character such an inherent sense of falsehood, and so ready a talent for the perversion of truth, that we fear even the dread of capital punishment would not effectually eradicate this favourite and habitual vice. We know of no mortal torture that would prevent or deter them from indulging this propensity; indeed, so strong is the predilection in some Negroes for the perversion of facts, that even where they expect reward for a 'plain unvarnished tale', they generally find more difficulty in relating the real truth, than in uttering a lie. Those who have had the longest and most frequent intercourse with Negroes are aware that theft and lying are amongst their most besetting sins: And that to discover the truth through means of Negro evidence is one of the most hopeless tasks any manager can undertake. The most clever and intelligent Negro is usually the most deceitful and we have seen some with art enough to baffle the most expert lawyer that ever put question . . .[59]

Lewis, after detecting one of his slaves lying for no apparent reason, remarked that 'I am assured that unless a Negro has an interest in telling the truth, he always lies—in order to "keep his tongue in practice" '.[60] Even Madden, an anti-slavery writer and strong sympathizer of the slave had to admit that they were pathological liars.

The evasiveness of the slave was also expressed in his peculiar mode of arguing, the essence of which seemed to have been to stray from the point as far as possible. It was this quality which was partly referred to as 'congo

[58] T. Cooper, *Facts Illustrative of the Condition of the Negro Slaves in Jamaica* (London, 1824), p. 14. According to Rev. R. Bickell (*The West Indies as They Are; or a Real Picture of Slavery* . . . [London, 1825], p. 94), 'As soon as they are born they go away and speak lies.'

[59] *Jamaica Journal & Kingston Chronicle*, Vol. 2, No. 32.

[60] Lewis, *op. cit.*, p. 129.

saw'. It could be one of the most exasperating experiences that a white person might have with a slave and one strongly suspects that its primary purpose was deliberate annoyance. Edwards has a detailed account of this trait[61] and Lewis gives several amusing instances. McNeill acidly remarked that:

> . . . a Negro, without much violence of metaphor, may be compared to a bad pump, the working of which exhausts your strength before you can produce a drop of water.[62]

Another frequently noted trait of Quashee was distrustfulness, allied to which was a strong grain of conservatism. 'They are so accustomed to be the subject of exaction', wrote Mathison, 'that every innovation, though intended for their benefit, gives rise to a suspicion that it is intended for their oppression'.[63]

Quashee was also extremely capricious, a quality noted by many writers. Beckford observed that:

> Negroes are capricious, the recurrence of everyday life will evince. Give them a house ready built, they will not inhabit it—a ground ready cleared, they will not work it— if you study their convenience, their ease, and happiness, they will be discontented—they must have everything their own way; and would sooner complain of a good overseer, than not covet an exchange by the risk of one who is bad.[64]

The laziness of quashee became proverbial and hardly needs any documentation here.[65] Quashee was, in addi-

[61] Edwards, *op. cit.*, Bk. 4, p. 100.
[62] McNeill, *op. cit.*, p. 15.
[63] G. Mathison, *Notices Respecting Jamaica, 1808–09–10* (London, 1811), p. 101.
[64] Beckford, *op. cit.*, p. 90.
[65] The classic exposition of the stereotyped view of Quashee's laziness was written several years after slavery by Thomas Carlyle in his 'An Occasional Discourse on the Nigger Question', *Fraser's*, Vol. XL (1849), pp. 667–79.

tion, extremely childlike, a quality which Lady Nugent, among others, often remarked on.[66] Quashee was also, from all reports, gay, happy-go-lucky, frivolous and cheerful. To Stewart, 'He is patient, cheerful, and commonly submissive, capable at times of grateful attachments where uniformly well treated, and kind and affectionate toward his kindred and offsprings'.[67] And Sir John Keane found it 'a most extraordinary thing' that 'they are always singing, and seem excessively delighted'.[68] But Quashee's darker traits were stressed just as often. He was revengeful, harbouring grudges for a long time; when placed in positions of authority he was likely to be extremely cruel and tyrannical; he was 'possessed of passions not only strong but ungovernable . . . a temper extremely irascible; a disposition indolent, selfish and deceitful; fond of joyous sociality; riotous mirth and extravagant show'.[69]

In addition, the contemporary accounts almost all attribute an element of stupefaction to Quashee, and an almost complete lack of judgment. Quashee somehow managed to do everything wrongly. Repeated attempts at correction were doomed to failure. Lewis, despite his fondness for his slaves, wrote toward the end of his journal that, 'Somehow or other, they never can manage to do anything quite as it should be done. If they correct themselves in one respect today, they are sure of making a blunder in some other manner tomorrow'.[70] This stupidity was often quite consciously feigned, as Madden makes clear:

> It is a difficult thing to get a Negro to understand anything which he does not wish to hear; the more you try to explain a matter that is disagreeable to him, the more incapable he appears of comprehension; or if he finds

[66] Frank Cundall, ed., *Lady Nugent's Journal* (London, 1907); see for example p. 288.

[67] Stewart, *Account of Jamaica*, pp. 234–35.

[68] House of Lords Committee on Slavery, 1832, Evidence of Sir John Keane, *House of Lords Sessional Papers*, Vols. 106–7, p. 179.

[69] McNeill, *op. cit.*, p. 28.

[70] Lewis, *op. cit.*, p. 392.

this plan ineffectual, he endeavours to render the matter ridiculous; and his talent at rendering ridicule sarcastic is really surprising.[71]

On the other hand, several penetrating observers did not fail to notice the acuteness of the slave in judging the character of those about him. Phillippo noted, for example, that, 'so far from being more deficient in acuteness and discrimination than other men, none can penetrate more deeply than the Negro into the character, or form an opinion of strangers with greater correctness and precision'.[72]

That Quashee existed there can be no doubt. The problem is to ascertain how real, how meaningful, this psychological complex was in the life of the slave. A full answer to this question would involve a digression into existential and role psychology which is outside the confines of this work.[73] We may, however, make a few tentative observations.

Quashee may be said to have existed on three levels. First, as a stereotyped conception held by the whites of their slaves; secondly, as a response on the part of the slave to this stereotype; and thirdly, as a psychological function of the real life situation of the slave. All three levels of Quashee's existence were closely related and mutually reinforced each other.

Let us begin with the third level. The real life situation of the slave, as we have shown, was one in which there was a complete breakdown of all major institutions—the family,

[71] R. R. Madden, *Twelve Months' Residence in the West Indies during the Transition from Slavery to Apprenticeship* (2 vols.; Philadelphia, London, 1835), Vol. 2, pp. 155–56.

[72] J. M. Phillippo, *Jamaica: Its Past and Present State* (London: John Snow, 1843), p. 204. Similarly it was often remarked by American slave owners that 'a Negro understands a white man better than the white man understands the Negro' (Ulric B. Phillips, *American Negro Slavery*, p. 327).

[73] For an extremely suggestive analysis of similar personality complexes as Quashee, see R. D. Laing's discussion of 'The false-self system' in Chapter 6 of his book, *The Divided Self*. See also J. P. Sartre's analysis of 'bad faith' in his *Being and Nothingness*.

marriage, religion, organized morality. This situation was made worse by the fact that the white group offered no alternate mores and institutions, but were just as disorganized socially as they were. There could be no kind of guiding principle, then, in the socialization of the slave, except that of evasion, which he learned from hard experience. The habitual laziness of the slave was also largely the function of his work situation. From early childhood he was stimulated to work, not by the expectations of reward, but entirely by the threat of punishment. Naturally, he grew to hate work and could only be industrious if forced to. The happy-go-lucky irresponsibility of the slave could also be explained in terms of his upbringing, especially with regard to males when we recall the demoralizing effect of slavery on them.

But the complexity of Quashee cannot be completely explained in situational terms. The explanation of the element of evasiveness and dissemblance, the pathological lying, must be sought elsewhere. To some extent this was to be found in the stereotype the whites had of Quashee.[74] This stereotype undoubtedly possessed what Prothro and Milikian have called a 'kernel of truth' about the real situation. But stereotypes, as the above writers pointed out, also reflect the 'characteristics of the individuals holding stereotypes or the state of politico-economic relations between groups'.[75] The same principle holds for the plantocrats of Jamaican slave society. The outright brutality and unrestrained exploitation of the system made even the most hardened plantocrat desirous of a system of rationalization. Certain aspects—usually either those which were the worst,

[74] 'Stereotyping may be defined as the tendency to attribute generalized and simplified characteristics to groups of people in the form of verbal labels and to act towards the members of these groups in terms of these labels' (W. E. Vinacke, 'Stereotyping among National-Racial Groups in Hawaii: a Study in Ethnocentricism', *Journal of Social Psychology*, Vol. 30 [1949]).

[75] Prothro and Milikian, 'Studies in Stereotype: Familiarity and the Kernel of Truth', *Journal of Social Psychology*, Vol. 41 (1955).

or the most easily patronized—of the personality traits of the slaves were therefore seized upon and elaborated into a generalized body of 'truths' about the Negro.

At this point, Merton's concept of the 'self-fulfilling prophecy' becomes useful. As he wrote: 'The systematic condemnation of the outgrouper continues largely irrespective of what he does; more, through a freakish exercise of capricious judicial logic, the victim is punished for the crime'.[76] Since masters had absolute control over their slaves, it was not difficult for them to create the conditions that would actualize the stereotypes they had of these slaves.

The self-fulfilling prophecy, however, has a further dimension which Merton failed to point out. It is the fact that the subordinate group, in addition to being forced into situations which fulfil the stereotype of the superordinate group, also responds directly to these stereotypes by either appearing to, or actually internalizing them. The slave, in fact, played upon the master's stereotype for his own ends. Playing the stereotype had three broad functions.

First, with his acute sensitivity, the slave easily saw that although the master might consciously protest at his stupidity or frivolity or whatever Quashee trait he was playing up, he was nonetheless, inwardly pleased by the slave offering further proof of his rationalizations. From the slaves' point of view, this was a direct appeal to, and exploitation of, the inevitable see-what-I-mean mentality of their masters.[77]

---

[76] R. K. Merton, *Social Theory and Social Structure*, p. 186.

[77] The American psychologist Allport identified this kind of behaviour as 'clowning'. He wrote: 'And if the master wants to be amused, the slave sometimes obligingly plays the clown . . . Richard Wright in *Black Boy* describes the coloured elevator man who wins his way by exaggerating his Negro accent, and affecting the traits ascribed to his racial group: begging, laziness, and tall tales. His passengers give him coins and make him a pet'. Allport also speaks of 'protective clowning', a perfect example of which was the 'spook' personality among Negro soldiers, of whom he writes: 'A spook can't be hurt; he can't

Secondly, by playing the stereotype, the slave both disguised his true feelings (which it was his cardinal principle never to reveal since no one, least of all the master, could be trusted)[78] and had the psychological satisfaction of duping the master. The well known Jamaican Negro proverb, 'Play fool to catch wise', well sums up this form of stereotype playing.[79]

Thirdly, if the slaves strongly resented an overseer or book-keeper and wanted to get rid of him, in the majority of cases they could achieve their objective by simply being the perfect Quashee—stupid, bungling, exasperating and completely inefficient. Long has left us a penetrating account of the overseer-slave relationship which illustrates all three types of stereotype playing:

. . . Their principal address is shown in finding out their master's temper, and playing upon it so artfully as to bend it with most convenience to their own purposes. They are not less studious in sifting their master's representative, the overseer; if he is not too cunning for them, which they soon discover after one or two experiments, they will easily find means to overreach him on every occasion, and make his indolence, his weakness, or sottishness, a sure prognostic of some comfortable term of idleness to them; but if they find him too intelligent, wary and active, they leave no expedient untried, by thwarting his plans, misunderstanding his orders, and reiterating complaints against him, to ferret him out of his post; if this will not succeed,

---

be downed; he doesn't talk back, but he can't be coerced. He will come right through doors and walls whatever you do; he has a sassy if silent invulnerability' (G. W. Allport, *The Nature of Prejudice* [Cambridge, Mass.: Addison-Wesley, 1954], p. 148).

[78] There is the problem, however, of deciding exactly what the true feelings of the slave were. This goes to the heart of the problem of deciding where the difference lies between *conscious* role playing and *natural* role playing. See Elkins' discussion in *Slavery*, pp. 131–33.

[79] See also I. Anderson and F. Cundall, *Jamaica Negro Proverbs* [1927] (Wilmington, Del.: Mellifont Press, 1970), in particular, Nos. 263–68, 536, and 544.

they perplex and worry him, especially if he is of an impatient, fretful turn, till he grows heartily sick of his charge, and voluntarily resigns it. An overseer therefore, like a prime minister, must always expect to meet with a faction, ready to oppose his administration, right or wrong; unless he will give the reins out of his hands, and suffer the mob to have things their own way; which if he complies with, they will extol him to his face, condemn him in their hearts, and very soon bring his government to disgrace.[80]

[80] Long, *op. cit.*, Bk. 4, p. 405.

3.

As a vivid contrast with slave circumstances, an English officer stationed in Surinam in the late eighteenth century here portrays the daily round of the slave-owning planter. The description is generalized (we are not even told what crops are grown on the estate), but the features of plantation life—the multiplicity of servants, the hierarchical relations between planter and overseer, the casual sadism of the daily round, and the lavish and frequent hospitality to relieve its boredom—which the author describes would fit any large plantation in the Caribbean.

In 1772 JOHN G. STEDMAN, half-Dutch, half-English, joined a relief force sent out to quell a slave rebellion in Surinam. During his years there he gradually grew more sympathetic to the slaves and the freed blacks. Like many travelers to the West Indies, Stedman was overwhelmed by the contrast between the lavish beauty of the tropics and the harshness and cruelties of the slaves' existence.

A Planter's Day*
John G. Stedman

A planter in Surinam, when he lives on his estate (which is but seldom, as they mostly prefer the society of Paramaribo [the capital]), gets out of his hammock with the rising sun, *viz.* about six o'clock in the morning, when he makes his appearance under the piazza of his house; where his coffee is ready waiting for him, which he generally takes with his pipe, instead of toast and butter; and there he is attended by half a dozen of the finest young slaves, both male and female, of the plantation, to serve him; at this *sanctum-sanctorum* he is next accosted by his overseer, who regularly every morning attends at his levee, and having made his bows at several yards distance, with the most profound respect informs his Greatness what work was done the day before; what negroes deserted, died, fell sick, recovered, were bought or born; and, above all things, which of them neglected their work, affected sickness, or had been drunk or absent, &c.; the prisoners are generally present, being secured by the negro-drivers, and instantly tied up to the beams of the piazza, or a tree, without so much as being heard in their own defence; when the flogging begins, with men, women, or children,

Narrative, of a Five Years' Expedition, Against the Revolted Negroes of Surinam, in Guiana, on the Wild Coast of South America; from the year 1772 to 1777: Elucidating the History of That Country, and Describing Its Productions, 2 vols., London, J. Johnson, 1806, pp. 56–61.

* [Editors' title]

without exception. The instruments of torture on these occasions are long hempen whips, that cut round at every lash, and crack like pistol-shot; during which they alternately repeat, "*Dankee, massera*" (Thank you, master). In the mean time he stalks up and down with his overseer, affecting not so much as to hear their cries, till they are sufficiently mangled, when they are untied, and ordered to return to their work, without so much as a dressing.

This ceremony being over, the dressy negro (a black surgeon) comes to make his report; who being dismissed with a hearty curse, for *allowing* any slaves to be sick, next makes her appearance a superannuated matron, with all the young negro children of the estate, over whom she is governess; these, being clean washed in the river, clap their hands, and cheer in chorus, when they are sent away to breakfast on a large platter of rice and plantains; and the levee ends with a low bow from the overseer, as it begun.

His worship now saunters out in his morning dress, which consists of a pair of the finest Holland trowsers, white silk stockings, and red or yellow Morocco slippers; the neck of his shirt open, and nothing over it, a loose flowing night-gown of the finest India chintz excepted. On his head is a cotton night-cap, as thin as a cobweb, and over that an enormous beaver hat, that protects his meagre visage from the sun, which is already the colour of mahogany, while his whole carcass seldom weighs above eight or ten stone, being generally exhausted by the climate and dissipation. To give a more complete idea of this fine gentleman, I . . . present him to the reader with a pipe in his mouth, which almost every where accompanies him, and receiving a glass of Madeira wine and water, from a female quaderoon slave, to refresh him during his walk.

Having loitered about his estate, or sometimes ridden on horseback to his fields, to view his increasing stores, he returns about eight o'clock, when, if he goes abroad, he dresses, but if not, remains just as he is. Should the first take place, having only exchanged his trowsers for a pair of thin linen or silk breeches, he sits down, and holding out one foot after the other, like a horse going to be shod, a negro boy puts on his stockings and shoes, which he also buckles, while another dresses his hair, his wig, or shaves his chin, and a third is fanning him to keep off the musquitoes. Having now shifted, he puts on a thin coat and waistcoat, all white; when under an umbrella, carried by a black boy, he is conducted to his barge, which is in waiting for him with six or eight oars, well provided with fruit, wine, water, and tobacco, by his overseer, who no sooner has seen him depart, than he resumes the command with all the usual insolence of office. But should this prince not mean to stir from his estate, he goes to breakfast about ten o'clock, for which a table is spread in the large hall, provided with a bacon ham, hung-beef, fowls, or pigeons broiled; plantains and sweet cassavas roasted; bread, butter, cheese, &c. with which he drinks strong beer, and a glass of Madeira, Rhenish, or Mozell wine, while the cringing overseer sits at the farther end, keeping his proper distance, both being served by the most beautiful slaves that can be selected;—and this is called breaking the poor gentleman's fast.

After this he takes a book, plays at chess or billiards, entertains himself with music, &c. till the heat of the day forces him to return into his cotton hammock to enjoy his meridian nap, which he could no more dispense with than a Spaniard with his *siesta,* and in which he rocks to and fro, like a performer on the slack-rope, till he falls asleep, without either bed or covering; and during which time he is fanned by a couple of his black attendants, to keep him cool, &c.

About three o'clock he awakes by natural instinct, when having washed and perfumed himself, he sits down to dinner, attended as at breakfast by his deputy governor and sable pages, where nothing is wanting that the world can afford in a western climate, of meat, fowls, venison, fish, vegetables, fruits, &c. and the most exquisite wines are often squandered in profusion; after this a cup of strong coffee and a liqueur finish the repast. At six o'clock he is again waited on by his overseer, attended as in the morning by negro-drivers and prisoners, when the flogging once more having continued for some time, and the necessary orders being given for the next day's work, the assembly is dismissed, and the evening spent with weak punch, sangaree, cards and tobacco.—His worship generally begins to yawn about ten or eleven o'clock, when he withdraws, and is undressed by his sooty pages. He then retires to rest, where he passes the night in the arms of one or other of his sable sultanas (for he always keeps a seraglio) till about six in the morning, when he again repairs to his piazza walk, where his pipe and coffee are waiting for him; and where, with the rising sun, he begins his round of dissipation, like a petty monarch, as capricious as he is despotic and despicable.

Such absolute power indeed cannot fail to be peculiarly delightful to a man, who, in all probability, was in his own country, Europe, a—nothing.

But, in this colony, this is too frequently the case, where plantations are sold upon credit, and left (by the absent proprietor) to the appraisers, who, by selling cheap, have generally an understanding with the buyer.

These are the planters who are the pest of the colony; such as the fine gentleman just described, who, while he lives at the above rate, pays nobody, under pretence of bad crops, mortality amongst the slaves, &c. but like an upstart rascal massacres the negroes by double labour, ruins and pillages the estate of all its productions, which he clandestinely sells for ready money, makes a purse, and runs away. Exceptions, however, take place in every circumstance of life; and I have known many planters in Surinam as good men as I ever would desire to be acquainted with . . .

As for the ladies, they indulge themselves just as much, by giving way to their unbounded passions, and especially to the most relentless barbarity. But while I can bear witness to the exalted virtues of such a woman as Mrs. Elizabeth Danforth, now Mrs. Godefrooy, and a few more whose characters shine with treble lustre, I shall draw a veil over all the imperfections, too common to their sex in this climate. Before I drop this subject, however, I must attest, that hospitality is in no country practised with greater cordiality or with less ceremony, a stranger being every where at home, and finding his table and his bed at whatever estate necessity or choice may occasion him to visit. This is the more to be regarded, as no inns are to be met with in the neighbourhood of any of the Surinam rivers.

4.

This description of the whites of Saint-Domingue, originally published in 1797, forms part of a general study of that colony by a white from another French West Indian colony. It describes and differentiates among the various European residents and the native-born whites (Creoles). This selection shows how constant association with slaves affected the white Creole personality, and it complements Patterson's similar discussion from the slave point of view.

MÉDÉRIC-LOUIS-ÉLIE MOREAU DE SAINT-MÉRY, a second-generation Creole from Martinique, was an astute observer and chronicler of every aspect of West Indian life. A lawyer and judge in the Antilles, he was active in Paris in both cultural and political affairs and occupied prominent positions, both before and after the French Revolution, as historian, *littérateur,* and administrator.

Whites in a Slave Society*
Médéric-Louis-Élie Moreau de Saint-Méry

Material in brackets was deleted by the author from the
first printed edition but restored by the compilers of the
1958 edition.

In places where men come to dwell together over a long
period of time, [some special system of association
emerges, with rules governed by local conventions. In the
absence of extraordinary or rare events, the system endures without sensible change, because the few individuals
who come to join the group and those who are born into
it adopt its usages; strictly speaking, it is just a family, more
or less numerous.] They seem almost completely amalgam-
ated, and members of the society at large all share similar
and easily identifiable traits. But in colonial establishments
recently created by successive emigrations, the signs of a
genuine ensemble are not to be seen: instead these societies are shapeless mixtures subject to diverse influences;
and this lack of cohesion is especially marked when a great
colony is made up of individuals who have come there in
search of a clime distant and wholly different from their

*Description topographique, physique, civile politique et his-
torique de la partie française de l'Isle Saint-Dominique*, 3 vols.,
pp. 29–44. Originally published in Philadelphia by the author,
1779. Republished in Paris, Société de l'Histoire des colonies
Françaises et Librairie Larose, 1958. Translated by Marquita
Riel and David Lowenthal. Copyright © 1973 Lambros Comitas
and David Lowenthal.

* [Editors' title]

own, because then each person adheres to many usages
of the country he has left behind, only slightly modified
and adapted to the country he has come into. How much
more is this the case when, in the newly adopted country
where they find themselves thrown together as by chance,
the settlers are surrounded by slaves!

In line with these facts, which give the customs of the
American colonies their particular character, I shall try to
elucidate what specifically distinguishes the French settlers
of Saint-Domingue.

Pirates accustomed to looking for their wants amid the
perils of the sea, if necessary at gun point, and Buccaneers,
terrors of the forest whose inhabitants they destroyed,
could not help but be ferocious and sanguinary in their
behavior.

Yet it was such men, descendants of many nationalities,
whom metropolitan Speculators after the French conquest
sought to tame and subordinate to their own personal interests. Absurd on the face of it, this plan could only have
succeeded through a leader of the most extraordinary
qualities. The *Compagnie des Îles de l'Amérique* found
such a leader.

In fact, no one more greatly influenced the customs of
the fearless conquerors of French Saint-Domingue than
d'Ogeron, who succeeded in transforming them into
farmers. To instil in them the essential qualities, d'Ogeron
invoked the aid of the seductive sex, who everywhere
sweeten men and render them more sociable. He sent over
to France for interesting girls, mostly timid orphans, to
tame these proud men who were used to rebellion and to
transform them into sensitive husbands and virtuous
fathers. In this way, Saint-Domingue acquired a native
population, which began to consider it (St.-D.) their own
true country.

When these first settlers began to liberate themselves
from the exploitation of the commercial companies, and
when the harassment they encountered in selling their tobacco forced them to substitute other crops for it, their
circumstances became easier. Tranquil and contented,

they saw their means of subsistence increase. Soon, well-off without being opulent, they led a life all the more enviable because they had not yet learned to regard luxuries as necessities. These colonial mores long held sway even among the soldiers, who everywhere tend to set themselves apart from other citizens. But here, any soldier could aspire to become a farmer. Except for the frequent turnover of governors and the influence of political events on their fate, the Islanders had no reason to envy the inhabitants of the mother country.

But this peaceful happiness itself became a cause of significant change. Settlers enriched through well-planned agriculture now sought other occupations for their children. They had to be sent to France to acquire an education appropriate to their future state. Those who came back to the island brought with them tastes which could not be satisfied there. Sometimes they could not give up penchants already strongly confirmed; or perhaps they were ashamed of the simple customs of their parents. Hence, their aversion toward their birthplace, a kind of lassitude in which they viewed themselves only as transients in a country where they were sometimes forced to stay for their entire lives. Hence, their unconcern for the good and prosperity of a country from which they wished to extract only the means of living far away. Hence, the high price paid for pleasures which were multiplied merely because they failed to bring satisfaction.

To this misfortune, which made most of the Colonists aliens in the land that gave them birth, still another was added. Their taste for dissipation and their extravagant spending, which made them highly visible, created an exaggerated impression of the Colony. A country whose production could maintain such unrestrained luxury had to be considered an inexhaustible mine; and the Europeans' lust for gold led them to go and seek their share of these immense treasures. That a deadly climate killed most of them deterred few, for nothing was seen but the booty brought back by those who returned.

However, the Colony seemed to satisfy much ambition,

and in 1738 it was entrusted to two administrators whose collaborative talents made it even more important. Their happiest thought was to induce the inhabitants to use the water, which ran off untapped in the vast plains, to increase the fertility of the soil. Channels in which ran a stream of gold, so to speak, were then opened up everywhere, fructifying valuable crops. Better roads were constructed, and the different parts of the Colony enabled to communicate with each other. Under Larnage and Maillart's paternalistic administration, the population doubled, because the settlers remained in the Colony and Europeans continued to be attracted to it.

But this new level of civilization, coupled with other events, also altered customs during the second colonial era.

The loss of some of our colonies during the war of 1756 aroused fears for the others, and regimental and other troops were sent out to assure the maintenance of French dominion. It was thus that Saint-Domingue received many battalions in 1762. But the defenders of the nation are not the guardians of its virtues: the mores of Saint-Domingue were proof of this. Excessive indulgence spread throughout the Colony and affected every walk of life, above all where women were concerned, and marriages ruled by gold and vanity multiplied at a scandalous rate. Thus, while external enemies caused no loss, the Colony defended itself less well against the evil example of those who saw to its safety. Since then another war, whose principal cause and seat were in America, has increased the troubles of Saint-Domingue by multiplying the troops, the sailors, and even the adventurers whom these agitated times seem to bring out, for the depravity of custom is a real source of troubles.

In the present condition of the French Colony, the white population is no more than one-quarter Creole, that is, born on the Island, and moreover, most of these are women. The remainder is made up of Europeans from different parts of France, mixed with some foreigners and Creoles from other colonies.

We will speak first of the Europeans, since they were the

founders of the Colony. From the beginning, the French there included a great many folk from Normandy, the first navigators of the Windward Islands, whose influence is still evident in many domestic customs and in many words of the Creole patois.

CONCERNING THE EUROPEANS WHO INHABIT SAINT-DOMINGUE

At the time of their landing, Europeans who come to Saint-Domingue have a rough ordeal to bear in common. When a man has left home in the hope of an envisaged fortune on the American shore, and finds himself isolated and without resources there, he would like to go back; but it is too late. Everyday needs, hard to satisfy because everything is expensive, are multiplied; the future assumes a hideous guise, the temper turns sour; the burning fever of this torrid climate comes, and death is often the end of undertakings which are as brief as they are foolish. But the Mother Country has its idlers, its daredevils, its credulous, perhaps its dangerous men, who will not be lacking in this land which devours them, and which also beckons to men of precious skills, unemployed in Europe, who come from far and wide to practice their activities and talents in which the New World glories.

When the arriving European has a retreat from which he can consider the future without worry, he must attend to the dictates of fashion. He does not require heavy fabrics, but rather light ones; he wants fine and therefore very expensive linen, whose simplicity he enhances with striking jewelry. This is the first thing he has to do with his profits or credits: spend it on proper colonial attire. Not to wear it, is to downgrade oneself or to assume the tone of a censor in a land whose rule is to listen to none.

Another concern, no less important, is to boast about one's origin in order to impress. In that way one compensates for reality, and this kind of invention is quite successfully practiced. At the least, one must keep one's origin secret when it is not a noble one, and for some envious

person who found it out in the Mother Country to reveal
the truth is indeed too much to bear. In Saint-Domingue
one slips easily into the habit of believing oneself ennobled
by the mere fact of residence on the island. In fact, some
Europeans break off family relationships, avoid every
family contact when they are back in France, and take
care to shun places where their humble backgrounds are
known. Finally, they choose an heir in the Colony, to
protect their reputation against the shame which would
spread if unrefined relatives showed up to collect the inheritance.

One of the most dangerous pitfalls for those arriving in
Saint-Domingue is the widespread passion for gambling.
This is a place where a man builds his own happiness on
the misfortune of others, where he is called generous for
knowing how to make an often desperate being contract
debts which are dignified by the sacred name of honor,
and where he forgets that he is husband, father, and
citizen.

But if one escapes this contagion, it is more difficult to
resist the lures of another passion, the germ of which nature takes pleasure in putting into every heart. One does
not find in Saint-Domingue, as in the great European cities,
the disgusting spectacle of a sex attacked by the one
which must know how to defend itself in order to em-
bellish its defeat; but neither is one protected by the public
decency which preserves morality in places where one
blushes at the depravity of large cities. Migrants are mostly
at the age when desires are ebullient; they have sometimes
just escaped the annoying supervision of their parents and,
suddenly on their own, they are exposed to the most dangerous seduction, since its source is in themselves. A proven
courage would be needed to escape such a danger, and it
is so often said in Saint-Domingue that the climate forbids
any hope of victory, that little effort is made to dispute it.
Hence, one indulges one's natural inclinations and, counting life more in terms of pleasure than of duration, one
rapidly reaches the point of self-destruction.

Gluttony is still a common vice in Saint-Domingue. Although the tempestuous abandon of old, heralding the loss of reason, has been banned from the table, one always entertains in the Creole fashion, that is, with profusion. On the other hand, as the great heat saps vitality, one believes in restoring it with highly seasoned food.

In Saint-Domingue everything takes on a character of opulence, which astounds the Europeans. The crowd of slaves who await orders or even signals from just one man give a sense of importance to whoever commands them. A wealthy man owes it to himself to have four times as many servants as he needs. Women especially are skilled at surrounding themselves with a useless coterie, taken from among their own sex. And what is hard to reconcile with the envy that these brown servants sometimes arouse in their mistresses, is the amount of care the latter take in choosing pretty ones and in dressing them elegantly: so much does pride dictate everything! A European's supreme pleasure being to be served, he will rent slaves while waiting until he can own them.

Upon arrival in Saint-Domingue, one feels remote from almost everybody there. The only possible conversation is about one's intentions to leave the place, for the general mania is to speak of returning or of going to France. Everyone repeats that he is leaving "next year," and considers himself only a transient in a land which is so often his last refuge. This unfortunate idea is so embedded that people deny themselves the small comforts that make life pleasant. The inhabitant sees himself as camping on a fortune of many millions; his residence is that of a tenant whose lease is about to expire; his luxuries, for he needs some, consist of domestic servants and of good eating, and one would think that he is living in a rooming house.

To this description of customs which can be called general, it is necessary to add one that pertains specifically to white Creoles. Numerous causes, in particular the action of the constantly burning sun, produce modifications in the inhabitants of the torrid zone which make them different from the inhabitants of the temperate zones.

CONCERNING THE WHITE CREOLES

Americans who were born in Saint-Domingue and who are called *Creole* (a name common to all those born in the colony) are usually well built and of good height. Their features are regular, but their faces lack the coloring with which nature brightens and embellishes complexions in cold climates. Their glance is expressive and even indicates a kind of pride, which can prejudice one against them at first sight.

Free of the torture of swaddling clothes, their limbs seldom show any deformity. The temperature, again favoring them, gives them an agility which fits them for all physical exercise, for which they have as much inclination as aptitude.

The rapid development of their physical capacities, the continual spectacle of rebirth enriching their country through an ever-active and fertile principle, the constant sight of the element that separates them from the rest of the Universe: everything concurs to give the Creoles active imaginations and quick minds. These favorable gifts would ensure success in any enterprise, did not this facility itself become an obstacle by producing love of variety, and if these gifts, of which nature is so generous in their childhood, did not often change into troubles for them and objects of astonishment for observers.

Various circumstances concur to deprive young Creoles of their early advantage over children of other climes: in the first place, the blind and excessive love of parents who indulge their children's desires and who believe that love precludes the least resistance. There is no fancy that is not gratified; no whim that is not excused; no fantasy that is not satisfied, but rather it is inspired; finally, no shortcoming that is not left to time to correct—time which sometimes suffices to make them incorrigible.[1]

[1] Everybody knows this anecdote imputed to a Creole child and which characterizes a large number of them.—"Mon vlé

Yet happy is the Creole child whom good health protects from an ill-fated occasion of total exposure to the over-indulgence of his parents. For if his life is threatened, if his health is precarious, he cannot escape the misfortune of becoming an object of idolatry. All the vile symptoms of his disease are, in the eyes of his parents, proof of supposed desires which they believe he lacks the strength to express. Then they improvise for him, giving vent to the most extravagant ideas; and if the constitution of the Creole child, stronger than the obstacles that a slavish devotedness sets against him, surmounts the physical ailment, the perhaps indestructible germs of a moral disease threaten the rest of his days.

Add to these disadvantages those stemming from the habit of being surrounded by slaves, and of needing only one look to have everything yielded to him. No despot has had more attentive homage nor more constant adulators than the Creole child. Each slave is subjected to the fluctuations of his temper, and his childish tantrums only too often trouble domestic tranquillity, for he can command any injustice his ungovernable will desires.

Finally, even in his games, the Creole child is reduced to being only a tyrant. Put among little slaves who are condemned to obey his slightest whim, or, what is even more revolting, to suppress all of their own, he will not tolerate the least opposition. What he sees, he wants; what is shown to him, he demands; and if one of his small playmates by ill fate resists him, he becomes angry. Everybody hastens to answer his screams, and those of the hapless child designed by color for submission soon make it known that he has been forced to yield and perhaps punished for disobedience and his lack of an instinct of servitude.

It is nevertheless in these acts of shameful despotism that the well being of some slaves often has its source; because if the Creole child shows a predilection for certain slaves, they are assured of a better lot. In the event the Creole

gnon zé.—Gnia point.—A coze ça mon vlé dé.”—“I want an egg.—There are none.—If that's the case, I want two.”

child adopts another child and they grow up together, th
latter, depending on its sex, will one day become the objec
or the minister of his master's pleasures. The influence h
then acquires will shield him, and other slaves he want
to protect, from the injustices of his master.

However, these circumstances, which could stifle all th
germs of virtue in the Creole soul, and to which shoul
be added the dangers which accompany the blessings o
wealth, would matter little if a supervised education coun
tered all these enemies of his well being. Removed fron
privilege and retaining from his early tendencies only a de
gree of energy and high spirits, which attentive and intelli
gent teachers could transform into virtues, the American
already favored in his physical constitution, would ceas
to be condemned to mediocrity.

But it is in precisely this respect that the Creole fate is
to be lamented. Consigned in France mainly to the care
of those to whom they are foreigners or to profiteers wh
often sell them inferior services at a high price, they can
not even hope to profit from the imperfect education offered by the colleges to which they are sent. Nobody stimu-
lates them, nobody encourages them. Unable to desire success for its own sake, they count in boredom the days
already spent away from home and with impatience count
those that still remain. Their parents are mentioned only
to flatter their vanity, which, instead of winning them approbation, makes them believe that they are always worthy
of it. The mention only awakens the memory of parental
indulgence, and the comparison of their past circumstances
with their present state of neglect is certainly not conducive
to inflame them with the desire to study, the rewards of
which are in the future.

In this way most Creoles, whether in the Colony or in
France, reach the age when they must make their entrance
into social life. To destroy any hope of their becoming estimable, it is enough to whet their appetites for consumption
and for pleasures of a kind that sometimes mark the soul
more deeply than any excess, and finally to constrain them
on only one point, precisely the one which it would seem

should be free: the choice of a profession. This choice is made according to pride of the father, even though he is two thousand leagues away.

Everything leads us to believe that an education, whose first concern should be to understand the young Creoles and their inclinations, would foster the aptitudes they exhibit in their early childhood, but which are progressively lost under a system whose sad uniformity is everywhere apparent. Indeed, some Creoles have fulfilled the expectations they aroused, because they have found a profound interest that becomes a vehicle and a reward for the one who knew how to inspire it. There are even some who have overcome the obstacles surrounding them. Why, in a country where exotic growths excite so much interest and care, is there only indifference toward those transplanted there that have already proved the effects of a beneficial climate, whose fruits would so well reward the labor of any industrious and respectable cultivator!

It is because these facts were overlooked, that the Americans have been reproached with being good at nothing. To begin with, the point they started from should have been noted, that is, that in order to learn Sciences and Letters, and consequently to love them, they had to expatriate themselves. It would then have been realized that this requirement in itself placed Creoles in circumstances whose disadvantages of which could not be compensated by the influence of their climate, which critics have preferred to view as promoting their physical aptitudes at the expense of their mental. Hence, some learned absurdities which enrich *Recherches sur les Américains,* and which the American genius, Franklin, has forever confounded [for the sole reason that he was born in America].

The Creole who has never left Saint-Domingue, where he cannot receive any education, and the Creole who comes back to his native land, after his education has been neglected in France, are thenceforward totally under the sway of this active and ebullient imagination with which, as I have said, they are endowed by under a burning sun, following the dangerous indulgence of their parents and the ease with which their wishes became laws for their slaves. What dangers for a time of life when the passions compete for a heart predisposed to feel acutely both their impact and their turmoil!

It is then that the Creole, losing sight of everything that is not apt to satisfy his passions and disregarding everything that does not bear the mark of pleasure, abandons himself to the whirlwind that is about to carry him off. Deliriously infatuated with dancing, music [parties, and everything that beguiles and feeds his desires], he seems to exist only for voluptuous pleasures.

How difficult it is for such inclinations not to become disastrous in a place where it is so uncustomary to control them! How is it possible to curb a passionate temperament where the only preoccupation of a large number of women, the offspring of white men and female slaves, is to avenge themselves with the weapons of love for being condemned to degradation? Thus, passions exert all their power in the hearts of most Creoles, and when at last [the ills they have begotten or] the feebleness of old age arrives, it does not always extinguish desire, the cruelest of all passions.

It can truly be said that everything concurs to mold the well-known impetuous, lively, and fickle Creole temper, rendering them so unfit for marriage, in which happiness can only be fashioned by mutual constancy. Made jealous by their vanity, they are tormented by the fear of unfaithfulness, of which they themselves are the prime examples. Yet, happy is the betrayed wife who, while suffering the insult of being under suspicion, is not sometimes condemned to endure before her very eyes the rival who robs her of the tokens of love solemnly avowed her.

The faults of the Creole, among which must be included a passion for gambling, are nevertheless redeemed by a host of estimable qualities. Sincere, affable, generous to the point of ostentation, confident, courageous, reliable friends and good fathers, they are exempt from the crimes which degrade humanity: the annals of a colony as large as Saint-Domingue provide scarcely any Creole names to inscribe on the list of criminals. How easy it would be to make the inhabitants of this prosperous Colony as meritorious as any now cited as inimitable models.

One of the principal virtues of the Creole is hospitality. What I have said of their longing to go to France should suffice to prove that there is little social life in Saint-Domingue, and that this transient disposition is certainly not conducive to making it pleasant. This is reason enough to welcome, on the estates, travelers who can vary the usual monotony. In a vast land of great wealth, where there are no posthouses, where a small number of inns cater only to those without relations in the Colony, hospitality takes on the quality of generosity, which does honor to those who practice it. Some planters devote more than 30,000 livres to horses, carriages, and coachmen for the convenience of those who need to go from place to place in the Colony. But why not deceive oneself? It would greatly embarrass the Europeans to reveal the lengths to which the planters exert themselves, the difficulties they incur on their behalf. Despite this unhappy experience, a man acknowledged as the friend of one lone planter can still undertake a tour of the Colony, and if his personal qualities make him likable, he is certain to take away regrets from all the places where successive introductions would have made him welcome.

The Creole character is also visible in the way they travel. Little horses of mediocre appearance are made to carry sedan chairs or *cabriolets* at speeds of three or even four leagues an hour. This rate of speed underscores the Creole habit of demanding [energetically] and of being obeyed promptly. The coachman who knows his master's nature [incessantly spurs on his steeds], shares his impatience, and takes pride in not being outdistanced. Horses are still an article of luxury for the planter; so much so that on the least pretext a messenger on horseback is dispatched who, by the rapidity of his progress and the screams with which he urges on his sweat-covered mount, could be taken for a courier bearing news of an event of interest to the whole Colony.

The Creoles of Saint-Domingue are less subject than the

Europeans to the diseases of their climate. But a premature
adolescence, the abuse of pleasures, perhaps this infection,
whose origin is by now the only thing about which America
and Europe might disagree, often enough suffice to destroy
the most robust constitution. Thus the moment is sped when
the Creole needs to make use of the indifference with which
he envisages the cessation of life, owing to the frequent
sight of death [in a land it decimates].

But let us leave this dismal picture, to sketch the character of the most affecting portion of the human species.

CONCERNING WHITE CREOLE WOMEN

To delicacy of features, the Creole women of Saint-
Domingue add the trim figure and elegant bearing that seem
to be the attributes of women in warm countries. Seldom
endowed with the harmony and strict regularity which essentially constitute beauty, their faces almost always tender
a combination, more seductive and more difficult to describe, which is called character; and if beautiful women
can readily be found in Greece and Georgia, Saint-
Domingue supplies pretty ones.

The great lively eyes of Creole women display a happy
contrast of a soft languor and a lively vivacity. Did not
the harsh climate make their fresh complexion so fleeting,
it would be hard to resist a look in which tenderness and
a kind of gaiety mix without blending. Capable of using
with exquisite taste the subtle resources that dress can offer,
without any artificial counterfeits, Creoles helped by these
[fresh] charms, know how to keep the ascendency nature
has given them.

Clad as lightly as the climate demands, they appear even
more free in all their movements and most apt to awaken
the thought of sensual delight, all the more seductive owing
to the languid character of all their action.

The state of idleness in which Creole women are reared,
the almost constant heat they suffer, the pampering to which
they are perpetually subjected, the effects of an active imagination and a precocious development; all produce an ex-

treme sensitivity in their nervous system. From this sensitivity itself stems their indolence, allied with vivacity, in a temperament at bottom somewhat melancholy.

However, any single desire suffices to reinspire them with energy. Used to making imperious demands, they are angered by obstacles; and as soon as these disappear, their listlessness reappears. Without seeking to emulate the desirable skills it would be so easy for them to acquire, they nevertheless covet them spitefully as soon as anyone else possesses them. But what distresses them most, is the preference one of them can gain over the others through the charms of appearance. It is even easy to suspect this antipathy, born of secret rivalry, when one notices how seldom Creole women seek to be together, although they pour out caresses whenever they meet by chance.

Creole women carry to excess their love for their children. It is they especially who inspire them with the most peculiar fancies. I have said enough about how their blindness is fatal to these children toward whom they start behaving like [real] mothers only when they agree to send them to France, in the hope that they will receive there a liberal education. They are also [very] fond of their parents, and lavish on them the most sweetest marks of affection.

Love, this need or rather this tyrant of sensitive souls, reigns over those of Creole women. Lovable because of their own sensitivity and their natural charms, without deception or artifice, they follow their inclination which, to perfect the happiness of those who are its object, should perhaps depend more on sense.

It must however be added that if love sometimes leads Creole women astray, their enduring attachment to their guilty choice would redeem their fault were it not a permanent offense to decency.

Happy is the Creole women for whom marriage oaths have been vows of love! Cherishing her husband as a lover, her faithfulness, more commonly the fruit of her listless prudence than of virtue, which implies battles and a victory, will ensure their joint tranquillity. But if the husband has no other rights than those of duty, let him dread, while despotically exercising these rights, to disregard those of his consort; his example could be followed.

It follows from their loving disposition, that the loss of the man to whom they were tied leads almost immediately to a new engagement. Hence, we can apply to them what M. Thibault de Chanvallon has said about Creole women of another colony: "There is no widow who, despite her affection for her children, does not soon erase by a new marriage the name and memory of the man whom she seemed to love so desperately." Perhaps there is no other country where second marriages are as common as in Saint-Domingue, and women are to be seen there who have had seven husbands.

The Creole woman's attachment is mixed with jealousy, and in spite of her indifference toward a husband who is hers by convention alone, she cannot forgive his unfaithfulness. She becomes furiously angry at everything she can possibly suspect. Jealousy [which afflicts the Universe] has killed Creole women who could not bear inconstancy in the men they doted upon. They are even capable of preferring the death of the beloved to his love; so much does this detestable passion distort everything, even the very sentiment from which it springs!

Frenetic dancing is so attractive to Creole women that they surrender to it entirely, despite the heat and their weak constitutions. This exercise seems to brighten their existence, and they know only too well what new charms it adds to an expressive face and to a graceful figure, so that they seek it ardently. It makes them forget the languidness they seem to cherish. They can even be heard beating time with strict precision, but without stiffness. Finally, such is the state of trance into which dancing throws them that a foreign spectator would think that this pleasure utterly dominates their souls. Moreover, in seeing at a ball that the departure of a few women becomes a signal for the others to stop dancing, one could imagine that, forming only a single family, they enjoy this entertainment only to the exten-

they all share it. How lamentable that this impulse of apparent affection requires a new ball to reappear!

Creole women love to sing. Their soft voices are admirably suited to light and tender tunes; but the sentimental ballad pleases them most. Its plaintive tones seem made to encourage their languid disposition and they accentuate them with a sincerity that seduces the heart after having charmed the ear.

Solitude is very pleasing to Creole women, who willingly live alone, even in the middle of the city. It gives them an expression of timidity which does not leave them when in company, where they exhibit few charms, unless they have learned in France to appreciate an amiability which they know how to render affecting.

Creole women are very temperate. Chocolate, candies, especially coffee with milk: that is their nourishment. But a taste that seems stronger than their will still induces them to refuse healthy foods and to prefer salted meat imported from Europe, together with the local dishes, prepared in a bizarre fashion and known by even more bizarre names. Fresh water is their usual beverage, but they sometimes prefer a lemonade made of sugar syrup and lemon juice. Creole women eat hardly at all during meals, but indiscriminately whenever they feel like it, giving way to the most depraved appetites.

Protracted sleep, the inactivity in which they live, all manner of lapses from the regular regime, ill-chosen food, intense passions almost always in play; such are the sources of the evils that menace Creole women, and the reasons their charms wither so quickly. Radiant like flowers, they also last only as long.

Another cause of the rapidity with which Creole women lose both their power to please and their health is the pernicious custom of marrying them before nature has completed their growth. Mothers before they have become mature women, they give life only by shortening their own. Generally fertile, sustaining pregnancy without disease and childbirth without accident, they deceive themselves about

these advantages which are due solely to the weaknesses
of their organs.

I can almost visualize the astonishment of learning that
in a country where maternal love is an exalted virtue, in-
fants suckle at a strange breast. It is only too true that if
there are few Creole women who attempt to feed their children, very few succeed in fulfilling this duty. Weak by constitution and because the age of motherhood has been hastened, weak because they destroy their stomachs and
because the climate and perhaps hereditary defects have
made their nervous systems very sensitive, Creole women
are reduced to soliciting from their slaves the sacrifice of
their offspring to keep alive the child to whom they [Creole
women] could only give life. But their children are breast-
fed under their supervision, they contend for caresses from
the wet nurse who is almost always freed as a payment for
her good offices; at length the mothers compensate through
their care and their solicitude for their incapacity to supply
a need whose neglect is often mercilessly punished in other
climates.

Creole women receive no education in Saint-Domingue,
and when they are judged in the light of this observation,
it is surprising to find they have such good sense. Their
native intelligence, free of prejudices, stamps them with
strength of character which, if it helps lead them astray in
whatever irrational thing they desire, lends their well-guided
resolves a steadfastness some peevish traducers had maintained their sex was incapable of.

One can with assurance ask Creole women for advice,
as long as it concerns feelings or scruples. Endowed with
a tact often better than our principles, they naturally incline towards what is best. Proud, shocked by anything de
basing, despising, even more than men, degraded men, the
Creole woman feels keenly insults toward one she loves.
He must renounce her affection if he is able to swallow
an insult; she will never listen to the sighs of a coward
and would rather weep on his grave.

It is unfortunately only too easy to prove to them tha
one is worthy of them in this respect. The best evidence

of the dearth of social intercourse in Saint-Domingue is the false sense of honor that still dominates opinion there. In a land where luck raises up so many rivals, it is difficult to assume the polite façades which are perhaps the first protections of personal safety. The habit of giving orders to slaves and of finding nothing but submission necessarily makes for rather haughty tempers, and as defenders of their own homes Colonists seem to be dominated by a prejudice as old as the Colony; it gives even magistrates the appearance of warriors.

Creole women are also naturally affable, generous, compassionate toward everything that is marked by misfortune and sorrow, but they sometimes forget these virtues when it comes to their domestic slaves.

Who would not be revolted at the sight of a refined woman, whom the recital of a lesser misfortune than the one she is about to inflict would cause to shed tears, presiding over the punishment she has ordered! Nothing equals the anger of a Creole woman punishing the slave whom her husband has perhaps forced to sully the conjugal bed. In her jealous fury she knows only how to devise means to satisfy her vengeance.

These horrible scenes which are very rare are becoming still more so from day to day. Maybe even Creole women will in time cast off their inclination toward harsh domination, to which they became habituated in early childhood. Making it a point to bring up and educate many of them in France, the influence of books which praise domestic virtues and which they read with emotion will doubtless bring about this happy revolution. Already Creole women are finding pleasure in easing the lot of slaves near them; already they are lavishing on all their slaves' children attentions that they formerly disdained. There is more than one respectable Creole woman whose first concern upon arising is to go and visit the infirmary on her property, and to see that the ailments of the Negroes are allayed and their pains soothed. Sometimes their dainty hands even prepare medications while consolations flow from their persuasive lips.

Charming sex! Such is your legacy: sweetness and kind-

ness. Nature molded you to temper man's pride, to capti-
vate him, to make pleasant for him the dream of life. Do
not disdain to reign by the means nature has given you. The
founder of a religion, while painting in strokes of fire a
place of eternal delight, felt that to arouse enthusiasm, you
should be depicted in this sweet and lovely abode, and he
has captivated us with this truly enchanting scene!

I do not claim, in this picture of the character of the
Whites of Saint-Domingue, to have put in every characteristic, but only to suggest the main principles on which it
is based. In the remainder of *Description de la partie française* there will be given more than one circumstance bearing on customs and characters of the inhabitants of Saint-
Domingue, more than one remarkable exception, more than
one subject of praise or blame, and the attentive Reader
will not always need to have them pointed out, to be struck
by them. He must already realize that in a Colony, where
each man with his own vices and virtues directs his steps
toward the temple of fortune according to his views, his
needs, and the circumstances, there must be palpable differences, even absolute unlikenesses [although one single ambition here brings together individuals from all over the
world].

5.

Free colored West Indians, seen here through the eyes of an eighteenth-century Jamaican white, led lives of continual aggravation, remote in status from both white and slave. This account, written in 1774, is extracted from a classic study of Jamaica. The free-colored inhabitants are viewed in terms of the problems they posed for the whites, who were at the same time their progenitors, rivals, and lovers. Conceiving these associations dangerous to white purity and mastery, the author fulminates against local practices concerning half-breeds.

A Jamaican resident for twelve years, EDWARD LONG served as judge in the local vice-admiralty court, but ill-health forced him to leave the island before his book was published. Despite its racial bias, this account provides a clear picture of social and economic conditions in the island.

Freed Blacks and Mulattos
Edward Long

(handwritten annotations: "① Manumitted — couldn't vote")

There were three classes of freed persons here. The lowest comprehended those who were released from slavery by their owner's manumission, either by will or an instrument sealed and delivered, and registered either in the toll-book or the secretary's office. They were allowed no other mode of trial, than the common slaves, that is, "by two justices and three freeholders"; for they were not supposed to have acquired any sense of morality by the mere act of manumission; so likewise they were not admitted evidences against white or other free-born persons, in the courts of justice, nor to vote at parochial nor general elections.

The second class consisted of such as were free-born. These were allowed a trial by jury, and might give evidence in controversies at law with one another, and in criminal cases; but only in civil cases against white persons, or against freed-persons, particularly endowed with superior privileges.

The third contained such as, by *private acts* of assembly, became entitled to the same rights and privileges with other English subjects born of white parents, except that they might not be of the council nor assembly; nor judges in any of the courts, nor in the public offices, nor jurymen.

History of Jamaica, or, General Survey of the Ancient and Modern State of That Island, 3 vols., pp. 320–36. Originally published in London by T. Lowndes, 1774; available as Cass Library of West Indian Studies No. 12, London, Frank Cass, 1970.

Some of them are likewise precluded from voting at elections of assembly-members. There are not any considerable numbers who have enjoyed the privileges annexed to this latter class; they have chiefly been granted to such, who were inheritors of large estates in the island, bequeathed to them by their white ancestor.

The freedom of the two former classes was much enlarged in 1748, when a law passed, allowing the manumitted, as well as free-born, to give evidence against any freed-persons enjoying the liberty of white subjects, provided, in respect to the manumitted, they have received their freedom six months at least antecedent to the time of their offering such evidence; and if they should be convicted of wilful and corrupt perjury, they are made liable to the same punishment, as the laws of England inflict on this offence.

Thus it appears, that they hold a limited freedom, similar to that of the Jews; and it has been often suggested by very sensible men, that it is too circumscribed, more especially in reference to those who have large patrimonies in the island; who, without any probable ill consequence, might be permitted to have a vote in the vestry, and at the election of members to serve in the assembly; to write as clerks in some of the offices; and hold military commissions in the Black and Mulatto companies of militia; which privileges I will not dispute: but, for many reasons, it were better to confer them on particular or select persons, of good education and morality, than to extend them by a general law to many, who, it must be confessed, are not fitly qualified for this enlargement.

The descendants of the Negroe blood, entitled to all the rights and liberties of white subjects, in the full extent, are such, who are above three steps removed in the lineal digression from the Negroe *venter* exclusive; that is to say, real *quinterons,* for all below this degree are reputed by law *Mulattos.*

The law requires likewise, in all these cases, the sacrament of baptism, before they can be admitted to these privileges. Some few other restrictions are laid on the first and second class. No one of them, except he possesses a settlement with ten slaves upon it, may keep any horses, mares, mules, asses, and neat cattle, on penalty of forfeiture. This was calculated to put a stop to the practice of slaughtering the old breed on commons, and putting their own marks upon the young.

But two justices may license any such freed-person to keep such stock, during good behaviour.

They who have not a settlement, as just mentioned, must furnish themselves with certificates of their freedom, under the hand and seal of a justice, and wear a blue cross on the right shoulder, on pain of imprisonment.

If convicted of concealing, enticing, entertaining, or sending off the island, any fugitive, rebellious, or other slave, they are to forfeit their freedom, be sold, and banished.

These are the principal ordinances of the laws affecting the common freed-persons; whence the policy of the country may be easily measured. The restraints, so far as they are laid upon the lowest order just emerged from servitude, and who have no property of any consequence, seem very justifiable and proper; but in respect to the few who have received a moral and Christian education, and who inherit fortunes considerable enough to make them independent, they may be thought capable of some relaxation, without any prejudice to the general welfare of the colony; for it deserves serious reflection, that most of the superior order (for these reasons) prefer living in England, where they are respected, at least for their fortunes; and know that their children can enjoy *of right* all those privileges, which in Jamaica are withheld from their possession.

The slaves that most commonly gain a manumission here from their owners, are

1. Domesticks, in reward for a long and faithful course of service.

2. Those, who have been permitted to work for themselves, only paying a certain weekly or monthly sum; many of them find means to save sufficient from their earnings, to purchase their freedom.

3. Those who have effected some essential service to the public, such as revealing a conspiracy, or fighting valiantly against rebels and invaders. They have likewise generally been requited with an annuity, from the public treasury, for life.

Some regulation seems expedient, to give the first mentioned the means of acquiring their freedom, without the temptation of converting it into licentiousness.

In Antigua, every white person who bestows this boon upon his slave, accompanies it with some further grant, enabling him to enjoy his new station with advantage to himself and the community. The law there compels all these freed-men, who have not lands wherewith to form a settlement, to enter themselves into the service of some family. In Jamaica, where land is a cheap commodity, this is not the case. The Negroe receives his manumission, but not always a provision for his future subsistence; this defect therefore impels many of them to thefts and other illegal practices, for a maintenance. A liberty of this species is baneful to society; and it seems to be the proper object of legislature, to make these acts of private bounty subservient to, instead of leaving them subversive of, the publick good.

From five to ten acres of ground might very well be spared upon any planter's estate. Five acres of good soil are abundantly sufficient for one such freed Negroe. It may be said, that such a condition, tacked to these grants, would hinder men from rewarding their faithful slaves with liberty; but, on the other hand, in a publick view, it is better that the Negroe should continue an honest and industrious slave, than to be turned into an idle and profligate freeman. All however that is here meant is, that, in imitation of the Antigua law, all those freed-men, who have neither lands to cultivate, nor trade to follow, should be obliged to enroll themselves in some white family, as domesticks; a list should annually be taken, and registered, of all the classes, and their occupations annexed to their names.

I come now to speak of the Mulattoes and other casts, who (in common parlance) all pass under that appellation.

Upon enquiry of the assembly, in the year 1762, into the devises made by last wills to Mulatto children, the amount in reality and personalty was found in value between two and three hundred thousand pound. They included four sugar estates, seven penns, thirteen houses besides other lands unspecified. After duly weighing the ill consequences that might befall the colony, by suffering real estates to pass into such hands, a bill was passed, "to prevent the inconveniences arising from exorbitant grants and devises made by white persons to Negroes and the issue of Negroes, and to restrain and limit such grants and devises"; this bill enacted, that a devise from a white person, to a Negroe or Mulatto, of real and personal estate, exceeding in value 2000 *l.* currency, should be void. It has been objected by many, and with great warmth, to this law, "that it is oppressive in its effect, tending to deprive men of their right to dispose of their own effects and acquisitions, in the manner most agreeable to their inclinations". It may not be improper, therefore, to examine a little into the fair state of the question. That it is repugnant to the spirit of the English laws, is readily granted, and so is *Negroe slavery*: the question therefore arising from this comparison will be, Is there or not a local necessity for laying many restraints in this colony, where slave-holding is legally established, which restraints do not exist, nor are politically expedient, in England, where slavery is not tolerated? It is a first principle, and not to be controverted, in political and civil as well as in moral government, that if one person does any act, which if every other or even many others of the same society were to do, must be attended with injurious consequences to that society, such an act cannot in the nature of things be legal nor warrantable. All societies of men, wherever constituted, can subsist together only by certain obligations and restrictions, to which all the individual members must necessarily yield obedience for the general good; or they can have no just claim to those rights, and that protection, which are held by all, under this common sanction.

In countries where rational freedom is most enjoyed, as

in England, the laws have affixed certain bounds to men's passions and inclinations, in numberless examples; so a succession to estates there is regulated more according to the rules of policy, and the good of the community, than to the *law of nature,* simply considered; therefore, although a man may be desirous, nay, thinks he has a natural right, to determine who shall enjoy that property from time to time after his death, which he acquired by his industry while living, the law of England, abhorring perpetuities as hurtful to the society, defeats this purpose, and readily gives its assistance to bar such entails.

The right of making devises by will was established in some countries much later than in others. In England, till modern times, a man could only dispose of one third of his moveables from his wife and legitimate children; and, in general, no will was permitted of lands till the reign of Henry the Eighth, and then only a certain portion; for it was not till after the Restoration, that the power of devising real property became so universal as at present. The antient law of the Athenians directed that the state of the deceased should always descend to his legitimate children; or, on failure of such lineal descendants, should go to the collateral relations. In many other parts of Greece they were totally discountenanced. In Rome they were unknown till the laws of the twelve tables were compiled, which first gave the right of bequeathing; and among the Northern nations, particularly the Germans, testaments were not received into use. By the common law of England, since the conquest, no estate, greater than for term of years, can be disposed of by testament, except only in Kent and in some antient burghs, and a few particular manors, where their Saxon immunities by particular indulgence subsisted. And though the feudal restraint on alienations by deed vanished very early, yet this on wills continued for some centuries after, from an apprehension of infirmity and imposition on the testator *in extremis*; which made such devises suspicious. Every distinct country has different ceremonies and requisites to make a will compleatly valid; and this variety may serve to evince, that the right of making wills and disposing of property after death is merely a creature of the civil or municipal laws, which have permitted it in some countries, and denied it in others; and even where it is permitted by law, it is subjected to different restrictions, in almost every nation under Heaven. In England, particularly, this diversity is carried to such a length, as if it had been meant to point out the power of the laws in regulating the succession to property; and how futile every claim must be, that has not its foundation in the positive rules of the state.[1] In the same kingdom, the institution of marriage is regarded as one of the main links of society, because it is found to be the best support of it. A promiscuous intercourse and an uncertain parentage, if they were universal, would soon dissolve the frame of the constitution, from the infinity of claims and contested rights of succession: for this reason, the begetting an illegitimate child is reputed a violation of the social compacts, and the transgressors are punishable with corporal correction.[2] The civil codes were so rigorous, that they even made bastards incapable, in some cases, of a gift from their parents. The detestation in which they have been held by the English laws is very apparent, and may be inferred from the spirit of their several maxims: as, "Hæres *legitimus* est quem *nuptiæ* demonstrant &c."[3] "*Cui pater est populus,* non habet ille patrem."[4] "Qui ex *damnato* coitu nascuntur, inter liberos non computentur." So they are likewise styled "*filii nullius,*"[5] because their real father is supposed to be uncertain, or unknown. The lenity however of the English law at present, is satisfied only with excluding them from inheritance, and with exacting a competent provision for their maintenance, that they may not become chargeable upon the publick.

[1] Blackstone.
[2] 18 Eliz. 7 Jac. 1.
[3] A legitimate child is he that is born after wedlock.
[4] The offspring of promiscuous conjunctions has no father. Marriage ascertains the father.
[5] Bastards are not endowed with the privilege of children. No man's children.

The institution of marriage, is doubtless of as much concern in the colony, as it is in the mother country: perhaps more so; because a life of celibacy is not equally hurtful in the latter, who may draw recruits to keep up her population, from the neighbouring states of Europe. But the civil policy of the two countries, in respect to successions to property, differ very materially; so that, if three fourths of the nation were slaves, there can be no question but that the law of last wills would be modified to a different frame, perhaps carried back again to the antient feudal doctrine of non-alienation, without consent of the lord; which restraint was suited to the policy of those times, when villeinage prevailed. A man's right of devising his property by will ought justly, therefore, from the constitution of our West India colonies, to be more circumscribed in them, than is fitting in the mother state. A subject (for example) in Jamaica ought not to bequeath his whole personal estate, which may be very considerable, to a slave; and, if he should do so, it is easy to conceive that it would be utterly repugnant to the civil policy of that island. The Jamaica law permits the putative father to leave, what will be thought, a very ample provision, in order to set his bastard forward in the world; and in all cases where the father, having no legitimate kin to whom he may be willing to give his property, where that property is large, and his illegitimate child may be, by the polish of a good education, and moral principles, found well deserving to possess it; there can be no question, but he might be made legitimate and capable of inheriting, by the power of an act of assembly; since the same thing has been done in similar cases in England, by act of the parliament. It is plain, therefore, the policy of the law only tends to obviate the detriment resulting to the society, from foolish, and indiscriminate devises; leaving in the breast of the legislature to ratify others particularly circumstanced, and which might not be so likely to produce the same inconveniences. It is a question easily answered, whether (supposing all natural impediments of climate out of the way) it would be more for the interest of Britain, that Jamaica should be possessed

and peopled by white inhabitants, or by Negroes and
Mulattos? — Let any man turn his eyes to the Spanish
American dominions, and behold what a vicious, brutal,
and degenerate breed of mongrels has been there produced,
between Spaniards, Blacks, Indians, and their mixed progeny; and he must be of opinion, that it might be
much better for Britain, and Jamaica too, if the white men
in that colony would abate of their infatuated attachments
to black women, and, instead of being "grac'd with a
yellow offspring not their own,"[6] perform the duty incumbent on every good cittizen, by raising in honourable wedlock a race of unadulterated beings. The trite pretence of
most men here, for not entering into that state, is "the
heavy and intolerable expences it will bring upon them."
This, in plain English, is nothing more than expressing their
opinion, that society shall do every thing for them, and
that they ought to do nothing for society; and the folly of
the means they pursue to attain this selfish, ungrateful purpose, is well exposed, by the profusion and misery into
which their disorderly connexions often insensibly plunge
them. Can we possibly admit any force in their excuse,
when we observe them lavishing their fortune with unbounded liberality upon a common prostitute? when we see
one of these votaries of celibacy grow the abject, passive
slave to all her insults, thefts, and infidelities; and disperse
his estate between her and her brats, whom he blindly
acknowledges for his children, when in truth they are entitled to claim twenty other fathers? It is true, the issue of a
marriage may sometimes lie under suspicion, through the
loose carriage of the mother; but on which side does the
weight of probability rest, on the virtue of a wife, or
the continence of a prostitute?

Very indigent men may indeed, with more colour of
propriety, urge such an argument in their defence; but the
owner of a large fortune possesses what is a visible demon-
stration, to prove the fallacy of his pretence. Such a man is
doubtless as able to maintain a wife, as a mistress of all the

6 Pitt's Virgil's *Aeniad*, vi, 293.

vices reigning here; none are so flagrant as this of concubinage with white women, or cohabiting with Negresses
and Mulattas, free or slaves. In consequence of this practice we have not only more spinsters in comparison to the
number of women among the natives (whose brothers
or male relations possess the greatest part of their father's
patrimony) in this small community, than in most other
parts of his majesty's dominions, proportionably inhabited;
but also, a vast addition of spurious offsprings of different
complexions: in a place where, by custom, so little restraint is laid on the passions, the Europeans, who at home
have always been used to greater purity and strictness of
manners, are too easily led aside to give a loose to every
kind of sensual delight: on this account some black or
yellow *quasheba* is sought for, by whom a tawney breed
is produced. Many are the men, of every rank, quality,
and degree here, who would much rather riot in these
goatish embraces, than share the pure and lawful bliss derived from matrimonial, mutual love. Modesty, in this respect, has but very little footing here. He who should presume to shew any displeasure against such a thing as simple
fornication, would for his pains be accounted a simple
blockhead; since not one in twenty can be persuaded, that
there is either sin or shame in cohabiting with his slave.
Of these men, by far the greatest part never marry after
they have acquired a fortune; but usher into the world a
tarnished train of beings, among whom, at their decease,
they generally divide their substance. It is not a little curious, to consider the strange manner in which some of them
are educated. Instead of being taught any mechanic art,
whereby they might become useful to the island, and enabled to support themselves, young *Fuscus,* in whom the
father fondly imagines he sees the reflected dawn of paternal genius, and Miss *Fulvia,* who mamma protests has a
most delicate ear for music and French, are both of them
sent early to England, to cultivate and improve the valuable talents which nature is supposed to have so wantonly
bestowed, and the parents, blind with folly, think they have
discovered. To accomplish this end, no expence nor pains

are spared; the indulgent father, big with expectation of the future *eclat* of his hopeful progeny,

> . . . disdains
> The vulgar tutor, and the rustic school,
> To which the dull cit' sends his low-born fool.
> By our wise sire to London are they brought,
> To learn those arts that high-bred youths are taught;
> Attended, drest, and train'd, with cost and care,
> Just like some wealthy duke's apparent-heir.

Master is sent to Westminster, or Eaton, to be instructed in the elements of learning, among students of the first rank that wealth and family can give: whilst Miss is placed at Chelsea, or some other famed seminary; where she learns music, dancing, French, and the whole circle of female *bon ton*, proper for the accomplishment of fine women. After much time and money bestowed on their education, and great encomiums, year after year, transmitted (by those whose interest it is to make them) on their very uncommon genius and proficiency, at length they return to visit their relations. From this period, much of their future misery may be dated. Miss faints at the sight of her relations, especially when papa tells her that black *Quasheba* is her own mother. The young gentleman too, after his introduction, begins to discover that the knowledge he has gained has only contributed to make him more susceptible of keen reflections, arising from his unfortunate birth. He is soon, perhaps, left to herd among his black kindred, and converse with *Quashee* and *Mingo,* instead of his school-fellows, *Sir George,* or *My Lord*; while mademoiselle, instead of modish French, must learn to prattle gibberish with her cousins *Mimba* and *Chloe*: for, however well this yellow brood may be received in England, yet here so great is the distinction kept up between white and mixed complexions, that very seldom are they seen together in a familiar way, though every advantage of dress or fortune should centre with the latter. Under this distinction, it is impossible but that a well-educated Mulatta must lead a very unpleasant kind of a life here; and justly may apply to her reputed father what Iphicrates said of his, "After all your pains, you have made me no better than a slave; on the other hand, my mother did everything in her power to render me free." On first arriving here, a civilized European may be apt to think it impudent and shameful, that even bachelors should publickly avow their keeping Negroe or Mulatto mistresses; but they are still more shocked at seeing a group of white legitimate, and Mulatto illegitimate, children, all claimed by the same married father, and all bred up together under the same roof.[7] Habit, however, and the prevailing fashion, reconcile such scenes, and lessen the abhorrence excited by their first impression.

To allure men from these illicit connexions, we ought to remove the principal obstacles which deter them from marriage. This will be chiefly effected by rendering women of their own complexion more agreeable companions, more frugal, trusty, and faithful friends, than can be met with among the African ladies. Of some probable measures to effect this desireable purpose, and make the fair natives of this island more amiable in the eyes of the men, and

[7] Reason requires, that the master's power should not extend to what does not appertain to his service. Slavery should be calculated for utility, not for pleasure. The laws of chastity arise from those of nature, and ought in all nations to be respected. If a law, which preserves the chastity of slaves, be good in those states where an arbitrary power bears down all before it, how much more so will it be in monarchies! and how much more still in republics! The law of the Lombards has a regulation which ought to be adopted by all governments. "If a master debauches his slave's wife, the slave and his wife shall be free"; an admirable expedient, which, without severity, lays a powerful restraint on the incontinency of masters. The Romans erred on this head: they allowed an unlimited scope to the master's lust; and, in some measure, denied their slaves the privilege of marrying. It is true, they were the lowest part of the nation; yet there should have been some care taken of their morals, especially as, in prohibiting their marriage, they corrupted the morals of the citizens.

So thinks the inimitable Montesquieu. And how applicable these sentiments are to the state of things in our island, I leave to the dispassionate judgement of every man there, whether married or single.

more eligible partners in the nuptial state, I have already ventured my sentiments. A proper education is the first great point. A modest demeanour, a mind divested of false pride, a very moderate zeal for expensive pleasures, a skill in economy, and a conduct which indicates plain tokens of good humour, fidelity, and discretion, can never fail of making converts. Much, indeed, depends on the ladies themselves to rescue this truly honourable union from that fashionable detestation in which it seems to be held; and one would suppose it no very arduous task to make themselves more companionable, useful, and esteemable, as wives, than the Negresses and Mulattas are as mistresses: they might, I am well persuaded, prove much honester friends. It is true, that, if it should be a man's misfortune to be coupled with a very profligate and extravagant wife, the difference, in respect to his fortune, is not great, whether plundered by a black or by a white woman. But such examples, I may hope, are unfrequent without the husband's concurrence; yet, whenever they do happen, the mischief they occasion is very extensive, from the apprehensions with which they strike multitudes of single men, the viler part of whom endeavour to increase the number of unhappy marriages by every base art of seduction; while others rejoice to find any such, because they seem to justify their preference of celibacy, or concubinage. In regard to the African mistress, I shall exhibit the following, as no unsuitable portrait. All her kindred, and most commonly her very paramours, are fastened upon her keeper like so many leeches; while she, the chief leech, conspires to bleed him *usque ad deliquium.* In well-dissembled affection, in her tricks, cajolements, and infidelities, she is far more perfectly versed, than any adept of the hundreds of Drury. She rarely wants cunning to dupe the fool that confides in her; for who "shall teach the wily African deceit?" The quintessence of her dexterity consists in persuading the man she detests to believe she is most violently smitten with the beauty of his person; in short, over head and ears in love with him. To establish this opinion, which vanity seldom fails to embrace, she now and then affects to be jealous,

laments his ungrateful return for so sincere a passion; and,
by this stratagem, she is better able to hide her private
intrigues with her real favourites. I have seen a dear companion of this stamp deploring the loss of her deceased
cull with all the seeming fervency of an honest affection, or
rather of outrageous sorrow; beating her head; stamping
with her feet; tears pouring down in torrents; her exclama-
tions as wild, and gestures as emphatic, as those of an
antient Roman orator in all the phrensy of a publick ha-
rangue. Unluckily, it soon appeared, that, at this very time,
she had rummaged his pockets and escrutoire; and con-
cealed his watch, rings, and money, in the feather-bed
upon which the poor wretch had just breathed his last. And
such is the mirror of almost all these conjunctions of white
and black! two tinctures which nature has dissociated, like
oil and vinegar. But, as if some good was generally to arise
out of evil, so we find, that these connexions have been
applauded upon a principle of policy; as if, by forming
such alliances with the slaves, they might become more
attached to the white people. Perhaps, the fruit of these
unions may, by their consanguinity with a certain number
of the Blacks, support some degree of influence, so far as
that line of kindred extends: yet one would scarcely suppose it to have any remote effect; because they, for their
own parts, despise the Blacks, and aspire to mend their
complexion still more by intermixture with the Whites. The
children of a White and Quateron are called English, and
consider themselves as free from all taint of the Negroe
race. To call them by a degree inferior to what they really
are, would be the highest affront. This pride of amended
blood is universal, and becomes the more confirmed, if they
have received any smattering of education; for then they
look down with the more supercilious contempt upon those
who have had none. Such, whose mind has been a little
purged from the grossest ignorance, may wish and endeavour to improve it still more; but no freed or unfreed
Mulatto ever wished to relapse into the Negroe. The fact is,
that the opulent among them withdraw to England; where
their influence, if they ever possessed any, ceases to be of

any use. The middle class are not much liked by the Negroes, because the latter abhor the idea of being slaves to the descendants of slaves. And as for the lower rank, the issue of casual fruition, they, for the most part, remain in the same slavish condition as their mother; they are fellow-labourers with the Blacks, and are not regarded in the least as their superiors. As for the first-mentioned, it would probably be no disservice to the island, to regain all those who have abandoned it. But, to state the comparison fairly, if their fathers had married, the difference would have been this; their white offspring might have remained in the colony, to strengthen and enrich it: the Mulatto offspring desert and impoverish it. The lower class of these mixtures, who remain in the island, are a hardy race, capable of undergoing equal fatigue with the Blacks, above whom (in point of due policy) they ought to hold some degree of distinction. They would then form the centre of connexion between the two extremes, producing a regular establishment of three ranks of men, dependent on each other, and rising in a proper climax of subordination, in which the Whites would hold the highest place. I can foresee no mischief that can arise from the enfranchisement of every Mulatto child. If it be objected, that such a plan may tend to encourage the illicit commerce of which I have been complaining; I reply, that it will be more likely to repress it, because, although the planters are at present very indifferent about the birth of such children upon their estates, knowing that they will either labour for them like their other slaves, or produce a good price, if their fathers should incline to purchase them; yet they will discountenance such intercourses as much as lies in their power (when it shall no longer be for their interest to connive at them), and use their endeavours to multiply the unmixed breed of their Blacks. Besides, to expect that men will wholly abstain from this commerce, if it was even liable to the severest penalties of law, would be absurd; for, so long as some men have passions to gratify, they will seek the indulgence of them by means the most agreeable, and least inconvenient, to themselves. It will be of some advantage, as things are circumstanced, to turn unavoidable evils to the benefit of society, as the best reparation that can be made for this breach of its moral and political institutions. A wise physician will strive to change an acute distemper into one less malignant; and his patient compounds for a slight chronic indisposition, so he may get relief from a violent and mortal one. I do not judge so lightly of the present state of fornication in the island, as to suppose that it can ever be more flourishing, or that the emancipation of every Mulatto child will prove a means of augmenting the annual number. The retrieving them from profound ignorance, affording them instruction in Christian morals, and obliging them to serve a regular apprenticeship to artificers and tradesmen, would make them orderly subjects, and faithful defenders of the country. It may, with greater weight, be objected, that such a measure would deprive the planters of a part of their property; and that the bringing up so many to trades and mechanic arts might discourage white artificers.

The first might be obviated, by paying their owners a certain rate *per* head, to be determined by the legislature. The second is not insurmountable; for few or none will be master-workmen; they will serve as journeymen to white artificers; or do little more than they would have done, if they had continued in slavery; for it is the custom on most estates at present to make tradesmen of them. But, if they were even to set up for themselves, no disadvantage would probably accrue to the publick, but the contrary. They would oblige the white artificers to work at more moderate rates; which, though not agreeable perhaps to these artificers, would still leave them an ample gain, and prove very acceptable to the rest of the inhabitants; for to such a pitch of extravagance have they raised their charges, that they tax their employers just what they think fit; each man of them fixes a rate according to his own fancy, unregulated by any law; and, should his bill be ever so enormous or unjust, he is in no want of brother tradesmen in the jury-box to confirm and allow it. I shall not here presume to dictate any entire plan for carrying this scheme into effect. This must be left to the wisdom of the legislature, and be made consistent with the abilities of the treasury. In general only I may suppose, that for every such child, on its attaining the age of three years, a reasonable allowance be paid to the owner: from that period it becomes the care of the public, and might be provided for, at a cheap rate, until of an age fit for school; then be instructed in religion; and at the age of twelve apprenticed for the term of four years; after this, be regimented in his respective district, perhaps settled near a township; and, when on militia or other public duty, paid the same subsistence *per* day, or week, that is now allowed to the Marons [Maroons]. The expediency must be seen of having (as in the French islands) such a corps of active men, ready to scour the woods upon all occasions; a service, in which the regulars are by no means equal to them. They would likewise form a proper counter-balance to the Maron Negroes; whose insolence, during formidable insurrections, has been most insufferable. The best way of securing the allegiance of these irregular people must be by preserving the treaty with them inviolate: and, at the same time, awing them into the conservation of it on their part by such a powerful equipoise, composed of men dissimilar from them in complexion and manners, but equal in hardiness and vigour.

The Mulattos are, in general, well-shaped, and the women well-featured. They seem to partake more of the white than the black. Their hair has a natural curl; in some it resembles the Negroe fleece; but, in general, it is of a tolerable length. The girls arrive very early at the age of puberty; and, from the time of their being about twenty-five, they decline very fast, till at length they grow horribly ugly. They are lascivious; yet, considering their want of instruction, their behaviour in public is remarkably decent; and they affect a modesty which they do not feel. They are lively and sensible, and pay religious attention to the cleanliness of their persons: at the same time, they are ridiculously vain, haughty, and irascible. They possess, for the most part, a tenderness of disposition, which leads them to do many charitable actions, especially to poor white per-

sons, and makes them excellent nurses to the sick. They
are fond of finery, and lavish almost all the money they
get in ornaments, and the most expensive sorts of linen.
Some few of them have intermarried here with those of
their own complexion; but such matches have generally
been defective and barren. They seem in this respect to be
actually of the mule-kind, and not so capable of producing
from one another as from a commerce with a distinct
White or Black. Monsieur Buffon observes, that it is nothing strange that two individuals should not be able to propagate their species, because nothing more is required than
some slight opposition in their temperaments, or some ac-
cidental fault in the genital organs of either of these two
individuals: nor is it surprising, that two individuals, of
different species, should produce other individuals, which,
being unlike either of their progenitors, bear no resemblance to any thing fixed, and consequently cannot produce any thing resembling themselves, because all that is
requisite in this production is a certain degree of conform-
ity between the form of the body and the genital organs
of these different animals. Yet it seems extraordinary, that
two Mulattos, having intercourse together, should be unable
to continue their species, the woman either proving barren,
or their offspring, if they have any, not attaining to maturity; when the same man and woman, having commerce
with a White or Black, would generate a numerous issue.
Some examples may possibly have occurred, where, upon
the intermarriage of two Mulattos, the woman has borne
children; which children have grown to maturity: but I
never heard of such an instance; and may we not suspect the lady, in those cases, to have privately intrigued
with another man, a White perhaps? The suspicion is not
unwarrantable, if we consider how little their passions are
under the restraint of morality; and that the major part,
nay, almost the whole number, with very few exceptions,
have been *filles de joye* before they became wives. As for
those in Jamaica, whom I have particularly alluded to, they
married young, had received some sort of education, and
lived with great repute for their chaste and orderly con-

duct; and with them the experiment is tried with a great degree of certainty: they produce no offspring, though in appearance under no natural incapacity of so doing with a different connexion.

The subject is really curious, and deserves a further and very attentive enquiry; because it tends, among other evidences, to establish an opinion, which several have entertained, that the White and the Negroe had not one common origin. Towards disproving this opinion, it is necessary, that the Mulatto woman should be past all suspicion of intriguing with another, or having communication with any other man than her Mulatto husband; and it then remains for further proof, whether the offspring of these two Mulattos, being married to the offspring of two other Mulatto parents, would propagate their species, and so, by an uninterrupted succession, continue the race. For my own part, I think there are extremely potent reasons for believing, that the White and the Negroe are two distinct species. A certain philosopher of the present age confidently avers, that "none but the blind can doubt it." It is certain, that this idea enables us to account for those diversities of feature, skin, and intellect, observeable among mankind; which cannot be accounted for in any other way, without running into a thousand absurdities.

6.

The free colored in another island, Saint-Domingue, are seen here from their own point of view rather than from that of the whites. The structure of a society rigidly controlled according to shades of color, the constant coercion of the free colored by whites jealous of their prosperity or fearful of their influence with the slaves, the hardships suffered by the free colored as revolution neared are all graphically portrayed in this chapter from the same study as the first selection on the slaves.

C. L. R. JAMES is identified on page 3.

The Free Colored in a Slave Society*
C. L. R. James

There was another class of free men in San Domingo, the
free Mulattoes and free blacks. Neither legislation, nor the
growth of race prejudice, could destroy the attraction of
the black women for the white men of San Domingo. It
was characteristic of all classes; the rabble on the shore-
front, the planter or overseer who chose a slave to pass the
night with him and drove her from his bed to the lash of
the slave-driver next morning; a Governor of the colony,
newly arrived from France, who was disturbed at finding
himself seized with a passion for the handsomest of his
four black maids.

In the early days every Mulatto was free up to the age of
24, not by law, but because white men were so few in
comparison with the slaves that the masters sought to bind
these intermediates to themselves rather than let them swell
the ranks of their enemies. In those early years race prejudice was not strong. The Negro Code in 1685 authorised marriage between the white and the slave who had
children by him, the ceremony freeing herself and her
children. The Code gave the free Mulattoes and the free
Negroes equal rights with the whites. But as the white
population grew larger, white San Domingo discarded the
convention, and enslaved or sold their numerous children

The Black Jacobins, New York, Random House (second edition, revised from the 1938 edition), 1963, pp. 36–44. Reprinted
by permission of the author.

* [Editors' title]

like any king in the African jungle. All efforts to prevent concubinage failed, and the Mulatto children multiplied, to be freed or to remain slaves at the caprice of their fathers. Many were freed, becoming artisans and household servants. They began to amass property, and the whites, while adding unceasingly to the number of Mulattoes, began to restrict and harass them with malicious legislation. The whites threw as much as possible of the burdens of the country upon them. On attaining their majority they were compelled to join the *maréchaussée*, a police organisation for arresting fugitive Negroes, protecting travellers on the high road, capturing dangerous Negroes, fighting against the maroons, all the difficult and dangerous tasks which the local whites might command. After three years' service in the *maréchaussée*, they had to join the local militia, provide their own arms, ammunition and accoutrements, and, without pay or allowance of any kind, serve at the discretion of the white commanding officer. Such duties as the forced upkeep of the roads were made to fall on them with extra severity. They were excluded from the naval and military departments, from the practice of law, medicine, and divinity, and all public offices or places of trust. A white man could trespass on a Mulatto's property, seduce his wife or daughter, insult him in any way he chose, certain that at any hint of resentment or revenge all the whites and the Government would rush out ready to lynch. In legal actions the decision nearly always went against the Mulattoes, and to terrorise them into submission a free man of colour who struck a white man, whatever his station in life, was to have his right arm cut off.

But by some fortunate chance, the amount of property that they could hold was not, as in the English islands, limited. Of fine physique and intelligent, administering their enterprises themselves without exhausting their fortunes in extravagant trips to Paris, they began to acquire wealth as master-artisans and then as proprietors. As they began to establish themselves, the jealousy and envy of the white colonists were transformed into ferocious hatred and fear.

They divided the offspring of white and black and intermediate shades into 128 divisions. The true Mulatto was the child of the pure black and the pure white. The child of the white and the Mulatto woman was a quarteron with 96 parts white and 32 parts black. But the quarteron could be produced by the white and the marabou in the proportion of 88 to 40, or by the white and the sacatra, in the proportion of 72 to 56 and so on all through the 128 varieties. But the sang-mêlé with 127 white parts and 1 black part was still a man of colour.

In a slave society the mere possession of personal freedom is a valuable privilege, and the laws of Greece and Rome testify that severe legislation against slaves and freedmen have nothing to do with the race question. Behind all this elaborate tom-foolery of quarteron, sacatra and marabou, was the one dominating fact of San Domingo society —fear of the slaves. The mothers of the Mulattoes were in the slave-gangs, they had half-brothers there, and however much the Mulatto himself might despise this half of his origin, he was at home among the slaves and, in addition to his wealth and education, could have an influence among them which a white man could never have. Furthermore, apart from physical terror, the slaves were to be kept in subjection by associating inferiority and degradation with the most obvious distinguishing mark of the slave —the black skin. Few of the slaves being able to read, the colonists did not hesitate to say openly: "It is essential to maintain a great distance between those who obey and those who command. One of the surest means of doing this is the perpetuation of the imprint that slavery has once given." No Mulatto, therefore, whatever his number of white parts, was allowed to assume the name of his white father.

But despite these restrictions the Mulattoes continued to make progress. By 1755, little more than three generations after the Negro Code, they were beginning to fill the colony, and their growing numbers and riches were causing alarm to the whites.

They lived (ran a report)[1] like their forebears, on the local vegetables, drinking no wine, confining themselves to the local liquors brewed from the sugar cane. Thus their personal consumption contributed nothing to the maintenance of the important trade with France. Their sober ways of living and their small expenditure enabled them to put away most of their income every year, they accumulated immense capital, and grew more arrogant as their wealth increased. They bid for all properties on sale in the various districts, and raised prices to such fantastic heights that the whites who were not wealthy could not buy, or ruined themselves by attempting to keep pace with them. Thus, in some districts, the finest properties were in the possession of the half-castes, and yet they were everywhere the least ready to submit to statute labour and the public dues. Their plantations were the sanctuary and asylum of the freedmen who had neither work nor profession and of numerous fugitive slaves who had run away from their gangs. Being so rich they imitated the style of the whites and sought to drown all traces of their origin. They were trying to get high commands in the militia. Those who had ability enough to make them forget the vice of their origin were even seeking places in the judiciary. If this sort of thing went on, they would soon be making marriages with distinguished families, which would bind these families in alliance with the slaves in the gangs, whence the mothers of these upstarts came.

This was no cantankerous croak from a jealous colonist. It was an official memorandum from the bureaucracy to the Minister. Increasing numbers, increasing wealth were giving the Mulattoes greater pride and sharpening their resentment against their humiliations. Some of them were sending their children to France to be educated, and in France, even a hundred years before the revolution, there was little colour prejudice. Up to 1716 every Negro slave who touched French soil was free, and after an interval of

[1] Pierre de Vaissière, *Saint-Domingue, 1629–1789* (Paris, 1909), p. 222.

fifty years another decree in 1762 reaffirmed this. In 1739 a
slave served as trumpeter in the royal regiment of Cara-
bineers; young Mulattoes were received in the military
corps reserved to the young nobility and in the offices of
the magistracy; they served as pages at court.[2] Yet these
men had to go back to San Domingo and submit to the dis-
criminations and brutality of the San Domingo whites. And
as the Mulattoes began to press against the barriers, white
San Domingo passed a series of laws which for maniacal
savagery are unique in the modern world, and (we would
have said up to 1933) not likely to be paralleled again in
history. The Council of Port-au-Prince, holding up the race
question as a screen, wanted to exterminate them. Thus
the whites could purge their system of a growing menace,
get rid of men from whom they had borrowed money, and
seize much fine property. The Council proposed to banish
all the half-castes up to the degree of quarteron to the
mountains ("which they would bring into cultivation"), to
forbid the sale of all property on the plains to half-castes,
to deny them the right of acquiring any house-property, to
force all those up to the degree of quarteron and all those
whites who had married people of colour to that degree, to
sell all their slaves within a year. "For," said the Council,
"these are dangerous people, more friendly to the slaves, to
whom they are still attached, than to us who oppress them
by the subordination which we demand and the scorn with
which we treat them. In a revolution, in a moment of tension, they would be the first to break the yoke which
weighed on them, the more because they are richer and are
now accustomed to have white debtors, since when they
no longer have sufficient respect for us." But the colonists
could not carry out these sweeping plans. The Mulattoes,
unlike the German Jews, were already too numerous, and
the revolution would have begun there and then.

The colonists had to content themselves with throwing
on these rivals every humiliation that ingenuity and malice
could devise. Between 1758 and the revolution the per-

[2] Lebeau, *De la condition des gens de couleur libres sous
l'ancien régime* (Poitiers, 1903).

secutions mounted.[3] The Mulattoes were forbidden to wear
swords and sabres and European dress. They were forbidden to buy ammunition except by special permission with
the exact quantity stated. They were forbidden to meet
together "on the pretext" of weddings, feasts or dances,
under penalty of a fine for the first offence, imprisonment
for the next, and worse to follow. They were forbidden to
stay in France. They were forbidden to play European
games. The priests were forbidden to draw up any documents for them. In 1781, eight years before the revolution,
they were forbidden to take the titles of Monsieur and Ma-
dame. Up to 1791, if a white man ate in their house, they
could not sit at table with him. The only privilege the
whites allowed them was the privilege of lending white
men money.

Short of insurrection, there was no way out of this. And
until the Bastille fell the efforts of the Mulattoes to emanci-
pate themselves assumed strange forms. De Vaissière has
unearthed a story, which we can understand better after
Hitlerism than we could have done before. In 1771 the
Sieur Chapuzet had obtained from the Council of Le Cap
a decree which gave him the privileges of a white man,
his obscure career preventing any questions being raised
about his origin. A little later he attempted to become an
officer in the militia. Four lieutenants in the militia of the
North Plain made minute researches into the records
and presented an exact genealogy of the Chapuzet family,
proving that a maternal ancestor, 150 years back, was a
Negro from St. Kitts. De Chapuzet defended himself, "in
law and in fact," in law because the power of deciding on
the status of a citizen was the prerogative of the Government and not of private individuals, in fact because in
1624 there were no Negroes in St. Kitts. Colonial history
was now the terrain. With extracts from the historians the
whites proved that there were slaves in St. Kitts in 1624.
Chapuzet admitted defeat and left for France.

[3] *Ibid.*; De Vaissière, *op. cit.*, ch. 3; Albert Savine, ed., *Saint-
Domingue à la veille de la Révolution: Souvenirs du Baron
de Wimpffen* (Paris, 1911), pp. 36–38.

Three years after, he returned, calling himself M. Chapuzet de Guérin, or familiarly M. le Guérin. Aristocrat at least in name, by means of a sponsor he again brought his case for being considered a white man before the courts. Once more he was defeated. But Chapuzet was a man of resource. He claimed that this ancestor, "the St. Kitts Negro", was no Negro, but a Carib, a free-born Carib, a member of "that noble race on whom the French and Spaniards had imposed the law of conquest." Chapuzet triumphed. In 1779 two decrees of the Council declared that his claims were justified. But he did not get his rank. The local officials dared not appoint him. Following the publication of the decrees, the people of colour abandoned themselves to such demonstrations of joy and foolish hopes that the consequences of Chapuzet's appointment might have been very dangerous. The doors of Chapuzet's lawyer were besieged with quarterons and other fair-skinned Mulattoes seeking to have their remote slave ancestors transformed into free and noble Caribs.

The advantages of being white were so obvious that race prejudice against the Negroes permeated the minds of the Mulattoes who so bitterly resented the same thing from the whites. Black slaves and Mulattoes hated each other. Even while in words and, by their success in life, in many of their actions, Mulattoes demonstrated the falseness of the white claim to inherent superiority, yet the man of colour who was nearly white despised the man of colour who was only half-white, who in turn despised the man of colour who was only quarter white, and so on through all the shades.

The free blacks, comparatively speaking, were not many, and so despised was the black skin that even a Mulatto slave felt himself superior to the free black man. The Mulatto, rather than be slave to a black, would have killed himself.

It all reads like a cross between a nightmare and a bad joke. But these distinctions still exercise their influence in

the West Indies to-day.[4] While whites in Britain dislike the
half-caste more than the full-blooded Negro, whites in the
West Indies favour the half-caste against the blacks. These,
however, are matters of social prestige. But the racial dis-
criminations in Africa to-day are, as they were in San
Domingo, matters of Government policy, enforced by bul-
lets and bayonets, and we have lived to see the rulers of a
European nation make the Aryan grandmother as precious
for their fellow-countrymen as the Carib ancestor was to the
Mulatto. The cause in each case is the same—the justification of plunder by any obvious differentiation from
those holding power. It is as well to remind the reader that
a trained observer travelling in the West Indies in 1935
says of the coloured men there, "A few at the top, judges,
barristers, doctors, whatever their shade of colour, could
hold their own in any circle. A great many more are the intellectual equals or superiors of their own white contempo-
raries."[5] Many of the Mulattoes and free blacks were back-
ward in comparison to the whites but their capacity was
perfectly obvious in San Domingo in the years before
1789. It took gunpowder and cold steel to convince the San
Domingo whites. And if, as we have seen, the most intelligent of them did not delude themselves about the materialist origins of their prejudice against the Mulattoes, we yet
will make a great mistake if we think that they were hypo-
crites when they claimed that a white skin guaranteed to
the owner superior abilities and entitled him to a monopoly
of the best that the colony afforded.

"Upon the different forms of property, upon the social
conditions of existence as foundation, there is built a su-
perstructure of diversified and characteristic sentiments,
illusions, habits of thought, and outlooks on life in general.
The class as a whole creates and shapes them out of its
material foundation, and out of the corresponding social
relationships. The individual in whom they arise, through
tradition and education, may fancy them to be the true

[4] Still true, in 1961.
[5] W. M. Macmillan, *Warning from the West Indies* (London,
1936), p. 49.

determinants, the real origin of his activities."[6] On this common derivation of prejudice, small whites, big whites and bureaucracy were united against Mulattoes. It had been so for one hundred and fifty years, and therefore it would always be so. But would it? The higher bureaucrats, cultivated Frenchmen, arrived in the island without prejudice; and looking for mass support used to help the Mulattoes a little. And Mulattoes and big whites had a common bond—property. Once the revolution was well under way the big whites would have to choose between their allies of race and their allies of property. They would not hesitate long.

[6] Karl Marx, *The Eighteenth Brumaire.*

7.

This article by a contemporary Jamaican historian deals not with any single group of West Indians, but rather with an issue in West Indian history affecting all of them. Absentee proprietorship became endemic throughout the colonial West Indies when sugar became the major crop: for more than two centuries, a large proportion of West Indian estates were owned by individuals who did not live there. The economic and social effects of absenteeism have been graphically described in such classics as Pitman's *The Development of the British West Indies* and Ragatz's *The Fall of the Planter Class in the British Caribbean*. This selection contends that earlier scholars exaggerated the effects of absentee ownership but finds the absentee *spirit* of crucial significance in any case: whether planters left the West Indies or remained there, the local atmosphere was poisoned by the feeling that the islands were not fit places to live. As a consequence, the West Indies have been continually drained of resources, both physical and human.

DOUGLAS HALL, Jamaican-born, took his doctorate at the London School of Economics and returned to the Caribbean to become first a tutor in the Extra-Mural Department at the University of the West Indies, then a member of the History Department, of which he is presently Professor and Head.

Absentee-Proprietorship in the British West Indies, to About 1850
Douglas Hall

In the draft report of the Select Committee on Sugar and Coffee Planting in 1848 the Chairman, Lord George Bentinck, commented on the evidence given before the Committee by Mr. Edwin Pickwoad, whose family owned property in St. Kitts:

> Mr. Pickwoad's first and great object appeared to be to establish one of Lord Grey's [the Secretary of State for the Colonies] great axioms, that a large portion of the distress of the British Sugar and Coffee Planting Colonies arises from the want of resident proprietors.[1]

Lord Grey was not alone in this opinion. There is hardly a commentator or an historian who, in describing the distresses of the West Indian colonies in the nineteenth century or earlier, does not point to absentee-proprietorship as a major source of trouble. It has been said that by the prevalence of absentee-ownership the colonies were drained of economic wealth, and denied a gentry who might have set a high example both in social life and in the performance of political and administrative duties. Because of absenteeism, it has been claimed, many estates were left to the management of men who were nearly

Jamaican Historical Review, Vol. 4, 1964, pp. 15–34. Used by permission of the author.
[1] Select Committee on Sugar and Coffee Planting, 1848. Supplement (No. 1) to the 8th Report. Draft of Report proposed by Chairman.

always incompetent and often dishonest, the moral ton
of colonial society was coloured by the example of inferio
residents whose lack of right principle was both obviou
and irreparable, the public administration lacked integrit
and was bedevilled by multiple office-holding, and th
profits of sugar went not to colonial economic develop
ment but to the financing of British commercial and in
dustrial growth and the conspicuous consumption abroa
of the absentee proprietors.[2]

The number and variety of the charges kindle the spar
of curiosity. The profuse, but scattered, information at ou
disposal provides specific illustrations of all the allege
ills listed above; and yet, something seems questionable i
our traditional belabouring of absenteeism. The ver
limited purposes of this paper are to suggest that our gen

[2] For an overall review of absenteeism see L. J. Ragatz "Ab
sentee Landlordism in the British Caribbean, 1750–1833," (Ag
ricultural History, Vol. 5, 1931, pp. 7–24), and, by the sam
author, The Fall of the Planter Class in the British Caribbean
1763–1833 (New York and London, 1928). See also reference
to absenteeism in Edward Long, The History of Jamaica (
vols.; London, 1774); Trelawney Wentworth, The West Indi
Sketch Book (2 vols.; London, 1834), Vol. 2, pp. 346–55; J
A. Thome and J. H. Kimball, Emancipation in the West Indie
(American Anti-Slavery Society, N.Y., 1838), passim; B. M'Ma
hon, Jamaica Plantership (London, 1839); J. J. Gurney, A Win
ter in the West Indies (2nd ed., London, 1840), p. 109; G. Scot
land, A Letter Addressed to the Public of Jamaica (Spanish
Town, Jamaica, 1847), p. 19; Rev. D. King, State and Prospect
of Jamaica (London, 1850), p. 146; W. G. Sewell, The Ordea
of Free Labour in the British West Indies (London, 1861), pp
37–38, 236–37; Eric Williams, Capitalism and Slavery (Univer
sity of North Carolina Press, 1944), p. 86; H. V. Wiseman, .
Short History of the British West Indies (London: Universit
of London Press, 1950), p. 89; W. L. Burn, The British Wes
Indies (London: Hutchinson's, 1951), p. 63; F. Henriques, Fam
ily and Colour in Jamaica (London: Eyre & Spottiswoode
1953), p. 20; Sir Alan Burns, History of the British West Indie
(London: Allen & Unwin, 1954), passim; Philip Curtin, Tw
Jamaicas (Cambridge: Harvard University Press, 1955), p. 15
R. Pares, Merchants and Planters. The Economic History Re
view Supplements, No. 4 (C.U.P. 1960) and his larger earlie
work, A West India Fortune (London: Longmans, Green
1950); and many others.

eralisations about absentee-ownership are not always well-founded, and that when we have come to learn more about the subject we may have to shed our remarks of generality and put them in more specific contexts of place and time.

Absentee-proprietorship in the British West Indies began, not with the sugar industry, but with the first English colonizations and the establishment of forms of proprietory government.[3] Thus, from the time of the earliest settlements in the Leeward Islands and in Barbados, there existed a distinction between 'colonists' and 'proprietors'. In later years, as other colonies in the West Indies were acquired by Britain by conquest or by cession, many large tracts of land were granted to people living in Britain who had been instrumental to the new acquisitions, or who for some other reason enjoyed the favour of the Crown or Parliament.[4] Thus, in a number of specific instances absentee-proprietorship was created by sovereign fiat, and the absentee-proprietor decided whether he should move westwards across the Atlantic, either to take up residence on his new property or merely to visit it.

Another source of absentee-ownership emerged and grew with the increasing profitability of sugar-production from the second half of the seventeenth century.[5] Resident colonists who became wealthy by the production of sugar decided whether they should move eastwards across the

[3] See J. A. Williamson, *The Caribbee Islands Under the Proprietary Patents* (Oxford, 1926), and R. Pares, *Merchants and Planters*, The Economic History Review Supplements, No. 4 (C.U.P. 1960).

[4] Bryan Edwards, *op. cit.*, Vol. I, p. 421, wrote indignantly of St. Vincent, ceded by the French in 1763: "The first measure of the English government in respect to this island, after the peace of Paris, was to dispose of the lands—I dare not say to the best advantage! for no less than 24,000 acres, being more than one-fourth part of the whole country, were gratuitously assigned over to two individuals (Mr. Swinburne had twenty thousand acres, and General Moncton four thousand . . .)".

[5] This source of absentee-ownership is the one which has most engaged the comment of writers. The fact is, however, that it was not the only important source, and the ways in which absentee-ownership occurred affected both the numerical and the financial strength of the absentees.

Atlantic to reside in, or merely to visit, the metropolitan country whence they or their fathers, probably in less opulent personal circumstances, had formerly migrated.

A third source of absentee-ownership originated in the inheritance by people resident in Britain of West India property. Whether these beneficiaries had been born in Britain or in the West Indies makes no difference. On the inheritance of estates in the colonies they were free to choose either to remain in Britain or to go and assume, or resume, residence on the estates.

Fourthly, in the later eighteenth century when the profitability of West India estates generally declined, another source of absenteeism became important as creditors in Britain came, however reluctantly, into possession of unprofitable West India estates on which they had lien.[6] Most of these creditors were merchants or commission agents dealing in West India produce, to whom the less fortunate or less able estate owners, whether resident or absentee, had become largely indebted.[7]

In all of these ways absentee-ownership in its most obvious form developed as proprietors of more and more West India property were, in the eighteenth century, to be found resident in Britain. But the different sources of absentee-ownership produced different kinds of absentees, and until further research provides some dependable opinion of the relative importance of the different sources, and of the total numerical strength and the wealth of the absentees at different times, generalisations will remain open to challenge.

Another important distinction, between 'absentee-owners' and 'absenteeism', should also be made. The ratio between the number of absent owners and the value of absentee-owned property was variable between different

---

[6] R. Pares, *A West-India Fortune* (London: Longmans, Green, 1950) Chap. XII, and Eric Williams, *Capitalism and Slavery*, Chap. 4.

[7] It is also likely, though I am unable to cite a specific illustration, that there were instances of resident owners, on the verge of insolvency, going to Britain to try by some means to repair their misfortunes and, though continuing in possession of their estates, remaining in Britain.

colonies and over periods of time. When discussing the consequences of absenteeism it is necessary to distinguish between (i) those following the absence from a colony of a significant number of people, and (ii) those following the absence of the owners of a significant portion of the real estate and the wealth of the colony. This important difference is not generally noted in the literature. More often than not, 'absenteeism', 'absentee-proprietorship' and 'absentees' have been indiscriminately censured.

Thus it has sometimes been implied that the ills generated in the West Indies by the absence of proprietors could have been remedied by the return of the absentees to residence on their estates.[8] In fact, return was in some cases impossible and in many instances would have been of doubtful efficacy.

Return was impossible for those absentees who owned property in two or more of the colonies. Obviously, wherever they might have chosen to reside they would have been classed as absentees from some other place.[9]

In other cases, particularly among the Jamaica absentees who owned properties far apart in that mountainous island, residence in, say, the parish of St. James would have for all practical purposes of estate-supervision, constituted absenteeism from, say, St. Thomas in the East or even from St. Catherine.[10]

[8] For instance, in W. L. Burn, *Emancipation and Apprenticeship in the British West Indies* (London: Jonathan Cape, 1937), pp. 28–30.

[9] The Codringtons (Barbados, Antigua, Barbuda), the Gladstones (British Guiana and Jamaica), the Colvilles (Jamaica and British Guiana) and the Warners (Antigua and Trinidad in the 1830's and previously in St. Kitts and Barbados) are a few examples of this "multiple-absentee-ownership".

[10] Matthew Lewis in his *Journal of a West India Proprietor* (London, 1834), p. 161, noted: "The short time allotted for my stay in the island makes it impossible to attend properly both to this estate [Hordley, in St. Thomas-in-the-East] and to Cornwall [in St. James] at this first visit, and therefore I determined to confine my attention to the negroes on the latter estate till my return to Jamaica." Lewis arrived in Jamaica on Jan. 1, 1816 and left on April 1 the same year. He returned in late January 1818 and left at the beginning of May. He died on the return voyage to England.

Moreover, even if at any given time every absentee owner had immediately returned to his property, or to one of his properties, the numerical flows of individuals into the various colonies would have differed. Quite clearly the broad consequences in any colony of any such return would have been as much dependent on the number, as on the wealth, of those returning. A return of two large proprietors might considerably reduce a previously significant absentee-ownership in a small colony, but could hardly be counted on to produce large social and administrative reform.

The following Table, showing the distribution, by acreages, of estates in the island of St. Vincent in 1801 and in 1827 suggests that generalisations about absentee ownership, even in that single island, over a period of 2: years are hardly likely to be acceptable.

ESTATES IN ST. VINCENT

	1801	182
150 acres and under	27	8
151 to 250 acres	32	2
251 to 450 acres	48	3
451 to 1,000 acres	17	2:
over 1,000	1	:
TOTAL	125	9

Sources: 1801: "An Account of the number of slaves employed and the quantity of produce grown on the Several Estates ir the Island of St. Vincent and its dependencies, from 1801 . . . to 1824, inclusive." Compiled from the Official Returns (Gazette Office, Kingstown, St. Vincent, 1825.)

1827: Chas. Shephard, *An Historical Account of the Island of St. Vincent* (London, 1831), Appendix, pp. vi–xxiii.

Neither source is entirely accurate, but they serve the present purpose by showing the general change, and by illustrating the inadequacy of our information, for in neither is there any attempt to distinguish between resident and absentee-owned estates.

In the redistribution of property which the Table shows there must, clearly, have been some change in the fortunes of resident and of absentee proprietors as well as in their numbers. Moreover, considering the period covered by the Table, it is reasonable to ask whether, in regard to any single colony, much more for the British West Indies as a whole, it is not likely that every war which seriously affected the West India colonies and their trade did not also affect the distribution of wealth among residents and absentees.

One further illustration will serve. In Antigua, in 1848, Francis Shand, an absentee-proprietor, West India Merchant and Shipowner in Liverpool, owned nine of that island's most productive estates. He also held five other estates under lease and was the consignee in Britain of the produce of 32 others. There were then 150 estates in Antigua. Mr. Shand, clearly, was an extremely important absentee-owner, but he had not always been an absentee. He had lived in Antigua from 1830 to 1841. Any statement about the effects of absenteeism in Antigua between 1830 and 1848 should surely take into account the movements of Mr. Shand. It should also take into account the financial status of Sir William Codrington and his father. The older Sir William, in the pre-emancipation days, had netted about £20,000 a year from his Antigua and Barbuda estates. The younger Sir William, never in Antigua, had inherited in 1843, and in 1848 when he was asked "You are a Proprietor in Antigua?" replied, "I am sorry to say I am one of those unfortunate individuals." He had reason for his gloom. The annual income was down to about £2,000.[11]

The charges against absentee proprietors have, for the most part, been stated in general terms, levelled not at particular individuals but at the whole body of absentees. Such wide indictments can be supported only if the whole body of absentees can be given common definition and

[11] Select Committee on Sugar and Coffee Planting, 1848. Evidence of Mr. Shand and Sir William Codrington.

characteristics. It has already been implied, however, tha
the absentees were a heterogeneous lot: some were Wes
Indian born, others had made their first appearance else
where; some had lived on their estates, others had neve
done so; some were completely ignorant of the details c
sugar-making and the sugar trade, whereas others ha
practical experience of both; some were genteel, othe
were not. Indeed, the only safe generalizations about the
are that they were all estate-owners, nearly all of them wer
white, and many of them were, or had at some time beer
wealthy.

Thus, the general accusations are weakened by lack of
recognisable accused person, and are frequently riddle
with contradiction as one view or other of 'the absentee
prevails. We are told, for instance, that absentees, thoug
greedy for the profits, were indifferent to the welfare o
their estates;[12] but we are also told that absentee
proprietors were the first to introduce new equipment an
new techniques of production.[13] It is suggested that th
absentees would, by residence on their estates, have forme
a genteel colonial élite;[14] but it is also emphasized tha
many of the absentee-proprietors in Britain squandere

[12] L. J. Ragatz, *The Fall of the Planter Class in the Britis
Caribbean, 1763–1833*, pp. 54–55.

[13] Select Committee on Sugar and Coffee Planting, 1848. Evi
dence of Benjamin Buck Greene, 6194–6196. His experience o
St. Kitts leads him to think that resident proprietors do not man
age their estates as well as absentees do by their attorneys
"There is not the same spirit of enterprise? [Ans.] They hav
neither the capital nor the energy, I think, of the agents tha
are sent out by the absentees . . ." [But compare the view o
Mr. Jelly of Westmoreland, Jamaica, on this point! See foot
note 30]. Mr. Greene went on to say of the absentees livin
in Britain, ". . . here we are on the *qui vive*, and every improve
ment that is made we try to adopt and send it out. They [th
resident owners] have to wait and see what others are doing
and their estates generally do not appear to be managed so wel
as those that are under the direction of active agents."

[14] J. H. Parry and P. M. Sherlock, *A Short History of th
West Indies* (London: Macmillan, 1956), p. 154.

their fortunes in vulgar display.[15] The truth is, of course, that any of these views can be illustrated by reference to particular absentees at particular times; but none can be sustained in reference to absentees as a group over a long period of years.

Now that some of the major pitfalls of generalization have been indicated, the specific charges outlined in the opening paragraphs may be more confidently examined.

The argument that absentee-ownership left the colonial estates to the supervision of incompetent resident managers is supported by many reports of the following kind:

> . . . we forthwith began to examine into matters, and in Gen[ll] find all things in disorder, the whole works a pott of nastiness and in Gen[ll] out of repair: the Mill hous half legg deep in dung and the posts sunk we judg wth rotteness it being nowhere tite for want of the shingles being new layd, in the boyling hous not a copper or a cooler cleaned out and in several places a man might have gon over his shews in Molases a very great waste of sugar under the Ranges and several pots of sugar both whole and peses y[t] wass ill boyld stood there but noe thought or resolution taken what to be done wth them . . . in short everywhere he [the estate manager] has bin consern'd you have bin horrably abus'd . . .[16]

But, quite clearly, reports of this nature deal not with absentee-ownership as such, but with the indifference or

---

[15] Eric Williams, *Capitalism and Slavery*, pp. 85–86. See also W. L. Mathieson, *British Slavery and its Abolition, 1823–1838* (London: Longmans, Green, 1926), pp. 56–57, where the author quotes Edward Long to support an argument that "Proprietors who had inherited their estates and lived on them made much the best slave-owners . . .", whereas some who had gone as children to be educated in Britain returned to the West Indies ". . . only to dissipate their property having gained no 'other acquisition than the art of swearing, drinking, dressing, gaming and wenching' . . .".

[16] R. M. Howard (ed.), *The Longs of Jamaica and Hampton Lodge* (2 vols.; London, 1923). Vol. 1, p. 46.

incompetence of managers in the colonies.[17] Resident owners would probably have been less indifferent, but there is no reason to suppose that they would all have been less incompetent, and some of the absentees were almost totally ignorant of the processes of sugar-making.

It may be argued that those planters who had become wealthy enough to leave their estates and establish residence in England must have been good planters rather than bad ones. There is probably some truth in this; but it is also arguable in general terms that profitability is a reliable indication of good management only when market conditions are hard and uncompromising. It does not require splendid competence to make a profit during a boom in a protected market such as the West Indians had for their sugar. The wealthy planters who went to live abroad were not necessarily good planters. The merchant-creditors who acquired estates by default and foreclosure, and residents abroad who became West India proprietors by inheritance, were even less likely to have been so.

Not all owners are good managers. That is a truism on which the concept and the managerial organization of competitive production and distribution rest; but it is not

[17] G. Eisner, *Jamaica, 1830–1930: A Study in Economic Growth* (Manchester University Press, 1961), p. 197, makes the interesting point that absentee-ownership ceased to be a disadvantage in the nineteenth century. Previously, "While production relied heavily on manual labour the main requirement of managers was an ability to organize and supervise labour". Later, with increasing mechanization, ". . . trained managers were needed. The amateur sugar planter—even at his best—no longer sufficed." Thus, the advantage of resident proprietorship was lost as the need grew for highly skilled supervision. I agree with her emphasis on managerial ability, but, as I indicate later on, I do not agree that estate-management in the eighteenth century was quite as straightforward a business as she suggests. A good indication of the problems of an estate attorney is given by Richard B. Sheridan, "Letters from a Sugar Plantation in Antigua, 1739–1758" in *Agricultural History*, Vol. 31, No. 3, 1957, pp. 3–23; and in the same author's "Samuel Martin, Innovating Planter of Antigua, 1750–1776" in *Agricultural History*, Vol. 3, No. 3, 1960, pp. 126–29.

always adequately considered in discussions of absentee-proprietorship. It is not enough to point to the inefficiencies of resident estate-managers; it should also be shown that the estate-owners themselves would have been less inefficient. Quite clearly, even an inefficient manager might do better for an estate than an owner who undertook management even more inefficiently.

Of more general validity is the proposition that the system of remuneration, by which the attorneys of absentees were paid each year in proportion to the quantity of sugar they shipped, encouraged agents to force production at the expense of the long-term welfare and productivity of the estate.[18] But even here generalization is dangerous for there were cases in which other systems of remuneration were used.[19] Nor is it true that attorneys were always paid. In Barbados and the Windward Islands their reward was sometimes taken in the patronage and influence given them by acceptance of an attorneyship.[20] Thus it seems unreasonable to blame absenteeism alone for the prevalence of a payment by production system. It would probably be more useful to examine further the view of the colonies, held both by resident and absentee planters, as

---

[18] Select Committee on the Commercial State of the West India Colonies, 1832. Evidence of Peter Rose, planter in Jamaica, 1613. "Attorney's charges are a matter of arrangement, generally a commission; some give two and a half per cent, and some five, and I have known as high as ten per cent." In Jamaica, there was a legally fixed rate of 6%, intended to penalize absentee-owners (but it did not bring them to residence in the colony). See William Dickson, *Mitigation of Slavery* (London, 1814), p. 226.

[19] Some absentees, like John Tollemache who owned estates in Antigua, paid their attorneys regular salaries. (Select Committee of 1848, Evidence of John Tollemache, M.P. 7815–7818 and 7890–7900). Tollemache had found his attorneys benefiting by substantial "hidden perquisites"; but taking of "perks" would not have been limited to attorneys who received salaries rather than payment by commission. See also Bryan Edwards, *History . . . of the West Indies* (1819), Vol. 2, p. 299, where he allows a salary of £200, local currency, a year to "Overseer's or Manager's salary".

[20] Dickson, *Mitigation of Slavery*, p. 226, footnote.

plantation colonies which existed in order to be exploited.
The costs of exploitation, in land exhaustion and in slave
mortality, were high, and wiser planters, whether resident
or absentee, realised this and tried to ensure a more careful use of their resources even at the sacrifice of some
measure of immediate gain.[21] But few eighteenth century
planters were concerned with the possibilities of increasing
yields by the discovery, invention, and employment of
better techniques or methods of production. Their efforts
in this direction were attenuated by the protection given
to British colonial muscovado sugar in the British
market,[22] by their use of slave-labour,[23] and by the general political and economic uncertainty which attended the
conditions of sugar production in the eighteenth and early
nineteenth centuries.[24] Until the ending of slavery in 1834
and the freeing of British trade in sugar in the 1840's and
1850's, West India planters, resident and absentee, were
convinced that the profitability of their estates was to be
maintained by political means rather than by managerial
or technical innovations. Their chief concern was to maintain their highly protected position in the British market
and to embarrass the commerce of their foreign rivals. In
this, the efforts of the absentees, who formed part of the

[21] This was the burden of many of the careful instructions
issued by planters to their estate attorneys or managers. See,
for example, John Pinney's strictures on the management of his
Nevis estates (R. Pares, *A West-India Fortune*, Chap. VI).

[22] Noel Deerr, *History of Sugar*, 2 vols. (London, 1949–50),
Vol. 2, p. 430. Duties on British Colonial and Foreign produced
muscovado sugar entering Britain (to the nearest penny per
cwt.).

Year	Br. Col.	Foreign	Year	Br. Col.	Foreign	Year	Br. Col.	Foreign
1698	2/10d	7/7d	1759	6/4d	19/5d	1797	17/6d	31/9d
1705	3/4d	11/5d	1782	11/9d	25/11d	1805	27/–	60/–
1747	4/10d	15/5d	1787	12/4d	27/2d	1830	24/–	66/2d

[23] Douglas Hall, "Slaves and Slavery in the British Caribbean" in *Social and Economic Studies*, Vol. 11, No. 4, Dec.
1962, pp. 305–18.

[24] Douglas Hall, "Incalculability as a Feature of Sugar Production during the Eighteenth Century", in *Social and Economic
Studies*, Vol. 10, No. 3, Sept. 1961, pp. 340–52.

politically powerful West India interest in Britain in the eighteenth century, were invaluable.[25] But it is also clear that if there had been fewer important absentee-owners their Parliamentary influence would have been smaller; and it might sooner have become necessary to look for greater efficiency in production.

Greater efficiency would have been good, but not easy to achieve. Sugar-making contains both a large agricultural and a large manufacturing enterprise with the vital and urgent link between them of harvesting and immediately transporting the sugar-canes from fields to factory. Scientific farming, greater industrial power, and quicker transport and communication systems were all to come in the nineteenth century. More relevant to the present discussion is the gradual change which, during the eighteenth and first half of the nineteenth centuries, came over estate-management.

The early absentees had left their estates under the general supervision of local residents who might, or might not, themselves have been planters.[26] The management of an eighteenth century sugar estate demanded a combination of skills and aptitudes rarely to be found in any single manager. There was need for agricultural knowledge and the ability to apply it, an acquaintance with the crude chemistry of eighteenth century sugar-making, a familiarity with the machinery and equipment of the factory, an understanding of the care of the livestock used as draught animals in fields and factory, some skill in the keeping of accounts and an awareness of price and production trends in the sugar market, and a capacity for right judgement in human relations in a slave-society. This last was almost impossible of achievement.[27] Small wonder, then, that so many resident owners and managers can be shown to have

[25] L. J. Ragatz, *The Fall of the Planter Class in the British Caribbean, 1763–1833*, p. 52; Eric Williams, *Capitalism and Slavery*, Chap. 4; J. H. Parry and P. M. Sherlock, *A Short History of the West Indies*, p. 154.

[26] R. Pares, *A West-India Fortune*, p. 20.

[27] Hall, "Slaves and Slavery in the British Caribbean."

been in some degree incompetent. In measuring them with blame it must be remembered that a main and obvious difference between them and the absentees was the simple fact that the latter were not resident.

As time went on and absentee-ownership generally increased, there began to appear in the colonies a class of professional estate-attorneys or managers,[28] some of whom were also planters on their own account. Among them, there were individuals who, as they gained in knowledge and experience, became recognised as experts in their business. By the middle of the nineteenth century there were estate-attorneys whose services were sought after by the absentee-owners of West India estates,[29] and these men, jealous of their reputations and justly proud of their acknowledged expertise, did not look kindly on any assumption that the best managerial abilities were to be found in Britain:

> Whether from ignorance or from sinister motives, such have been the misrepresentations made to the parties in 'the Mother Country', that in many instances the infatuation of the proprietors prompted them to send out managers who had never seen a cane in their lives; and one gentleman more planet-struck than this brethren, but who fortunately could afford the experiment, not contented

[28] In Jamaica an absentee's (or resident's) agent was called an *attorney*, in other islands he was usually called a *manager*. If an attorney did not reside on an estate of which he was in charge, there was usually a manager *overseer* (sometimes called a manager in Jamaica) who supposedly carried out the instructions of the attorney who, in turn, carried out the instructions of the proprietor. Under the overseers there were the *bookkeepers* who had nothing to do with the keeping of estate-books but were field or factory fore-men.

[29] For instance, Mr. John Davy and Dr. Swanston, both in St. Kitts in the 1830's and 1840's (Minutes of Evidence, Select Committee, 1848, Questions 16603, 16638–40); Mr. Simon Taylor in Jamaica in the late eighteenth century (Proceedings of the Hon. House of Assembly of Jamaica, on the Sugar and Slave-Trade, October, 1792. Printed by Order of the House, London, 1793); and Mr. Jelly of Westmoreland, Jamaica whose comments are quoted below.

with dismissing an attorney,—who by common co[...]
was allowed to be one of the best agriculturalists i[...]
county of Cornwall,—and that too, on the professed plea,
that he doubted whether his attorney would carry out
his insane projects, sent out to his numerous estates a
colony consisting of an attorney, overseers, and book-
keepers, all married men, replete with morality and
versed in ethics, but as innocent as the newly born babe
of all knowledge pertaining to the cane and its culture.
The result might have been foreseen; many of these un-
lucky strangers lacking all knowledge of the dangers of
a tropical sun, and having no experienced guide to direct
them, speedily died. The attorney, a clever and enterpris-
ing man in his way, threw up his commission in disgust,
and the upshot of this preposterous experiment was a loss
of at least ten thousand pounds to the proprietor.[30]

It is not easy to follow Mr. Jelly's argument that those who
combine high moral principle with ignorance of cane-
farming are prone to early death from sunstroke. Nonetheless, in his magnificent opening sentence, his grievance
is well-aired and nicely illustrates the hardening of a professional opinion among the planting attorneys.

There is one other aspect of the management of
absentee-owned estates which must be mentioned. It has
often been claimed that professional attorneys undertook
the supervision of far more estates than they could properly
manage. There is much evidence to support this view.[31]
Again, however, generalization is dangerous. An attorney
who was responsible for the supervision of two large estates might have had a more onerous task than another
who was responsible for the management of six small ones.
The number of estates in an attorney's charge was only
one matter among many others such as the size of the
estates in question, their distance from each other, the
topography of the area involved, the means of communica-

[30] Thomas Jelly, *A Brief Enquiry into the Condition of Jamaica* . . . (London, 1847), p. xi, Preface.
[31] This is well illustrated in L. J. Ragatz, *The Fall of the
Planter Class in the British Caribbean, 1763–1833*, pp. 54–55.

tion and transportation, the competence of subordinate managers, overseers, book-keepers and skilled workers, the prevailing relations between the 'managerial' personnel and the slaves, or after emancipation, the labourers on the properties, the technical and financial equipment and resources at the disposal of the attorney, and his power to make decisions affecting the management of the estates in his care.

The separation of function between owner and manager of an estate was not, during our period, clearly marked either by convention or by contract.

> The subject of absenteeism is a question open to discussion, which my limits will not allow me to enter upon. I may, however, take this opportunity to recommend to the serious attention of the absentee proprietors, the propriety of vesting the acting resident manager with the *planting power of attorney,* as a rule only to be departed from under particular circumstances.[32]

Much of the difficulty of management arose from the fact that owners did not always give their managers sufficient rein in decision-making. In some instances the owners interfered in detail, like Lord Howard de Walden who in the early 1840's sent a booklet of specific instructions to his managers in Jamaica;[33] but many of them did not interfere so intelligently. Moreover, because of the great time-lag due to slow trans-Atlantic communications, an absentee's decisions might be made in ignorance of the current state of his property, such decisions as were permitted to an attorney or manager might be made in ignorance of market conditions in Britain, or conflicting decisions might be made and acted upon by both parties—each unaware of the measures taken by the other.

[32] J. Maxwell, *Remarks on the Present State of Jamaica* (London, 1848), p. 15 (footnote).

[33] W. H. de [Howard de Walden], *General Instructions for Montpelier and Ellis Caymanas Estates in Jamaica,* 1852 (London).

The return of the absentees would have reduced the number of conflicting decisions but would have done little to remedy those other conditions which rendered the management of West India property difficult. It is not easy to accept a general proposition that the assumption of colonial residence and estate-management by the absentee-proprietors would have resolved the managerial problems of sugar production.[34] Indeed, the whole history of the growth of industry and of business administration points rather to the advantages of separation between ownership and management.

It has been alleged that absenteeism deprived the colonies of a social élite who would have set a guiding example in colonial private and public morality. This is a good example of question-begging. Absenteeism may have deprived the colonies of the residence of people who, by reason of their colour and their wealth, would have formed the élite; but whether such an élite would have enhanced

[34] There were resident proprietors, such as Charles John Moulton Barrett in Jamaica in the 1850's who ". . . had no liking for estate work, and taking up his residence on the pen property of Retreat in St. Ann, lived in retirement most of his time. To his younger brother Septimus, he gave the power of attorney for his estates". But Septimus' extravagance lost the property, Cinnamon Hill, to the family. See J. Shore and J. Stewart, *In Old St. James* (London: Bodley Head, 1952), p. 80. In a report on a small property in Barbados in 1836, the comment was made that "This Estate [Goodlands Plantation] is only now coming into order, this in consequence of Mr. Callender [the resident owner] having lately given up the management of it to . . . Mr. Rogers who conducts it extremely well . . ." (Public Record Office, London. C.O. 325/42. Quarterly Report of the Stipendary Justice for District A. Rural Division, 30th June 1836). In 1848, in his evidence before the Select Committee of Parliament, Benjamin Buck Greene remarked (6197) ". . . we have a correspondent of our own, who is a native of one of the islands, and I may mention that we have thought it necessary to give information to him as well as to others that we can no longer continue to make advances, beyond the value of the sugar which he sends us home, and he says it will stop his cultivation. He is a resident proprietor and employs an agent because he thinks that agent will do better for the estate than he can himself".

the moral tone of colonial high society is quite another matter.

Moreover, it seems reasonable to distinguish very clearly between those people who left the West Indies to reside in Britain, and those established residents in Britain who became, in one way or another, colonial absentee-proprietors. For the former there was a choice between resident-ownership and absenteeism, for the latter there would have been only a choice between absenteeism from Britain or absenteeism from a colony. By examining the motives of the former we may come closer to an understanding of the views of both descriptions of absentees.

Francis Bacon, about the end of the sixteenth century, when the West India islands were attracting those who thought to become rich by setting up a sugar plantation, wrote:

> He that hath wife and children hath given hostages to fortune; for they are impediments to great enterprises, either of virtue or mischief.[35]

Those who came to the sugar colonies to attempt a fortune seemed to prefer to travel light, unencumbered with familial obstacles to their enterprises. When a man had made his fortune he sought a wife to give him the heir who would inherit it. Whereas the quest for sexual adventure could be easily satisfied among the slave women and the poorer whites and free coloureds in a colony, the search for a wife generally led back to Britain. When whiteness of skin was one of the determinants of social excellence it was wiser, for those who wished to reach the top, whether as residents or abroad, to seek a wife whose complexion was clearly virgin, and whose pedigree was either rightfully emblazoned or easily embellished.

For the gentleman-owner of a productive and profitable estate, unless his soul was sold to the good tropical earth,

[35] Francis Bacon, "Of Marriage and Single Life," *The Essays of* . . . (London: Nelson).

a West India sugar colony in the eighteenth century offered few attractions for permanent residence.

Above all other motives behind the eastward voyage of the successful planter were the views of the colony as a place where a man might make his fortune, and of Britain as "home", where that fortune might be most comfortably and rewardingly spent.[36]

This implies the greatest weakness of the generalization that absenteeism drained the cream of society from the colonies. It was not so much true that absentee-owners were residents gone abroad as it was that residents in the colonies were temporarily, they hoped, absentees from Britain. In short, even the resident owners were, in orientation and in attitude, absentees. Their "home" was not in the West Indies, their degree of identification with colonial life and society was small and they hoped it would be fleeting.[37] To say that absenteeism skimmed the social cream is simply to put the matter misleadingly. The truth is that in British West Indian colonial society a man became a member of the élite only when he qualified as a potential absentee. Here is implied a distinction between the 'settler' who went to settle, and the 'adventurer' who went to make his fortune.

There have been attempts to distinguish between the behaviour in the colonies of the earliest 'settlers' and the following 'sugar-planters'. There have also been claims that as absentee-proprietorship grew in the eighteenth century so the social behaviour of the remaining residents was depraved. Lord Olivier, in his well-known account of Jamaica, quoted from an earlier work:

Imperfect as the records of the early years of our history are, enough remains to show that when the scum

[36] Bryan Edwards, *The History, Civil and Commercial, of the British West Indies* (5th ed., 5 vols.; London, 1819), Vol. I, p. 281: "Europeans who came to this island have seldom an idea of settling here for life. Their aim is generally to acquire fortunes to enable them to sit down comfortably in their native country; and, in the meanwhile, they consider a family as an incumbrance."

[37] Philip Curtin, *Two Jamaicas*, pp. 15–16, and 54–55.

which had floated on the surface of the first tide of conquest and immigration had drifted away, a large body
of colonists remained, whose ranks were continually aug-
mented, who sought to bring with them all that was precious in the social life of the country from which they
came, and who would in time have made Jamaica what
their countrymen were making of the New States of
America. This was not to be. Colonists gave place to
sugar planters. Sugar planters required slaves, and gradually the Island became a mighty aggregation of cane
fields, in which negroes toiled and white men were the
task-masters."[38]

Olivier then added his own comment:

I know no more striking illustration of the astonishing
contrast between the true Colonial ideal of what Jamaica
might have been made, and the blighting of that ideal
by the Island's conversion into a sphere of British capitalist exploitation, than the fact that whereas between
1667 and 1732 218 endowments were left in trust by
patriotic Jamaicans for the maintenance of schools and
churches (besides very many settlements by considerate
parents for the benefit of their illegitimate families) almost the whole of such property was embezzled during
the eighteenth century by its trustees . . .[39]

Gardner's distinction between 'colonists' and 'sugar-
planters' carries conviction, even though his previous suggestion of how Jamaica might have developed does not.
Olivier's opinion is less acceptable. The majority of the endowments to which he referred were paid for out of the
profits of sugar and were themselves products of that 'capitalist exploitation' against which he railed. Jamaica, taken
from the Spaniards in 1655 was, from 1660 onwards, developed as a sugar-plantation colony.

It is also open to question whether Olivier's 'patriotic
Jamaicans' might not be more accurately described as suc-

[38] W. H. Gardner, *History of Jamaica* (London, 1874).
[39] Olivier, *Jamaica; the Blessed Island* (London: Faber &
Faber, 1936), p. 19.

cessful proprietors in their usual state of *absence d'esprit*. Edward Long, in the 1760's remarked that it was an established custom "for every father here, who has acquired a little property, to send his children, of whatever complexion to Britain, for education. They go like a bale of dry goods, consigned to some factor, who places them at the school where he himself was bred, or any other that his inclination leads him to prefer."[40]

If propertied men endowed schools in Jamaica and at the same time sent their children to be placed in schools in Britain, then it is clear that the schools they endowed were not intended for their own children. This view is supported by current research;

> The intentions of the founders were open to interpretation. For the early foundations it could be assumed that less wealthy white children were supposed to be the beneficiaries; these were 'the poor children' or 'the poor boys and girls' of the various wills. The bequests were similar to those left in England in the eighteenth century to found charity schools for the poor of the locality on the death of the benefactor. The English charity school was concerned to give an elementary education of religious character as a preparation for life for working members of the respectable poor. The prospects were not equivalent for white children in Jamaica and Barbados, and few of the white estate employees or tradesmen in the towns would have appreciated such an educational offering for their children.[41]

Olivier's 'patriotic Jamaicans', it would appear, were less concerned with Jamaica than with acquiring the insignia of wealthy and benevolent Englishmen. Their foundations had little relevance to the needs of the island in which they were supposed to be doers of good things, and, it might be argued, were intended to increase their qualifications

[40] Edward Long, *The History of Jamaica*. I am grateful to my colleague Miss Shirley Gordon for giving me this reference.
[41] From a draft of Miss Shirley Gordon's history of West Indian education.

for absenteeism rather than to distinguish them as West India proprietors with a social conscience and the means to assuage it. Any contention that these people, whether resident or absentee, could have contributed to the growth of a sane and well-integrated colonial society is highly disputable.

Absenteeism did not deprive the colonies of a desirable social élite. It simply took from the colonies those people in whose view 'colonial élite' was a contradiction in terms and whose means permitted them to be élite rather than colonial.

It has been said in their defence that many of the absentees chose to leave the colonies because as sensitive and humane people they could not tolerate the daily rub with slavery.[42] A pity then, that their sensitivity did not radiate from their hearts to their pockets—but there have been many others equally determined to stand by their profits rather than by their principles.[43]

References to the social and political consequences of absenteeism point to the numerical scarcity in the colonies of people of a certain social class. Directly, therefore, they are concerned with the numbers of residents rather than with the numbers of absentees. The argument, really, is not that there were so many absentees, but that there were so few residents having sufficient claim to social eminence, and to political and administrative authority. But scarcity of residents of a certain social class may reflect an emigration of members of that class, a slow rate of population growth among that class, and an insufficient social mobility to allow the increase of that class by assimilations of new members from the general population.

In the British West Indies all these factors operated to limit the number of residents who might assume positions of social, political, and administrative leadership. Edward Long[44] gave estimates of the population of Jamaica as

---

[42] J. H. Parry and P. M. Sherlock, *op. cit.*, p. 153.

[43] Eric Williams, *op. cit.*, p. 86.

[44] *History of Jamaica*, Vol. I, pp. 376 ff. But estimates of populations in the West Indies in the eighteenth century vary

18,068 in 1673 (made up of 8,564 whites and 9,504 negroes), and 193,614 in 1774. The latter figure was broken down as follows:

WHITES:

Settled and resident	17,000
Transients	500
Soldiers and seamen	3,000
Annuitants and non-resident proprietors	2,000
Total	22,500

FREE PEOPLE OTHER THAN WHITES:

Maroons	500
Free Black and Coloured people	3,700
Total	4,200

SLAVES:

Mulatto	1,700
Negro	165,214
Total	166,914

These figures nicely illustrate the previous points. The number of absentee proprietors (even if we extend the figure to 10,000 to allow for their families[45]) was smaller than the number of resident settlers, and was about one-seventeenth of the total population. A comparison between the figures for 1673 and 1774 indicates a much more rapid growth of the negro than of the white population. The slower increase of whites reflected the aversion of fortune-seekers to the encumbrances of family in plantation colonies; the more rapid increase of negroes reflected the vast expansion of the slave-trade to feed the developing plantations with labour. But above all, the figures for

widely. R. M. Martin, *The English Colonies,* Vol. 4 (London, 1852), p. 93, gives the following figures for Jamaica in 1775: Whites—12,737, Free Coloured People—4,093, and Slaves—192,787.

[45] But note that the number of resident whites would not have included those children and others temporarily in Britain—though not as absentee-owners or annuitants.

1774 show that of a total population of over 190,000 about 170,000 had not the faintest hope of ever being reckoned among the élite or called to the slightest position in the public service of the colony.

The 500 maroons were concentrated in their own limited territory.[46] The 3,700 free black and coloured people, though often allowed the freedom of the boudoirs, were not received in the drawing-rooms of the whites, and until 1831 were ineligible for the vote or for the public service. The 167,000 slaves were capital equipment. Surely it is reasonable to say that slavery, and the social and civil disabilities of the free black and coloured people, rather than absenteeism, were to blame for the small numbers of 'qualified' people, and, consequently, for the general social and political malaise and its more specific features such as multiple office-holding and lack of integrity in high places. The oligarchic form of the colonial legislatures reflected the social and economic organization of slave-worked, sugar-plantation colonies. The smallness of the oligarchies was a consequence not only of the absence of some who would have qualified for membership, but, even more, of the refusal to recruit new membership locally through fear that the oligarchy might be broken.

Those who were debarred from high society and from public office were, however, permitted to enter trade and in that some did exceedingly well.[47] There has never been a complaint that absenteeism deprived the West Indies of a competent and successful merchant class, even though by the late eighteenth century many of the absentees were merchants.

Finally, there remains the larger claim that absentee-ownership drained wealth from the colonies; that the profits

[46] By the Articles of peace with the Maroons, March 1738. See Bryan Edwards, *History . . . of the West Indies*, Vol. I (Appendix), for a brief account taken from other sources.

[47] For information about the achievements of the "Free Black and Coloured People" see: C. H. Wesley, "The Negroes in the West Indies" in the *Journal of Negro History*, Vols. XVII (1932), pp. 51–66, and XIX (1934), pp. 137–71; J. A. Thome and H. J. Kimball, *Emancipation in the West Indies*.

of sugar went not to further economic development in the colonies, but to investment in the British home economy or to the financing of the conspicuous consumption of the absentee-proprietors.

In this paper consideration is limited to two basic questions: first, was there a drain of wealth from the colonies, and secondly, if there was, to what extent can it be attributed to the prevalence of absentee-ownership? There is unquestionable evidence that many absentees did indulge in extravagantly expensive, and sometimes vulgar display in Britain. There is less agreement about the investment of the profits of West Indian sugar in British economic growth. Adam Smith contended that the "monopoly of the colony trade" enriched only the merchants and distracted investment in British industry generally and in foreign commerce.[48] Eric Williams has presented much evidence to support the contrary view that the profits of sugar did find their way into the financing of the industrial revolution in Britain.[49]

There seems, consequently, little need here to remarshall the argument that there was indeed a flow of wealth from the colonies to Britain; whether for re-investment in 'the colony trade', or for investment in British industrial development, or for conspicuous consumption—which is obviously related to trade and industry which supply the goods to be conspicuously consumed.

All that remains, then, is the need to examine in greater detail the possible meaning of a 'drain of wealth', and to discover whether, in the period under review, absenteeism can be blamed for it.

The financing and marketing of British West Indian sugar production in the eighteenth and early nineteenth centuries were complicated businesses. The flows of money or bullion between Britain and the colonies, in either direction, were insignificant. Within the colonies payments were

[48] *The Wealth of Nations* (New York: Cannan Edition, Random House, 1937), pp. 557–606, on colonies.
[49] *Capitalism and Slavery*, Chap. 5, on British industry and the triangular trade.

made in produce, in the various 'local currencies', composed of small quantities of British or foreign coin which circulated there,[50] and in bills of exchange on British merchant or commission houses to which estates consigned their produce. Payments in Britain were made out of the proceeds of sales of crops forwarded from the estates to their consignees there, or in debit accounts with consignees. Consignees in Britain performed a multitude of services for West Indian planters, both resident and absentee. They received, stored, and sold sugar and other produce; they kept estate accounts; they made payments to the estate's creditors and to the holders of annuities chargeable on the profits; they made purchases on behalf of the estate, and to satisfy the personal needs of resident planters and their families; as we have already seen, they sometimes received the children of resident planters; and they were the bankers of the planters insofar as they held their current credit and debit balances. In a number of cases these merchants or commission agents were also absentee-proprietors.[51]

The wealth which flowed from the West Indies to Britain was in the form of produce, not money. It came from the estates of resident and of absentee-proprietors. When it was sold in Britain some of the proceeds went in payment of the costs of production and marketing, some went in payment for exports of all kinds from Britain to the colonies, and some went in payment of planters' debt. None of this can be said to have constituted a drain on the wealth of the colonies except insofar as 'the monopoly of the colony trade' raised the prices of goods, services, and credit to the planters.

To the extent that the planters were paying the price of

---

[50] Sidney Mintz, "Currency Problems in Eighteenth-Century Jamaica and Gresham's Law", in R. A. Manners, ed., *Process and Pattern in Culture* (Chicago: Aldine, 1964).

[51] For example: the Beckfords, Hibberts, and Pennants of Jamaica; the Codringtons of Barbados and the Leeward Islands; the Kirwans, Dunbars, and Shands of Antigua; the Gladstones of British Guiana and Jamaica; the Pinneys of Nevis; and many others.

dependence on merchants who controlled their trade, there
was a drain; but this was as true for resident as for absentee proprietors. Moreover, British commercial regulations and tariffs, until the 1840's, gave high protection in
the British market to British colonial sugars. Thus the
estate-owners, whether resident or absentee, enjoyed a degree of monopoly power in the British market, and were
able to fetch a higher price for their sugars than would
otherwise have been the case.

In the circumstances, the strongest position was held by
those estate-owners who were also engaged in Britain as
West India merchants or commission agents for West India
produce. As proprietors and merchants they could serve the
interests of their different enterprises and elect, as market
conditions varied, to take their profits either as producers
or as middlemen. But it was not necessary to be an absentee to enjoy this advantage. A resident planter or his
family might control a merchant-house or commission
agency in Britain, just as an absentee might control property in the colonies.[52]

Indeed, it is difficult to distinguish between resident and
absentee-owners except on the obvious difference that the
former were, and the latter were not, resident in the colonies. It was upon a similar distinction that Mountifort Longfield, writing in the 1830's primarily on the Irish absentee
problem, based his view that:

If absenteeism be injurious, it must be in one or both
of these respects. Either the absentee proprietor inflicts
a positive injury upon his country by living abroad, and
drawing and spending his revenue there, or he injures
it in another manner negatively, depriving his country

[52] In Antigua, for instance, "At least 52 families had members
away from the island for protracted periods in the years from
1730 to 1775. Included among them were 20 London-West India
merchants, 12 members of parliament, one lord mayor of London, and nine titled persons." R. B. Sheridan, "The Rise of a
Colonial Gentry: Antigua 1730–1775" in *The Economic History Review*, Second Series, Vol. XIII, No. 3, 1961, p. 346.

of those services which he probably would perform if he were to reside at home.[53]

As far as the absentee-owners of West Indian property were concerned, it has previously been argued that most of them did not appear to regard the colonies as "home"; that the extent to which their absence deprived the colonies of services of value depended, very largely, on the quantitative as well as the qualitative aspects of absenteeism at any particular time, and that the colonial élites were deprived of significant membership as much by internal social and demographic factors as by absenteeism. If those arguments are acceptable, it remains necessary to examine further only the 'positive injury' of absenteeism as defined above.

In this, however, a now familiar point again recurs. Absentee owners did indeed draw and spend their revenues abroad; but so too did the resident proprietors. The financial and marketing organization of sugar production was such that planters' accounts and balances were kept in Britain. Earnings were spent in Britain because the earners were either resident in Britain or resident in tropical agricultural islands, devoted to the production of export staples, and dependent on imports of British goods of all kinds to support life and labour on the tropical plantations. The profits of sugar, whether resident or absentee-owned, did not go to the founding of colonial banks, or to the subscription of loans in the colonies for local colonial enterprise, or to any other projects for local development, because Britain was the financial capital, the commercial entrepôt, and the industrial provider. Any colonial endeavour that seemed likely to threaten or to weaken British metropolitan interests was discouraged.

The whole object of the European nations in acquiring colonies in the late fifteenth to the late eighteenth centuries was to increase the wealth of the metropolitan country.

[53] Mountifort Longfield, *Three Lectures on Commerce and One on Absenteeism*, Dublin 1835 (London School of Economics and Political Science Reprint, 1938).

This was to be achieved by the effective occupation of territories which were regarded as being either rich in resources of value to the metropolitan country or strategically important in the military business of protecting empire or denying empire to others.

It was tobacco, then sugar and cotton, which made most of the West India islands desirable to Britain. Neither Crown nor Parliament had been much excited by the first settlements in Barbados and the Leeward Islands, until the first settlers began to produce tobacco in exportable quantity to a growing market in England. The subsequent turn to sugar cultivation enhanced the value of the islands, and Jamaica, soon after its capture, became 'the darling plantation' of Charles II.

Also contributing to their importance was the strategic value of islands such as Antigua, from which the French in the Windward Islands could be observed and, at times, harassed; Jamaica, lying almost between Cuba and Hispaniola, and between them and New Granada; and Trinidad, which, though a late eighteenth century British acquisition, had in the past been tempting as a good stepping stone to the Orinoco and "El Dorado".

The European view of tropical plantation colonies was that possession of them enriched the possessor. They yielded tropical produce desirable in colder Europe, and, since they were both tropical and agricultural, they provided markets for the products of European agriculture and industry. The European country which possessed the greatest and most productive of these plantations and bound their commerce to its own advantage consequently expected to reap the benefit of a rich trade and growing markets.

Clearly enough, it was the metropolitan view that the costs of acquiring and defending such plantations would be fully repaid by the wealth that possession of them would yield. Absentee-ownership entered not in the slightest degree into these reckonings. The device of early proprietory forms of government was contrived as a means of enabling first enterprise, not as a means of draining wealth. The growth of the sugar industry concurred with the decline of proprietory government and the emergence of loud local assemblies. The growth of the sugar industry also awakened the keen interest of Crown and Parliament in the ways and means of securing to England the wealth that English plantations would yield.

Even Adam Smith, whose 'Wealth of Nations' attacked the economic philosophy of the first British Empire, did not dispute that wealth had accrued from "the monopoly of the colony trade". He argued rather that the monopoly was restrictive, that the wealth had flowed not to Britain but to those British merchants in the colonial trade, and that the ending of the monopoly would yield a greater and a more general economic advantage by removing unwarrantable inducements to colonial commercial enterprise as against foreign trade and British industrial growth.

It is probably true that with or without absentee-ownership, wealth would have been drained from the colonies to Britain. The expectation of such a drain was one of the motives for the acquisition of 'tropical plantations'.

In conclusion, there is one small but important point which is sometimes overlooked in the general allegations against absentee-ownership. Wealth can be drained away only if there is wealth. The history of the British West Indies provides no picture of undisturbed prosperity. There have been times, for instance in the 1730's, the 1780's and in the post-Napoleonic War and post-emancipation periods, when West Indian property has been deeply depressed, and when the profits of sugar have been small for all but a few of the ablest or most fortunate producers. In such times the drain must have dwindled and perhaps dried up altogether, and there were years in which the drain flowed in reverse with absentee estate-owners investing their earnings from other sources in the maintenance of West India property until the sugar market improved.[54] If this be so, a 'net drain', one way or the other, should be determined only in account over a specified period of time.

[54] Gisela Eisner, *Jamaica 1830–1930, A Study in Economic Growth* (Manchester University Press, 1961), pp. 196–97.

It may be as well to end with a reminder. The purpose of this essay has not been to prove either that absentee-ownership was a good thing, or a bad thing; or that it did, or did not, reduce the wealth or prosperity of these territories. The purpose has been to plead that broad generalizations about the consequences of absentee-ownership are likely to be indefensible, and that a proper understanding of the importance of absentee-ownership in our history remains to be given by further careful research and assessment.

8.

This is the concluding essay of a series of articles commissioned for the New York *Times* in 1860, arguing that West Indian emancipation had been a success. The author asserts that freedom had benefited planters as well as former slaves; that production in most territories had increased rather than declined; and that an enhanced sense of general security augured well for the future of West Indian society. Seeking to put down slavery in the American South, the author painted West Indian emancipation *couleur de rose*. He alludes only briefly to the continuing subordination of the freed slaves to the planters, does not mention the decline of sugar, ignores the circumstances and effects of indentured immigration, and fails to notice the increasing acerbities among white, colored, and black that were soon to culminate in a bloody upheaval in Jamaica. But he saw, as did few other "objective" observers of the day, that where freedom of enterprise was really possible, freedom was not only real but immensely valuable.

Born in Quebec in 1829, WILLIAM G. SEWELL studied law but gave up his legal practice for journalism, which he followed in New York City until his death in 1862.

The Ordeal of Free Labor in the British West Indies
William G. Sewell

Bridgetown, Barbados, 1860.
I have endeavored, and I hope successfully, to show that each of the British West India colonies has had its own distinct and separate history, its own elements of prosperity, its own resources to develop, its own political and social evils to eradicate, its own policy to pursue, its own destiny to work out. I have endeavored to combat the error of judging the islands by rules that might apply to a continental dependency, and of tracing their depression, past or present, to the same or to a single origin. The fact that some islands need immigration, while others do not—that some are being colonized with Asiatics, while others are already densely peopled with Africans—points out the mistake of supposing their fortunes identical, or their cases exactly parallel. Emancipation, it is true, was granted to all at the same time and on the same conditions; but it was admitted to each island under different auspices, and breathed in each a different atmosphere. In Jamaica—where slavery was the primary formation upon which the social and political structures rested, and the revolution to be effected was most comprehensive—the change was resolutely and systematically opposed by a powerful plantocracy. Freedom, in Jamaica, was met and encountered at every point, and found, among the governing

The Ordeal of Free Labour in the West Indies, pp. 310–25; originally published in New York, Harper & Bros., 1861. Now available from Frank Cass, London, 1968.

classes, a very limited number of willing workers. In the small and comparatively unimportant island of Antigua, freedom was received by the monopolists of the day, if not with cordiality, at least as an innovation which they were forced to accept, and which merited, under the circumstances, a fair and impartial trial. Emancipation was an isolated experiment in each of the different colonies. Precedents and rules of action for one were no precedents or rules of action for another. *Here* there were obstacles to overcome and difficulties to surmount which *there* did not exist, or existed only in a mitigated form. Each colony was a field of battle upon which the banners of free labor and slave labor were flung to the winds; and while in some, where resistance was feeble, all trace of the contest has disappeared, and prosperity has revived, in others, where resistance was strong and determined, the exhaustion that follows a long war and a long reign of oppression weighs heavily upon a dispirited people. Let us not be deceived. Let us not misinterpret the true meaning of Jamaica's desolation at the present time. Let no one be so mad as to believe that it is the work of freedom. Let no one fancy that even an aristocracy were ruined by the system from which they so long and so stubbornly withheld their allegiance. Let no one question the victory, though its choicest fruits are yet to be reaped; let no one doubt that freedom, when it overturned a despotism and crushed a monopoly, unshackled, at the same time, the commerce, the industry, and the intelligence of the islands, and laid the foundations of permanent prosperity.

I have addressed myself exclusively to the argument of the planter, for his pretension is, in reality, the only one to be disputed. It could not have been expected that he would act otherwise than he did. It was his part to resist. The new system was meant to effect a radical change in plantation management, and it was only natural for the proprietor to look upon any change that he had not proved with distrust and aversion. His monopolies and his privileges were to be swept away, and he could not encourage the scheme that doomed them to destruction, and opened

to wide competition the field of profit he had hith
clusively enjoyed. Many of the planters went dow
the privileges and the monopolies by which alone
had managed to keep afloat; but are the Act of Emancipation and the abolition of a protective tariff to be condemned because they tore down the veil of fictitious prosperity and exposed a helpless bankruptcy? Are these West
India colonies ruined in their sugar interest, or any other
interest, because some five hundred third-rate sugar-
planters had not the stamina, pluck, capital, strength, wit,
or what you please, to stand alone when the props of favoritism and partial legislation were removed? If free labor
be tested by any other gauge than that of sugar-production,
its success in the West Indies is established beyond all cavil
and beyond all peradventure. If the people merit any consideration whatever—if their independence, their comfort,
their industry, their education, form any part of a country's
prosperity—then the West Indies are a hundred-fold more
prosperous now than they were in the most flourishing
times of slavery. If peace be an element of prosperity—
if it be important to enjoy uninterrupted tranquillity and
be secure from servile war and insurrection—then the
West Indies have now an advantage that they never possessed before it was given them by emancipation. If a
largely-extended commerce be an indication of prosperity,
then all the West Indies, Jamaica alone excepted, have
progressed under a system of free labor, although that
system hitherto has been but imperfectly developed.

I have endeavored to convey a correct idea of the
depreciation of commerce and the decline of sugar-
cultivation in Jamaica; and I have also endeavored to show
that this depreciation is an exception to the present general prosperity of the British West Indies—that it com-
menced before emancipation was projected, and can be
traced directly to other causes than the introduction of
freedom. Long before Mr. Canning, in his place in Parliament, became the unwilling organ of the national will,
and explained, in terms not to be mistaken, that the demand of the British people for the liberation of the slaves

could no longer be resisted, West India commerce was in the most alarming state of depression, owing to the heavy outlay and expenditure that a system of slave labor imperatively required. Testimony pointing directly and overwhelmingly to this conclusion has been given by planters themselves—by men put forward as the special champions of the planting interest—and fills a score of Parliamentary Blue-books. Upon their statements the report of the select committee on the condition of the West India colonies, printed in 1832, declared that "there was abundant evidence of an existing distress for ten or twelve years previous." That report described an impending, if not an actual ruin that we look for in vain at the present day. Jamaica, in 1860, and she only in the one particular of sugar-cultivation, is the single British island whose industry and enterprise remain, as we are told they formerly were, exhausted and paralyzed.

Let us appeal once more to figures. The colony of British Guiana, for four years prior to emancipation, exported an annual average of 98,000,000 lbs. of sugar, while, from 1856 to 1860, its annual average export rose to 100,600,-000 lbs. The colony of Trinidad, for four years prior to emancipation, annually exported an average of 37,000,000 lbs. of sugar, while, from 1856 to 1860, its annual average export rose to 62,000,000 lbs. The colony of Barbados, for four years prior to emancipation, annually exported an average of 32,800,000 lbs. of sugar, while, from 1856 to 1860, its annual average export rose to 78,000,000 lbs. The colony of Antigua, for four years prior to emancipation, exported an annual average of 19,500,000 lbs. of sugar, while, from 1856 to 1860, its annual average export rose to 24,400,000 lbs. This is a total exhibit of 265,000,-000 lbs. annually exported now, instead of 187,300,000 lbs. before emancipation, or *an excess of exports, with free labor, of seventy-seven million, seven hundred thousand pounds of sugar*.

In the matter of imports, we find that the colony of British Guiana, between the years 1820 and 1834, imported annually to the value of $3,700,000; that the an-

ual imports of Trinidad, during the same period, averaged
in value $1,690,000; that the imports of Barbados aver-
aged in value $2,850,000; and those of Antigua $600,000.
In the year 1859 the imports of Guiana were valued at
$5,660,000; those of Trinidad at $3,000,000; those of Barbados at $4,660,000; and those of Antigua at $1,280,000.
The total exhibit represents an annual import trade, at the
present time, of the value of $14,600,000, against $8,840,-
000 before emancipation, or *an excess of imports, under
a free system, of the value of five million, seven hundred
and sixty thousand dollars.*

In the exports I have made mention of sugar only; but
if all other articles of commerce be included, and a comparison be instituted between the import and export trade
of the colonies of Guiana, Trinidad, Barbados, and Antigua under slavery, and their trade under freedom, the
annual balance in favor of freedom will be found to have
reached already FIFTEEN MILLIONS OF DOLLARS at the very
lowest estimate.

This large increase in the trade of four out of the five
principal West India colonies is sufficient, I think, to demonstrate (were there no other evidence at hand) that free
labor, with which four have prospered, can not alone be
held responsible for the decline of the fifth. The increase
of sugar-production also demonstrates the improved industry of the islands to a very remarkable extent; for it
must be remembered that the agricultural force now engaged in cane-cultivation is scarcely more than half of
what it was in times of slavery, when the energies of the
whole population were directed to this single end. One
of the most natural and legitimate results of emancipation
was to allow every man to do what seemed to him best—to
achieve independence if he could—to pursue, in any case,
the path of industry most agreeable to his tastes, and most
conducive to his happiness. When we look at the vast
political and social structure that has been demolished—
the new and grander edifice that has been erected—the
enemies that have been vanquished—the prejudices that
have been uprooted—the education that has been sown

broadcast, the ignorance that has been removed—the in
dustry that has been trained and fostered—we can no
pause to criticise defects, for we are amazed at the progres
of so great a revolution within the brief space of twenty
five years. Those who have never lived in a slave country
little know how the institution entwines itself round the
vitals of society and poisons the sources of political life
The physical condition of the slave is lost in the contempla-
tion of a more overwhelming argument. Looking at the
question from a high national standpoint, it is, comparatively speaking, a matter of temporary interest and minor
importance whether the bondsman is treated with kindness
and humanity, as in America, or with short-sighted brutality, as in Cuba. It is the influence of the system upon
the energies and the morality of a people that demands
the calmest and most earnest consideration of patriots and
statesmen. The present is, perhaps, not so much to be
condemned as the future, from which all eyes are studi-
ously averted, is to be dreaded. An act of the British Parliament, and a vote of twenty millions sterling, were sufficient to release 800,000 slaves; but no act of the British
Parliament could thus summarily remove the curse that
slavery had bequeathed to these islands, and had left to
fester in their heart's core. Time only could do that; time
has not done it yet.

I have endeavored to show—and I hope successfully—
that the experiment of free labor in the West Indies has
established its superior economy, as well as its possibility
Not a single island fails to demonstrate that the Creoles or
African descent, in all their avocations and in all their
pursuits, work, under a free system, for proper remuneration, though their labor is often ignorantly wasted and
misdirected. *That* arises from want of education, want of
training, want of good example. I have not sought to
justify the maudlin sympathy that the mere mention of
these people seems to excite in certain quarters, nor have
I advocated their interests to the detriment of any other
interest whatever. I have simply maintained, from evidence
before me, that the right of one class to enjoy the wages

nd fruits of their labor, does not and can not injuriously
ffect the rights of any other class, or damage, as some
oolishly pretend, a country's prosperity. An ethnological
ssue, quite foreign to the subject, has been dragged into
he argument. No one can deny that, up to the present
ime, the African, in intelligence, in industry, and in force
f character, has been, and still is, the inferior of the
European; but it is a tremendous mistake to suppose that
is intelligence can ever be quickened, his industry sharp-
ned, or his character strengthened under slavery; and it
s worse than a mistake to consign him to slavery for de-
ects that slavery itself engendered, or to condemn him
ecause the cardinal virtues of civilization did not spring
nto life upon the instant that the heel of oppression was
emoved. With the destiny of the West Indies the welfare
f these people is inseparably bound up, and it is as wrong
o overlook their faults as to deny that they have pro-
ressed under freedom, or to doubt that, by the spread of
ducation and under the dominion of an enlightened gov-
rnment, they will become still more elevated in the scale
f civilization. Those who are not afraid of the confession
vill admit that the West Indian Creole has made a good
ght. The act of emancipation virtually did no more than
lace liberty within his reach. Actual independence he
ad to achieve for himself. All untutored and undisci-
lined as he was, he had to contend against social preju-
ice, political power, and a gigantic interest, before he
ould enjoy the boon that the act nominally conferred
pon him. The planter was bred to the belief that his
usiness could only be conducted with serf labor, and he
lung to the fallacy long after serf labor had been legally
bolished. Witness the land tenure which still exists in a
nitigated form throughout all the West Indies, and re-
uires the tenant, on peril of summary ejection, to give
is services exclusively to his landlord. The instinct of
elf-interest—the faintest desire for independence—would
rompt any one to reject such a bondage. Yet this rejec-
ion is the sole accusation brought against the negro—this
he only ground upon which he has been condemned. I

have endeavored to point out the two paths that lay open to the West Indian Creole after the abolition of slavery. The one was to remain an estate serf and make sugar for the planter; the other was to rent or purchase land, and work for estates, if he pleased, but be socially independent of a master's control. I endeavored to follow these two classes of people in the paths they pursued—the majority who have become independent, and the minority, who have remained estate laborers—and I have shown that the condition of the former is infinitely above the condition of the latter. Is this any where denied? Can any one say that it was not the lawful right of these people thus to seek and, having found, to cherish their independence? Can any one say that, by doing so, they wronged themselves, the planters, or the government under which they lived? Can any one say that they are to blame if, by their successful attempts to elevate themselves above the necessitous and precarious career of labor for daily hire, the agricultural field force was weakened, and the production of sugar diminished? Yet this is the fairest case that can be made out for the oligarchies of these West India islands. They have denounced the negro for his defective industry; but what, we may ask, have they themselves done—in what have *they* given proof of their nobler civilization and higher intelligence? Surely a most important duty devolved upon them. They were the privileged aristocracy, the landed proprietors, the capitalists, the rulers of the colonies—as they still are. Their political power was supreme; yet what have they done, not for the permanent prosperity of the islands—for the question need not be asked—but in behalf of their own special interests? They arraigned the negro for deserting their estates and ruining their fortunes, when they themselves were absentees, and were paying the legitimate profits of their business to agents and overseers. They offered the independent peasant no pecuniary inducement, or its equivalent, to prefer their service; but they attempted to obtain his work for less remuneration than he could earn in any other employment. They never cared for the comfort or happiness of their tenants, or

ought to inspire them with confidence and contentment. They made no effort to elevate labor above the degraded level at which slavery left it, and they never set an example to their inferiors of the industry that is still needed in the higher as well as in the lower classes of West Indian society. Enterprise never prompted them to encourage the introduction of labor-saving arts. Yet these were measures that demanded the action of an enlightened legislature and the consideration of an influential proprietary long before scarcity of labor became a subject of complaint. Instead of averting the evil they dreaded, they hastened its consummation, and injured their cause still more deeply by the false and evasive plea that the idleness of the Creole was the cause of a commercial and agricultural depression that they had brought entirely on themselves. Is it any argument against the industry of the laboring classes of America that a large proportion annually become proprietors, and withdraw from service for daily hire? Yet this is precisely what the West India Creole has done; this is the charge on which he has been arraigned—this is the crime for which he has been condemned.

I do not think it can be doubted that a want of confidence between employer and employed, engendered altogether by the mistaken policy of the governing classes, contributed largely to the prolonged depression of the West Indies—a depression from which most of them, under the advantages of free labor, have greatly recovered within the last ten years. Many of the old sources of evil and complaint have been abolished; some still live. Absenteeism is prevalent, and hypothecation, in Jamaica more especially, weighs heavily upon the agricultural interest. But the West Indian planter now generally admits the superior advantages of free labor, and is careful to avoid the grosser errors into which his predecessors fell. Landed property is changing hands, and new men are building up, upon a broader and sounder basis than that of slavery, the most important interest of these islands. The storm of a great adversity has passed over. There is

no longer a struggle to wring from an unwilling plantocracy an admission in favor of freedom. That belongs to
the history of the battle of independence, which, in these
colonies, was nobly fought and triumphantly won; and if I
have recalled the contest to mind, it was not to revive old
grievances, but to illustrate truth, and vindicate the policy
of freedom. The mode by which those colonies that need
labor are to be supplied with an intelligent and industrious
population is the practical question of the day. It certainly
would neither be wise nor just to oppose, by legislation or
otherwise, the abstraction of labor from estates so rapidly
going on. Nothing could be adduced to illustrate more
forcibly the progress of the people. The abstraction did
not commence until some years after emancipation—until
those who had been able to save money began to purchase land and cultivate for themselves. This is the great
West Indian problem. It has been so complicated and dis-
torted that its most familiar acquaintances scarcely know
what to believe; but, divested of such foreign incum-
brances as "defects of African character," and other similar stuff and nonsense, it is simply a land question, with
which race and color have nothing whatever to do. The
same process goes on in the United States, in Canada, in
Australia, and in all new countries where land is cheap
and plentiful and the population sparse. The laborer soon
becomes a proprietor; the ranks of the laboring force are
rapidly thinned; and the capitalist is compelled to pay high,
it may be extravagant wages. In the West Indies the capitalist refuses to pay high wages; he thinks that the control
of the labor market is one of his rights. He imagines, and
upon what ground I can not comprehend, that farming
in these colonies should yield much larger profits than
farming any where else. He calls it "planting," and fancies
that there ought to be a wide social distinction between the
man who grows cane or cotton and the man who grows
potatoes and parsnips. God save the mark! Does any one
dream that if West India planters stuck to their business
like English farmers, and possessed one half of their practical ability and industry, the agricultural and commercial

interests of the islands would have ever suffered from emancipation? The profits of sugar-cultivation, according to the planter's creed, must be large enough to yield the proprietor, though an absentee, a comfortable income, and pay large salaries besides to overseers and attorneys; otherwise estates are abandoned, and the sugar interest is "ruined." These expectations might have been realized in the days of the old monopoly; they certainly are not realized now, and never can be realized again, unless the British people recede from their principles of free trade and free labor. If labor in the West Indies is high—so high that sometimes the planter can not afford to pay the price demanded—he is not worse off than the capitalist in all new countries. His attempt to keep the people day laborers, and to check the development of a natural law, is foolish and wicked. There is but one remedy for this abstraction from estate-labor, and that remedy is immigration. It must be a constant immigration as long as land is cheap and plentiful, for the immigrants themselves—and notoriously the Portuguese, whose industry was once the theme of the planter's praise and exultation—forsake the laboring ranks, and become proprietors and tradesmen as soon as they are released from their contracts of service. It must be a colonizing immigration, or permanent prosperity can never be reaped. It must be a free immigration, violating in no points of theory and in no details of practice the grant of liberty conferred by the Act of Emancipation upon these islands and their populations forever. This immigration has been placed within the reach of all the colonies that required it, though the jealous fears of the British people have prompted them to withhold from the local governments its entire direction and control. By this immigration the planters of Trinidad and Guiana have greatly profited, while the planters of Jamaica, exceptional again, with languishing energies and paralyzed enterprise, have derived no more benefit from the labor they imported than from the Creole labor they profess to have lost, but which, in reality, they recklessly squandered.

Truth, we are told, will prevail, and freedom, we know,

is truth. Howsoever people may differ on questions of political liberty, into which inequalities of birth, race, position, and intelligence are permitted to enter, modern civilization has recognized and ratified the inalienable right of men to the wages of their industry, to the happiness they have toiled for, and to the independence they have earned. Here is the true field of equality, where rank, or race, or intellect has no chartered precedence. From the day when this great principle was admitted throughout the British West Indies their true prosperity may be dated. For freedom knows no favoritism; her honors are not crowded upon a privileged class, her aid is not limited to a particular interest. The act of British emancipation has been widely abused; but its detractors must live among the people it disenthralled if they would learn the value at which it *can* be estimated. Time, which develops the freedom that act created, adds continually to its lustre; and long after England's highest achievements in arts or in arms shall have been forgotten, this grant of liberty shall testify to the grandeur of her power and to the magnanimity of her people. I have not assumed, in aught I have written, that the West Indian Creole is yet capable of self-government. I have simply endeavored to show that, under freedom, sources of industry and prosperity have been opened that, under slavery, would have remained closed forever. I have endeavored to show that, for the West Indies, freedom has been the best policy, though the moralist may condemn an argument that sets forth another motive for doing right than the sake of right itself. If emancipation did no more than relieve the West Indian slave from the supervision of a task-master I should have nothing left to say; for I admitted, at the outset, that the condition of the laboring classes was but one among many interests whose ruin, if personal liberty could ruin them, would make us disbelieve in truth itself. But freedom, when allowed fair play, injured the prosperity of none of these West Indian colonies. It saved them from a far deeper and more lasting depression than any they have yet known. It was a boon conferred upon all classes of society: upon planter and upon laborer; upon all interests: upon commerce and agriculture—upon industry and education—upon morality and religion. And if a perfect measure of success remains to be achieved, let not freedom be condemned; for the obstacles to overcome were great, and the workers were few and unwilling. Let it be remembered that a generation, born in the night of slavery, has not yet passed away, and that men who were taught to believe in that idol and its creations still control the destinies of these distant colonies. Reluctantly they learnt the lesson forced upon them; slowly their opposition yielded to the dawning of conviction; but, now that the meridian of truth has been reached, we may hope that light will dispel all the shadows of slavery, and confound the logic of its champions when they falsely assert that emancipation has ruined the British islands.

9.

Visiting the West Indies in 1888, an eminent British historian drew conclusions directly contrary to those of the previous selection. This chapter from Froude's book presents a white racist perspective on the consequence of freedom and self-government. The author's imperialist, chauvinist, and racially biased views were shared by many eminent Englishmen of the era—Thomas Carlyle's "Occasional Discourse on the Nigger Question," judging Negroes inherently incapable of self-rule and hence better off in a state of subjugation, is the best-known example of the genre. As the number of whites in the islands rapidly declined, Froude and like-minded Britons feared that local self-government might end in black rule after the Haitian model.

JAMES ANTHONY FROUDE, Regius Professor of History at Oxford, based his West Indian conclusions on limited observations and discussions confined mainly to West Indian officials. The combination of Froude's bias and his prestige made his book infamous throughout the Caribbean.

The Perils of Black Supremacy*
James Anthony Froude

As I was stepping into the boat at Port Royal, a pamphlet was thrust into my hand, which I was entreated to read at my leisure. It was by some discontented white of the island—no rare phenomenon, and the subject of it was the precipitate decline in the value of property there. The writer, unlike the planters, insisted that the people were taxed in proportion to their industry. There were taxes on mules, on carts, on donkeys, all bearing on the small black proprietors, whose ability to cultivate was thus checked, and who were thus deliberately encouraged in idleness. He might have added, although he did not, that while both in Jamaica and Trinidad everyone is clamouring against the beetroot bounty which artificially lowers the price of sugar, the local councils in these two islands try to counteract the effect and artificially raise the price of sugar by an export duty on their own produce—a singular method of doing it which, I presume, admits of explanation. My pamphleteer was persuaded that all the world were fools, and that he and his friends were the only wise ones: again a not uncommon occurrence in pamphleteers. He demanded the suppression of absenteeism; he demanded free trade. In exchange for the customs duties, which were to be abolished, he demanded a land tax—the very mention of which, I had been told by others, drove the black pro-

The English in the West Indies: or, The Bow of Ulysses, London, Longmans, 1888, pp. 277–87.

* [Editors' title]

prietors whom he wished to benefit into madness. He
wanted Home Rule. He wanted fifty things besides which
I have forgotten, but his grand want of all was a new currency. Mankind, he thought, had been very mad at al
periods of their history. The most significant illustration of
their madness had been the selection of gold and silver as
the medium of exchange. The true base of the currency
was the land. The Government of Jamaica was to lend to
every freeholder up to the mortgage value of his land in
paper notes, at 5 per cent interest, the current rate being
at present 8 per cent. The notes so issued, having the land
as their security, would be in no danger of depreciation,
and they would flow over the sugar estates like an irrigat-
ing stream. On the produce of sugar the fate of the island
depended.

On the produce of sugar? And why not on the produce
of a fine race of men? The prospects of Jamaica, the
prospects of all countries, depend not on sugar or on any
form or degree of material wealth, but on the characters
of the men and women whom they are breeding and rearing. Where there are men and women of a noble nature,
the rest will go well of itself; where these are not, there
will be no true prosperity though the sugar hogsheads be
raised from thousands into millions. The colonies are interesting only as offering homes where English people can
increase and multiply; English of the old type with simple
habits, who do not need imported luxuries. There is room
even in the West Indies for hundreds of thousands of them
if they can be contented to lead human lives, and do not
go there to make fortunes which they are to carry home
with them. The time may not be far off when men will be
sick of making fortunes, sick of being ground to pattern
in the commonplace mill-wheel of modern society; sick of
a state of things which blights and kills simple and original
feeling, which makes us think and speak and act under
the tyranny of general opinion, which masquerades as
liberty and means only submission to the newspapers. I
can conceive some modern men may weary of all this,
and retire from it like the old ascetics, not as they did into

the wilderness, but behind their own walls and hedges, shutting out the world and its noises, to inquire whether after all they have really immortal souls, and if they have what ought to be done about them. The West India Islands, with their inimitable climate and soil and prickly pears *ad libitum* to make fences with, would be fine places for such recluses. Failing these ideal personages, there is work enough of the common sort to create wholesome prosperity. There are oranges to be grown, and pines and plantains, and coffee and cocoa, and rice and indigo and tobacco, not to speak of the dollars which my American friend found in the bamboos, and of the further dollars which other Americans will find in the yet untested qualities of thousands of other productions. Here are opportunities for innocent industrious families, where children can be brought up to be manly and simple and true and brave as their fathers were brought up, as their fathers expressed it 'in the nurture and admonition of the Lord,' while such neighbours as their dark brothers-in-law might have a chance of a rise in life, in the only sense in which a 'rise' can be of real benefit to them.

* * * *

We took possession of those islands when they were of supreme importance in our great wrestle with Spain and France. We were fighting then for the liberties of the human race. The Spaniards had destroyed the original Carib and Indian inhabitants. We induced thousands of our own fellow-countrymen to venture life and fortune in the occupation of our then vital conquests. For two centuries we furnished them with black servants whom we purchased on the African coast and carried over and sold there, making our own profits out of the trade, and the colonists prospered themselves and poured wealth and strength into the empire of which they were then an integral part. A change passed over the spirit of the age. Liberty assumed a new dress. We found slavery to be a crime; we released our bondmen; we broke their chains as we proudly described it to ourselves; we compensated the owners, so far as money could compensate, for the entire dislocation of a state of society which we had ourselves created; and we trusted to the enchantment of liberty to create a better in its place. We had delivered our own souls; we had other colonies to take our emigrants. Other lands under our open trade would supply us with the commodities for which we had hitherto been dependent on the West Indies. They ceased to be of commercial, they ceased to be of political, moment to us, and we left them to their own resources. The modern English idea is that everyone must take care of himself. Individuals or aggregates of individuals have the world before them, to open the oyster or fail to open it according to their capabilities. The State is not to help them; the State is not to interfere with them unless for political or party reasons it happens to be convenient. As we treat ourselves we treat our colonies. Those who have gone thither have gone of their own free will, and must take the consequences of their own actions. We allow them no exceptional privileges which we do not claim for ourselves. They must stand, if they are to stand, by their own strength. If they cannot stand they must fall. This is our notion of education in 'manliness,' and for immediate purposes answers well enough. Individual enterprise, unendowed but unfettered, built the main buttresses of the British colonial empire. Australians and New Zealanders are English and Scotchmen who have settled at the antipodes where there is more room for them than at home. They are the same people as we are, and they have the same privileges as we have. They are parts of one and the same organic body as branches from the original trunk. The branch does not part from the trunk, but it discharges its own vital functions by its own energy, and we no more desire to interfere than London desires to interfere with Manchester.

So it stands with us where the colonists are of our race, with the same character and the same objects; and, as I said, the system answers. Under no other relations could we continue a united people. But it does not answer—it has failed wherever we have tried it—when the majority of the inhabitants of countries of which for one or other reason we have possessed ourselves, and of which we keep possession, are not united to us by any of these natural bonds, where they have been annexed by violence or otherwise been forced under our flag. It has failed conspicuously in Ireland. We know that it would fail in the East Indies if we were rash enough to venture the experiment.

* * * *

About the West Indies we do not care very earnestly. Nothing seriously alarming can happen there. So much, therefore, of the general policy of leaving them to help themselves out of their difficulties we have adopted completely. The corollary that they must govern themselves also on their own responsibilities we hesitate as yet to admit completely; but we do not recognise that any responsibility for their failing condition rests on us; and the inclination certainly, and perhaps the purpose, is to throw them entirely upon themselves at the earliest moment. Cuba sends representatives to the Cortes at Madrid, Martinique and Guadaloupe to the Assembly at Paris. In the English islands, being unwilling to govern without some semblance of a constitution, we try tentatively varieties of local boards and local councils, admitting the elective principle but not daring to trust it fully; creating hybrid constitutions, so contrived as to provoke ill feeling where none would exist without them, and to make impossible any tolerable government which could actively benefit the people. We cannot intend that arrangements the effects of which are visible so plainly in the sinking fortunes of our own kindred there, are to continue for ever. We suppose that we cannot go back in these cases. It is to be presumed, therefore, that we mean to go forward, and in doing so I venture to think myself that we shall be doing equal injustice both to our own race and to the blacks, and we shall bring the islands into a condition which will be a reproach and scandal to the empire of which they will remain a dishonoured part. The slave trade was an imperial monopoly, extorted by force, guaranteed by treaties, and our white West Indian interest was built up in connection with and in reliance upon it. We had a right to set the slaves free; but the payment of the indemnity was no full acquittance of our obligations for the condition of a society which we had ourselves created. We have no more right to make the emancipated slave his master's master in virtue of his numbers than we have a right to lay under the heel of the Catholics of Ireland the Protestant minority whom we planted there to assist us in controlling them.

It may be said that we have no intention of doing anything of the kind, that no one at present dreams of giving a full colonial constitution to the West Indian Islands. They are allowed such freedom as they are capable of using; they can be allowed more as they are better educated and more fit for it, &c. &c.

One knows all that, and one knows what it is worth in the half-elected, half-nominated councils. Either the nominated members are introduced merely as a drag upon the wheel, and are instructed to yield in the end to the demands of the representative members, or they are themselves the representatives of the white minority. If the first, the majority rule already; if the second, such constitutions are contrived ingeniously to create the largest amount of irritation, and to make impossible, as long as they last, any form of effective and useful government. Therefore they cannot last, and are not meant to last. A principle once conceded develops with the same certainty with which a seed grows when it is sown. In the English world, as it now stands, there is no middle alternative between self-government and government by the Crown, and the cause of our reluctance to undertake direct charge of the West Indies is because such undertaking carries responsibility along with it. If they are brought so close to us we shall be obliged to exert ourselves, and to rescue them from a condition which would be a reproach to us.

The English of those islands are melting away. That is

a fact to which it is idle to try to shut our eyes. Families who have been for generations on the soil are selling their estates everywhere and are going off. Lands once under high cultivation are lapsing into jungle. Professional men of ability and ambition carry their talents to countries where they are more sure of reward. Every year the census renews its warning. The rate may vary; sometimes for a year or two there may seem to be a pause in the movement, but it begins again and is always in the same direction. The white is relatively disappearing, the black is growing; this is the fact with which we have to deal.

We may say if we please, 'Be it so then; we do not want those islands; let the blacks have them, poor devils. They have had wrongs enough in this world; let them take their turn and have a good time now.' This I imagine is the answer which will rise to the lips of most of us, yet it will be an answer which will not be for our honour, nor in the long run for our interest. Our stronger colonies will scarcely attach more value to their connection with us if they hear us declare impatiently that because part of our possessions have ceased to be of money value to us, we will not or we cannot take the trouble to provide them with a decent government, and therefore cast them off. Nor in the long run will it benefit the blacks either. The islands will not be allowed to run wild again, and if we leave them some one else will take them who will be less tender of his coloured brother's sensibilities. We may think that it would not come to that. The islands will still be ours; the English flag will still float over the forts; the government, whatever it be, will be administered in the Queen's name. Were it worth while, one might draw a picture of the position of an English governor, with a black parliament and a black ministry, recommending by advice of his constitutional ministers some measure like the Haytian Land Law.

No Englishman, not even a bankrupt peer, would consent to occupy such a position; the blacks themselves would despise him if he did; and if the governor is to be one of their own race and colour, how long could such a connection endure?

No one I presume would advise that the whites of the islands should govern. The relations between the two populations are too embittered, and equality once established by law, the exclusive privilege of colour over colour cannot be restored. While slavery continued the whites ruled effectively and economically; the blacks are now free as they; there are two classes in the community; their interests are opposite as they are now understood, and one cannot be trusted with control over the other. As little can the present order of things continue. The West India Islands, once the pride of our empire, the scene of our most brilliant achievements, are passing away out of our hands; the remnant of our own countrymen, weary of an unavailing struggle, are more and more eager to withdraw from it, because they find no sympathy and no encouragement from home, and are forbidden to accept help from America when help is offered them, while under their eyes their quondam slaves are multiplying, thriving, occupying, growing strong, and every day more conscious of the changed order of things. One does not grudge the black man his prosperity, his freedom, his opportunities of advancing himself; one would wish to see him as free and prosperous as the fates and his own exertions can make him, with more and more means of raising himself to the white man's level. But left to himself, and without the white man to lead him, he can never reach it, and if we are not to lose the islands altogether, or if they are not to remain with us to discredit our capacity to rule them, it is left to us only to take the same course which we have taken in the East Indies with such magnificent success, and to govern whites and blacks alike on the Indian system. The circumstances are precisely analogous. We have a population to deal with, the enormous majority of whom are of an inferior race. Inferior, I am obliged to call them, because as yet, and as a body, they have shown no capacity to rise above the condition of their ancestors except under European laws, European education, and European authority, to keep them from making war on one another. They are docile, good-tempered, excellent and faithful servants when they are kindly treated; but their notions of right and wrong are scarcely even elementary; their education, such as it may be, is but skin deep, and the old African superstitions lie undisturbed at the bottom of their souls. Give them independence, and in a few generations they will peel off such civilisation as they have learnt as easily and as willingly as their coats and trousers.

Govern them as we govern India, with the same conscientious care, with the same sense of responsibility, with the same impartiality, the same disinterested attention to the well-being of our subjects in its highest and most honourable sense, and we shall give the world one more evidence that while Englishmen can cover the waste places of it with free communities of their own blood, they can exert an influence no less beneficent as the guides and rulers of those who need their assistance, and whom fate and circumstances have assigned to their care. Our kindred far away will be more than ever proud to form part of a nation which has done more for freedom than any other nation ever did, yet is not a slave to formulas, and can adapt its actions to the demands of each community which belongs to it. The most timid among us may take courage, for it would cost us nothing save the sacrifice of a few official traditions, and an abstinence for the future from doubtful uses of colonial patronage. The blacks will be perfectly happy when they are satisfied that they have nothing to fear for their persons or their properties. To the whites it would be the opening of a new era of hope. Should they be rash enough to murmur, they might then be justly left to the consequences of their own folly.

10.

No statement gave West Indians greater offense than Froude's assertion that Negroes were unfit to govern themselves. Within a few months, a rebuttal by a black Trinidadian exploded Froude's shallow self-contradictions. In this author's view, racial prejudice in the islands had notably declined since Emancipation, local whites were readily sharing administration with colored and black men, and Froude's fears of black revolution and retrogression were chimerical.

J. J. THOMAS, a brilliant journalist, teacher, and linguist of African descent, played a major role in Trinidad's intellectual and cultural life during the 1870s and 1880s and also wrote the first serious study of Creole grammar.

Froudacity Refuted*
J. J. Thomas

Last year had well advanced towards its middle—in fact it was already April, 1888—before Mr Froude's book of travels in the West Indies became known and generally accessible to readers in those Colonies.

My perusal of it in Grenada about the period above mentioned disclosed, thinly draped with rhetorical flowers, the dark outlines of a scheme to thwart political aspiration in the Antilles. That project is sought to be realised by deterring the home authorities from granting an elective local legislature, however restricted in character, to any of the Colonies not yet enjoying such an advantage. An argument based on the composition of the inhabitants of those Colonies is confidently relied upon to confirm the inexorable mood of Downing Street. Over-large and ever-increasing—so runs the argument—the African element in the population of the West Indies is, from its past history and its actual tendencies, a standing menace to the continuance of civilisation and religion. An immediate catastrophe, social, political, and moral, would most assuredly be brought about by the granting of full elective rights to dependencies thus inhabited. Enlightened statesmanship should at once perceive the immense benefit that would

Froudacity; West Indian Fables by James Anthony Froude, explained by J. J. Thomas, pp. 51–60. Originally published in London, T. Fisher Unwin, 1889. Available from New Beacon Books, London, 1969.

* [Editors' title]

ultimately result from such refusal of the franchise. The cardinal recommendation of that refusal is that it would avert definitively the political domination of the Blacks, which must inevitably be the outcome of any concession of the modicum of right so earnestly desired. The exclusion of the Negro vote being inexpedient, if not impossible, the exercise of electoral powers by the Blacks must lead to their returning candidates of their own race to the local legislatures, and that, too, in numbers preponderating according to the majority of the Negro electors. The Negro legislators thus supreme in the councils of the Colonies would straightway proceed to pass vindictive and retaliatory laws against their white fellow-colonists. For it is only fifty years since the White man and the Black man stood in the reciprocal relations of master and slave. Whilst those relations subsisted, the white masters inflicted, and the black slaves had to endure, the hideous atrocities that are inseparable from the system of slavery. Since Emancipation, the enormous strides made in self-advancement by the ex-slaves have only had the effect of provoking a resentful uneasiness in the bosoms of the ex-masters. The former bondsmen, on their side, and like their brethren of Hayti, are eaten up with implacable, blood-thirsty rancour against their former lords and owners. The annals of Hayti form quite a cabinet of political and social object-lessons which, in the eyes of British statesmen, should be invaluable in showing the true method of dealing with Ethiopic subjects of the Crown. The Negro race in Hayti, in order to obtain and to guard what it calls its freedom, has outraged every humane instinct and falsified every benevolent hope. The slave-owners there had not been a whit more cruel than slave-owners in the other islands. But, in spite of this, how ferocious, how sanguinary, how relentless against them has the vengeance of the Blacks been in their hour of mastery! A century has passed away since then, and, notwithstanding that, the hatred of Whites still rankles in their souls, and is cherished and yielded to as a national creed and guide of conduct. Colonial administrators of the mighty British Empire, the lesson which History has taught and yet continues to teach you in Hayti as to the best mode of dealing with your Ethiopic colonists lies patent, blood-stained and terrible before you, and should be taken definitively to heart. But if you are willing that Civilisation and Religion—in short, all the highest developments of individual and social life—should at once be swept away by a desolating vandalism of African birth; if you do not recoil from the blood-guiltiness that would stain your consciences through the massacre of our fellow-countrymen in the West Indies, on account of their race, complexion and enlightenment; finally, if you desire those modern Hesperides to revert into primeval jungle, horrent lairs wherein the Blacks, who, but a short while before, had been ostensibly civilised, shall be revellers, as high-priests and devotees, in orgies of devil-worship, cannibalism, and obeah—dare to give the franchise to those West Indian Colonies, and then rue the consequences of your infatuation! . . .

Alas, if the foregoing summary of the ghastly imaginings of Mr Froude were true, in what a fool's paradise had the wisest and best amongst us been living, moving, and having our being! Up to the date of the suggestion by him as above of the alleged facts and possibilities of West Indian life, we had believed (even granting the correctness of his gloomy account of the past and present positions of the two races) that to no well-thinking West Indian White, whose ancestors may have, innocently or culpably, participated in the gains as well as the guilt of slavery, would the remembrance of its palmy days be otherwise than one of regret. We Negroes, on the other hand, after a lapse of time extending over nearly two generations, could be indebted only to precarious tradition or scarcely accessible documents for any knowledge we might chance upon of the sufferings endured in these Islands of the West by those of our race who have gone before us. Death, with undiscriminating hand, had gathered in the human harvest of masters and slaves alike, according to or out of the normal laws of nature; while Time had been letting down on the stage of our existence drop-scene after drop-scene of years, to the number of something like fifty, which had been curtaining off the tragic incidents of the past from the peaceful activities of the present. Being thus circumstanced, thought we, what rational elements of mutual hatred should *now* continue to exist in the bosoms of the two races?

With regard to the perpetual reference to Hayti, because of our oneness with its inhabitants in origin and complexion, as a criterion for the exact forecast of our future conduct under given circumstances, this appeared to us, looking at actual facts, perversity gone wild in the manufacture of analogies. The founders of the Black Republic, we had all along understood, were not in any sense whatever equipped, as Mr Froude assures us they were, when starting on their self-governing career, with the civil and intellectual advantages that had been transplanted from Europe. On the contrary, we had been taught to regard them as most unfortunate in the circumstances under which they so gloriously conquered their merited freedom. We saw them free, but perfectly illiterate barbarians, impotent to use the intellectual resources of which their valour had made them possessors, in the shape of books on the spirit and technical details of a highly developed national existence. We had learnt also, until this new interpreter of history had contradicted the accepted record, that the continued failure of Hayti to realise the dreams of Toussaint was due to the fatal want of confidence subsisting between the fairer and darker sections of the inhabitants, which had its sinister and disastrous origin in the action of the Mulattoes in attempting to secure freedom for themselves, in conjunction with the Whites, at the sacrifice of their darker-hued kinsmen. Finally, it had been explained to us that the remembrance of this abnormal treason had been underlying and perniciously influencing the whole course of Haytian national history. All this established knowledge we are called upon to throw overboard, and accept the baseless assertions of this conjuror-up of inconceivable fables! He calls upon us to believe that, in spite of being free, educated, progressive, and at peace with all men, we

West Indian Blacks, were we ever to become constitution-
ally dominant in our native islands, would emulate in
savagery our Haytian fellow-Blacks who, at the time of
retaliating upon their actual masters, were tortured slaves,
bleeding and rendered desperate under the oppressors' lash
—and all this simply and merely because of the sameness
of our ancestry and the colour of our skin! One would
have thought that Liberia would have been a fitter standard
of comparison in respect of a coloured population starting
a national life, really and truly equipped with the requisites
and essentials of civilised existence. But such a reference
would have been fatal to Mr Froude's object: the annals
of Liberia being a persistent refutation of the old pro-
slavery prophecies which our author so feelingly rehearses.

Let us revert, however, to Grenada and the newly-
published *Bow of Ulysses,* which had come into my hands
in April, 1888.

It seemed to me, on reading that book, and deducing
therefrom the foregoing essential summary, that a critic
would have little more to do, in order to effectually exorcise
this negro-phobic political hobgoblin, than to appeal to
impartial history, as well as to common sense, in its application to human nature in general, and to the actual
facts of West Indian life in particular.

History, as against the hard and fast White-master and
Black-slave theory so recklessly invented and confidently
built upon by Mr Froude, would show incontestably—(*a*)
that for upwards of two hundred years before the Negro
Emancipation in 1838, there had never existed in one of
those then British Colonies, which had been originally discovered and settled for Spain by the great Columbus or
by his successors, the *Conquistadores,* any prohibition
whatsoever, on the ground of race or colour, against the
owning of slaves by any free person possessing the necessary means, and desirous of doing so; (*b*) that, as a consequence of this non-restriction, and from causes notoriously historical, numbers of blacks, half-breeds, and other
non-Europeans, besides such of them as had become possessed of their 'property' by inheritance, availed themselves

of this virtual license, and in course of time constituted a
very considerable proportion of the slave-holding section
of those communities; (c) that these dusky plantation-
owners enjoyed and used in every possible sense the identical rights and privileges which were enjoyed and used by
their pure-blooded Caucasian brother-slave-owners. The
above statements are attested by written documents, oral
tradition, and, better still perhaps, by the living presence
in those islands of numerous lineal representatives of those
once opulent and flourishing non-European planter-
families.

Common sense, here stepping in, must, from the above
data, deduce some such conclusions as the following. First
that, on the hypothesis that the slaves who were freed in
 1838—full fifty years ago—were all on an average fifteen
years old, those vengeful ex-slaves of today will be all men
of sixty-five years of age; and, allowing for the delay in
getting the franchise, somewhat further advanced towards
the human life-term of threescore and ten years. Again,
in order to organise and carry out any scheme of legislative and social retaliation of the kind set forth in the *Bow
of Ulysses,* there must be (which unquestionably there is
not) a considerable, well-educated, and very influential
number surviving of those who had actually been in bondage. Moreover, the vengeance of these people (also as-
suming the foregoing non-existent condition) would have,
in case of opportunity, to wreak itself far more largely and
vigorously upon members of their own race than upon
Whites, seeing that the increase of the Blacks, as correctly
represented in the *Bow of Ulysses,* is just as rapid as the
diminution of the White population. And therefore, Mr
Froude's 'Danger-to-the-Whites' cry in support of his anti-
reform manifesto would not appear, after all, to be quite
so justifiable as he possibly thinks.

Feeling keenly that something in the shape of the foregoing programme might be successfully worked up for a
public defence of the maligned people, I disregarded the
bodily and mental obstacles that have beset and clouded
my career during the last twelve years, and cheerfully

undertook the task, stimulated thereto by what I thought weighty considerations. I saw that no representative of Her Majesty's Ethiopic West Indian subjects cared to come forward to perform this work in the more permanent shape that I felt to be not only desirable but essential for our self-vindication. I also realised the fact that the *Bow of Ulysses* was not likely to have the same ephemeral existence and effect as the newspaper and other periodical discussions of its contents, which had poured from the press in Great Britain, the United States, and very notably, of course, in all the English Colonies of the Western Hemisphere. In the West Indian papers the best writers of our race had written masterly refutations, but it was clear how difficult the task would be in future to procure and refer to them whenever occasion should require. Such productions, however, fully satisfied those qualified men of our people, because they were legitimately convinced (even as I myself am convinced) that the political destinies of the people of colour could not run one tittle of risk from anything that it pleased Mr Froude to write or say on the subject. But, meditating further on the question, the reflection forced itself upon me that, beyond the mere political personages in the circle more directly addressed by Mr Froude's volume, there were individuals whose influence or possible sympathy we could not afford to disregard, or to esteem lightly. So I deemed it right and a patriotic duty to attempt the enterprise myself, in obedience to the above stated motives.

At this point I must pause to express on behalf of the entire coloured population of the West Indies our most heartfelt acknowledgements to Mr C. Salmon for the luminous and effective vindication of us, in his volume on *West Indian Confederation,*† against Mr Froude's libels. The service thus rendered by Mr Salmon possesses a double significance and value in my estimation. In the first place, as being the work of a European of high position, quite

† [Refers to *The Caribbean Confederation,* originally published by Cassell & Co., Ltd., 1888; see "Selected Readings" in this book.]

independent of us (who testifies concerning Negroes, not through having gazed at them from balconies, decks of steamers, or the seats of moving carriages, but from actual and long personal intercourse with them, which the internal evidence of his book plainly proves to have been as sympathetic as it was familiar), and, secondly, as the work of an individual entirely outside of our race, it has been gratefully accepted by myself as an incentive to self-help, on the same more formal and permanent lines, in a matter so important to the status which we can justly claim as a progressive, law-abiding, and self-respecting section of Her Majesty's liege subjects.

It behoves me now to say a few words respecting this book as a mere literary production.

Alexander Pope, who, next to Shakespeare and perhaps Butler, was the most copious contributor to the current stock of English maxims, says:

True ease in writing comes from Art, not Chance,

As those move easiest who have learnt to dance.†

A whole dozen years of bodily sickness and mental tribulation have not been conducive to that regularity of practice in composition which alone can ensure the 'true ease' spoken of by the poet; and therefore is it that my style leaves so much to be desired, and exhibits, perhaps, still more to be pardoned. Happily, a quarrel such as ours with the author of *The English in the West Indies* cannot be finally or even approximately settled on the score of superior literary competency, whether of aggressor or defender. I feel free to ignore whatever verdict might be grounded on a consideration so purely artificial. There ought to be enough, if not in these pages, at any rate in whatever else I have heretofore published, that should prove me not so hopelessly stupid and wanting in self-respect, as would be implied by my undertaking a contest in artistic phrase-weaving with one who, even among the foremost of his literary countrymen, is confessedly a master in that craft. The judges to whom I do submit our case

† [From *Essay on Criticism*, Part II.]

re those Englishmen and others whose conscience blends
vith their judgment, and who determine such questions as
his on their essential rightness which has claim to the first
ind decisive consideration. For much that is irregular in
he arrangement and sequence of the subject-matter, some
plame fairly attaches to our assailant. The erratic manner
n which he launches his injurious statements against the
hapless Blacks, even in the course of passages which no
more led up to them than to any other section of mankind, is a very notable feature of his anti-Negro production. As he frequently repeats, very often with cynical
aggravations, his charges and sinister prophecies against
the sable objects of his aversion, I could see no other course
open to me than to take him up on the points whereto I
demurred, exactly how, when, and where I found them.

My purpose could not be attained up without direct
mention of, or reference to, certain public employees in
the Colonies whose official conduct has often been the
subject of criticism in the public press of the West Indies.
Though fully aware that such criticism has on many occasions been much more severe than my own strictures,
yet, it being possible that some special responsibility may
attach to what I here reproduce in a more permanent
shape, I most cheerfully accept, in the interests of public
justice, any consequence which may result.

A remark or two concerning the publication of this rejoinder. It has been hinted to me that the issue of it has
been too long delayed to secure for it any attention in
England, owing to the fact that the West Indies are but
little known, and of less interest, to the generality of English readers. Whilst admitting, as in duty bound, the possible correctness of this forecast, and regretting the oft-
recurring hindrances which occasioned such frequent
and, sometimes, long suspension of my labour; and noting,
too, the additional delay caused through my unacquaint-
ance with English publishing usages, I must, notwithstanding, plead guilty to a lurking hope that some small
fraction of Mr Froude's readers will yet be found, whose
interest in the West Indies will be temporarily revived on

behalf of this essay, owing to its direct bearing on Mr
Froude and his statements relative to these Islands, contained in his recent book of travels in them. This I am
led to hope will be more particularly the case when it is
borne in mind that the rejoinder has been attempted by
a member of that very same race which he has, with such
eloquent recklessness of all moral considerations, held up
to public contempt and disfavour. In short, I can scarcely
permit myself to believe it possible that concern regarding
a popular author, on his being questioned by an adverse
critic of however restricted powers, can be so utterly dead
within a twelvemonth as to be incapable of rekindling
Mr Froude's *Oceana,* which had been published long
before its author voyaged to the West Indies, in order to
treat the Queen's subjects there in the same more than
questionable fashion as that in which he had treated those
of the Southern Hemisphere, had what was in the main
a formal rejoinder to its misrepresentations published only
three months ago in this city. I venture to believe that no
serious work in defence of an important cause or community can lose much, if anything, of its intrinsic value
through some delay in its issue; especially when written in
the vindication of Truth, whose eternal principles are beyond and above the influence of time and its changes.

At any rate, this attempt to answer some of Mr Froude's
main allegations against the people of the West Indies
cannot fail to be of grave importance and lively interest
to the inhabitants of those Colonies. In this opinion I am
happy in being able to record the full concurrence of a
numerous and influential body of my fellow-West Indians,
men of various races, but united in detestation of falsehood and injustice.

I THE NATURE OF THE
OCIAL ORDER

11.

This section on the general nature of West Indian societ opens with a classification of Jamaican social structure The author of the first selection is well known for his re finement of the concept of the plural society, a societa type first delineated by the economist J. S. Furnivall, em phasizing the role of control and force as opposed to con sensus as a unifying principle among social groups. Her the author examines the different forms of basic institu tions that characterize Jamaica's three socially significan population "sections"—essentially white, brown, and black

M. G. Smith's extension of pluralism in the West India context, best exemplified in a symposium on *Social an Cultural Pluralism in the Caribbean* and in his *The Plura Society in the British West Indies,* initiated a significan debate about West Indian societies in particular and, b extension, about other postcolonial societies. Not all Carib beanists accept Smith's pluralist viewpoint, but it has had salutary effect in raising fundamental theoretical question about the articulation of socioculturally diverse West In dian groups, about conflict and conflict resolution, an about social and political development and change in th region.

M. G. SMITH, a social anthropologist born in Jamaica was the recipient of an Island Scholarship; he took a

ndergraduate degree at McGill University and received
s doctorate at University College, London. He has done
xtensive field research in Jamaica, Grenada, and Car-
acou and also in Nigeria. Smith has been Research Fellow
nd Acting Director of the Institute of Social and Economic
esearch at the University of the West Indies, Jamaica,
nd a professor of anthropology at the University of Cali-
ornia, Los Angeles. Currently he is Professor of Anthro-
ology at University College, London.

The Plural Framework of Jamaican Society
M. G. Smith

Contemporary Jamaica is relatively complex and internally diverse. Although four-fifths of its population are black, and nine-tenths of the remainder are coloured persons of mixed ancestry, there are structurally significant groups of Chinese, Syrian, Jewish, Portuguese and British descent, and in several cases these ethnic groups are also differentiated by special statuses, organizations and occupational interests.

Apart from this racial complexity, Jamaica includes a number of significantly different ecological areas: the expanding urban area around Kingston; the sugar belts with their large plantations and landless labour force; the rural highlands settled by smallholders; and the tourist coast along the north shore. Community types and organization in each ecological area tend to be somewhat distinct. So do community interests, which now compete for influence on the island government. Of the 1.6 million persons who live in Jamaica, perhaps one-quarter are to be found in Kingston and the other main towns, and nearly one-half live in the hilly interior. The plainsfolk dependent on sugar probably exceed 400,000. Rural-urban differences are important already and will tend to become more so. The rate of population growth is very high.

Jamaica's racial diversity strikes the visitor immediately;

British Journal of Sociology, Vol. XII, No. 3, September 1961, pp. 249–62. Also available in *The Plural Society In the British West Indies*, University of California Press, 1965.

but local 'nationalism' has developed a convenient mythology of 'progress' according to which race differences are held to be irrelevant in personal relations. While it is difficult to state the precise significance of racial difference in a few words, it can be said categorically that race and its symbol colour do play a very important part in structuring relations between individuals within Jamaica, and the study of this aspect of local life can throw a great deal of light on the island-society.[1] Nonetheless, race concepts are cultural facts and their significance varies with social conditions.[2] To understand the local attitude to race, we must therefore begin with the society and its culture. Accordingly, in the following summary of Jamaican social structure, I shall avoid direct reference to ecological or racial differences as far as possible, while presenting a general account which incorporates this racial complexity fully within the frame of social and cultural difference. This procedure permits a shorter description than is otherwise possible, and reveals the basis of Jamaican thinking about race.

The most appropriate approach to the description of Jamaican society is that of institutional analysis. An institution is a form or system of activities characteristic of a given population. Institutional activities involve groups, and these groups generally have clearly defined forms of relations among their members. Moreover, institutional activities and forms of grouping are also sanctioned by normative beliefs and ideas, and social values are expressed in institutional rules. The basic institutions of a given population are the core of the people's culture; and since society consists of a system of institutionalized relations, a people's institutions form the matrix of their social structure. Thus the description of social structure consists in the analysis of the institutional system of the population under study.

[1] F. Henriques, *Family and Colour in Jamaica* (London: Eyre & Spottiswoode, 1953).
[2] M. G. Smith, *A Framework for Caribbean Studies* (Jamaica: University College of the West Indies, Extra-Mural Department, 1955).

In the following account of Jamaican social structure, I shall therefore describe the institutions of local society and their variety of alternative forms, as systematically and briefly as I can. In Jamaica, each institutional sub-system such as the family or religion is represented by a number of diverse alternatives. Moreover, each group of institutional alternatives characterizes a different segment of the local society. Although usually described as a social class, the population which practises a distinctive set of institutions is best described as a cultural or social section. The three distinctive institutional systems characteristic of contemporary Jamaica therefore define a society divided into three social sections. For initial reference, we may think of these sections as the white, the brown and the black, this being the order of their current and historical dominance, and the exact reverse of their relative numerical strength. Although these colour coefficients are primarily heuristic, they indicate the racial majority and cultural ancestry of each section accurately. The white section which ranks highest locally represents the culture of mid-twentieth-century West European society. It is the dominant section, but also the smallest, and consists principally of persons reared abroad from early childhood. The black or lowest section may include four-fifths of the population, and practises a folk culture containing numerous elements reminiscent of African societies and Caribbean slavery. The brown intermediate section is culturally and biologically the most variable, and practises a general mixture of patterns from the higher and lower groups. This mixture seems to involve a combination of institutional forms as often as institutional syncretism. Thus the culture of the middle section includes co-existent institutional alternatives drawn from either of the two remaining traditions, as well as those forms which are peculiar to itself.

Kinship institutions differentiate the three sections clearly. The general pattern of kinship throughout this society is bilateral, but its operative range increases as we move from the first section to the second, and its matrilateral range and emphasis are predominant among the

west group.[3] Differences in family types correspond with
ese differences in the kinship systems of the social sec-
ons; and these differences of family organization are both
rmal and functional. In the small dominant section,
milies have a bilateral authority structure, and are small,
ghtly-knit groups with important functions of status place-
ent and training. In the intermediate section, families
ave a patriarchal authority structure, the division of la-
our between husband and wife is quite distinctive, and the
omposition and range of the family are more various. In
e lowest-ranking section, family authority and responsi-
llity is modally matriarchal, and the composition of do-
estic units reflects the primacy of uterine kinship and
escent.

These sectional differences of family organization are
nked with other differences of mating pattern. The small
ominant section observes contemporary West European
orms of marriage. It includes more divorcees than bas-
ards. The intermediate section practises a creolized version
f Victorian marriage, and distinguishes men's legal and
legitimate issue most sharply. The third section typically
nates outside the context of marriage, which is usually
ostponed among them until middle age, very often after
he birth of grandchildren. In the top section, mating, mariage and cohabitation imply one another; and family and
ousehold normally coincide. At the opposite social ex-
reme, co-residence is certainly not a necessary condition
of mating, marriage even less so, and there is no equation
etween family, household and mating relation even as a
ocial ideal. In the intermediate section, the mating and
amily forms characteristic of the other two sections are
ften found together, men living with their wives and law-
ul issue respectably, apart from their current or former
nistresses and illegitimate children. These three differing
orms of domestic organization, mating, family, and kin-
hip are integrated as separate institutional systems which
differentiate the three social sections. Neither fully under-

[3] Edith Clarke, *My Mother Who Fathered Me* (London: Al-
en & Unwin, 1957).

stands or approves the kinship institutions of the others.

In their magico-religious systems, the three social sections are similarly differentiated. At one extreme, we find the agnostic attitudes characteristic of contemporary British society, and this religious agnosticism is coupled with operational faith and skill in modern science and administration, the dominant values of this world-view being those of materialism. At the other extreme, African-type ritual forms, such as spirit-possession, sacrifice, obeah or magic, are common, together with a liberal variety of beliefs in sorcery, witchcraft, divination, spirits and their manipulation, and several substitutes for *rites de passage*. Among the intermediate section, the typical religious form is denominational Christianity; and the church creed, ritual, theology, organization and modes of recruiting members differ remarkably from the corresponding revivalist forms which are current among the lowest section.[4] The fundamentalist world-view of this intermediate section contrasts sharply with the moral and cosmological systems of the other two. Basically, these three types of magico-religious systems are organized about competing principles of action and explanation. Agnosticism abides by materialist notions of causality, and is normally coupled with faith in science. Fundamentalist Christianity believes in an omnipotent Christian God, whose actions are morally perfect, and who can be appealed to but not manipulated. Revivalism and other Afro-Christian cults are based on a belief in good and bad spirits which can affect the living directly, and which may be manipulated for personal evil or good. In the agnostic view there is no room for revelation, but scientific method guides us to valid conclusions. In the fundamentalist view, the decisive revelations occurred long ago in Palestine, especially during the life of Christ. In Revivalism and other folk cults, revelation occurs presently through dreams, divination, omens, and especially through spirit possession with its prophecy 'in tongues'. Agnosticism is an outlook which has no institutional organization or

[4] G. E. Simpson, "Jamaican Revivalist Cults," *Social and Economic Studies,* Vol. 5, No. 4 (December, 1956).

membership. Denominational Christianity normally recruits members by infant baptism. Revivalism and other Afro-Christian cults do so by adult conversion and baptism. The priesthood and organization of Christian denominations differ in like measure from that of the revivalist groups.

Education also differentiates the three sections sharply; and there is a positive correlation between the differing sectional experiences of education on the one hand, and their differing magico-religious or kinship practices on the other. The small dominant section consists mainly of professionals with university training, of entrepreneurs and of landed proprietors, who could easily take such training if they wished, or finance it for their dependents independently. Members of the intermediate section normally undergo instruction in local secondary schools; while members of the third or lowest section have so far had little chance of formal education beyond the level of the elementary school. However, education and schooling are not co-terminous, and among all sections the informal component in education varies inversely in its significance with the amount of schooling received. Thus the peasant's lore of herbal medicines, proverbs, folk stories and the like, his skill in certain manual operations, and his knowledge of cultivation techniques have no parallel among the secondary school or college graduates. Thus the content as well as the form of these sectional educational experiences is quite dissimilar.

In adult life these differences find expression in differing occupational and employment patterns. The entrepreneur exercises managerial functions in personal or corporate organizations. The professional typically finds remunerative long-term appointment in some large corporation, such as government, or else conducts his own practice alone or in partnership. The secondary-school graduate whose education proceeds no further, typically finds clerical employment in business or government.

The great majority of Jamaica's school-leavers come from the elementary or primary schools, where tuition is

180 The Plural Framework of Jamaican Society

provided free by government, and where efforts at ensuring attendance sometimes involve compulsion. Most of these elementary schoolchildren later find manual employment on the farms in the rural areas or in menial capacities in the towns. Recent surveys by the Jamaica Social Welfare Commission indicate that a high proportion of those persons who have only had elementary school education are unable to read or write. Another recent survey by Dr. C. A. Moser points out that less than one-quarter of the children attending elementary schools do so for the full eight years of the course.[5] A fair proportion of rural and urban children simply do not attend school at all. Certain militant cult-groups such as the Ras Tafarites[6] condemn these elementary schools as agencies of sectional propaganda, in much the same terms as Dr. Madeline Kerr, who found that they produced disorganized personalities.[7]

In effect, the technology which adults manipulate varies with their early educational experience. In Jamaica, these sectional differences of occupation are in part effects of the differing contents and significance of informal education in childhood, in part they are due to the historical inequalities of formal education. The longer a child stays in school receiving formal education, and the greater the stress on his proficiency therein, the shorter and less significant his informal training. The professional is normally just as ignorant of the peasant's knowledge and skills, as is the latter of the former's speciality.

The economic system places special emphasis on the techniques and knowledge transmitted by formal education, and the resulting occupational groups enjoy differing rewards of income and status. Proprietors and professionals who receive the largest incomes also enjoy higher status than other occupational groups; unskilled or semi-skilled

[5] C. A. Moser, *A Study of Levels of Living with Special Reference to Jamaica* (London: H.M.S.O., 1957).

[6] G. E. Simpson, "Political Cultism in West Kingston," *Social and Economic Studies,* Vol. 4, No. 2 (June 1955), pp. 133–49.

[7] Madeline Kerr, *Personality and Conflict in Jamaica* (Liverpool: Liverpool University Press, 1952).

workers who receive very low incomes rank at the bottom of the occupational scales. These local scales of income and prestige are correlated with employment patterns; and, at least in recruitment, employment is closely related to the system of differential education. Thus the inequality of educational opportunities in Jamaica is an important condition of social and economic differentiation. The local system of differential education governs the distribution of those skills and aptitudes which are conditions of recruitment to occupations of different types. In this way the Jamaican educational system bolsters the social structure, and distinguishes three social sections.

The relation between the systems of occupational differentiation and education tends to be self-perpetuating, since the less-well-paid manual occupations do not allow parents to pay for their children's education at secondary schools. Moreover, children at elementary schools have not had adequate educational facilities or sufficient scholarship opportunities of free secondary education; these conditions have produced sufficient frustration to discourage many parents from sending their children to school regularly. Historically, the propertied sections of the Jamaican population have monopolized the local franchise on the basis of their educational and property qualifications. They have used their political influence to secure high government grants per pupil at the secondary schools while keeping expenditure on elementary education very low. Thus the differential allocation of political rights which was based on educational and economic differences was used by its beneficiaries to maximize the sectional differences in education which underlay these economic and political inequalities. Thus the educational system and the sectional order were integrated, and the one tended to perpetuate the other. Moreover, within Jamaica, the division of labour directly reflects these differences in the educational careers of the population, and serves to maintain them.

The three cultural sections already defined differ also in their economic institutions. Banking, currency, insurance, export-import commerce, and such large-scale agricultural undertakings as sugar or banana estates are controlled by that section which represents contemporary Western culture locally. Oversea marketing is controlled by oversea agencies, normally those of the metropolitan power. The forms of government finance and their development follow current metropolitan forms and changes. To a considerable degree, local branches of foreign economic organizations are managed by expatriates, or by persons of recent expatriate origin. Jews, Syrians, and Chinese are Jamaica's most important entrepreneurial groups; but the values which these groups attach to the maintenance of ethnic identity and cohesion only emphasize the extent to which economic control in Jamaica is separated from the 'native' population, or Creoles as they are called.[8]

If we consider employment, saving, property or marketing, the differing institutional forms and roles of the three Jamaican sections are equally clear. The top-ranking section consists of a hard core of employers and own-account professionals, together with superior civil servants, whose employment conditions are such that dismissal or demotion are virtually inconceivable. Most members of the intermediate section are themselves either employees of 'middle-income' status, or small proprietors, businessmen, farmers, contractors or such lesser professionals as teachers. The majority of this group are also themselves employers, hiring domestic labour and other types of service attendants by unwritten contracts and directing them in a personal fashion which involves heavy reliance on prompt dismissal and casual recruitment, but does not lend itself easily to trade-union action. In the lowest section, the typical employment status is a combination of wage and own-account work, and underemployment or unemployment is widespread. Such institutions as partnership, lend-day, and morning sport, which serve to redistribute labour on a cooperative reciprocal basis, are as distinctive and typical of the lower section as are the systems of regular or casual

[8] Simon Rottenberg, "Entrepreneurship and Economic Progress in Jamaica," *Journal of Inter-American Affairs,* Vol. 7, No. 2 (1953).

recruitment for task, job or daywork used by the first and second sections respectively.[9]

Saving and credit forms differ likewise. In urban areas, the lowest section saves either by means of African-type credit-thrift associations, such as 'partner' or 'susu';[10] or individually by loans to market vendors and others who 'keep' the money placed in their care while turning it over in trade; or cash is hoarded or put in government post office banks. For members of the lowest section credit facilities are usually available only from those shops and persons with whom they have regular business dealings. In the intermediate section, credit is obtained through solicitors against security in property or insurance, or by hire-purchase and other accounts with various firms. Among the dominant section, credit is sought overseas or through local branches of banks established overseas, and it is advanced by them typically on mortgage, in the form of trading materials and stock, or against produce designed for sale on the world market. Savings among the top section are mainly invested in stocks, business or land; at the intermediate level the main forms of investment are in houses purchased for rent; among the third section, animals or smallholdings predominate.

The three sections differentiated by these economic characteristics are also distinguished by the forms and roles of their economic associations. The dominant section is typically organized in employer associations, chambers of commerce, certain farmers' societies and the like. Some of these associations have long histories. The lowest section is now organized in trade unions and friendly societies, the former being of recent growth. The intermediate section has hitherto avoided explicit economic organizations of its own, and has also avoided direct participation in the conflict of labour and capital. Its membership in these unions and as-

[9] M. G. Smith, *Labour Supply in Rural Jamaica* (Kingston, Jamaica: Government Printer, 1956).

[10] W. R. Bascom, "The Esusu: A Credit Institution of the Yoruba," *Journal of the Royal Anthropological Society,* Vol. 72 (1952), pp. 63–69.

sociations is accordingly marginal; and in this respect its organization reflects its intermediate economic position. However, this intermediate section does control a number of important occupational societies, such as those for teachers, small farmers or civil servants, which represent its major economic interest-groups.

Property concepts and distribution also differentiate these three sections. Among the economically dominant section, property has the typical form of productive enterprise, such as commercial businesses, firms, factories, estates, or the like. Typically also these enterprises are limited liability companies, joint-stock or partnership organizations being in the majority, and in them the personalities of shareholders are sharply distinguished from their interests in the enterprise. Thus, for the dominant section, property principally connotes some interest or share in an enterprise, with corresponding rights to a fixed portion of the profits of its operation. Among the intermediate section, property is mainly held on an individual or family basis, by freehold or under mortgage; and it typically consists in land, homes and own-account enterprises, whether small businesses or professional practices. Among the lowest section, the dominant property form is 'family land', that is, land held without proper legal title, and without precise personal distribution of rights, by the members of a family and their dependants.[11] At this level also, personalty consists mainly of small stock, tools, clothes and the like, while the homes which their owners regard as realty have the legal status of 'chattels', being often movable structures, or otherwise of temporary character. The property concepts of each section are thus quite distinctive, those of the dominant section being defined mainly by company, contract and commercial law; while those of the intermediate section are governed by the law of real property and debt; and the property concepts of the lowest section require

[11] Edith Clarke, "Land Tenure and the Family in Four Communities of Jamaica," *Social and Economic Studies*, Vol. 1, No. 4 (August 1953), pp. 85–119.

such novel enactments as the 1955 Facilities for Titles Law to be accommodated to the prevailing legal code.

Similar differences characterize the sections in regard to marketing. Jamaican markets fall into three types: (*a*) the local shop or market, at which consumer meets vendor and in which 'the Chinaman' or the 'higgler' (market woman) are the specialist traders;[12] (*b*) intra-island produce marketing which is oriented to the collection of produce for shipment abroad, and wholesale shopkeeping which distributes imports; and (*c*) overseas import-export dealings which are controlled by large merchant houses that handle a variety of commodities travelling in either direction and typically operate a monopolistic system of commission agencies. There are also a number of recently developed crop associations, each exporting a particular commodity. The organization and processes of this large-scale overseas traffic are institutionally as different from those of the intra-island produce trade in their details of insurance, brokerage, shipping, customs, credit and commission agency, and in their relation to the world market, as is the local produce trade from the higgler-dominated trade in community markets. The specialist personnel who dominate each of these three different marketing systems are also drawn from a distinct social section.

The legal positions of the different sections are also different. Jamaican legal forms are typically imitations of the law of the metropolitan power. These imitations have been locally administered by British personnel. In their content and application Jamaican laws have hitherto reflected the interests of the dominant section in controlling the subordinate ones: and even today, when the political bases of this historical order have been partly removed, local laws relating to obeah, bastardy, praedial larceny, ganja and the like are sectional in their orientation, content and administration. The participation of the intermediate section in law-making and administration is relatively recent, and

12 Sidney W. Mintz, "The Jamaican Internal Marketing Pattern," *Social and Economic Studies*, Vol. 4, No. 1 (March 1955), pp. 95–103.

their typical role is still that of jurors or lawyers. Participation of the lowest section in legal administration has been limited to subordinate police capacities, while the local police and law courts have historically been administered by members of the dominant minority.

Both during and since slavery, the members of the lowest section of Jamaican society have tried to settle their community disputes by informal arbitration or adjudication, in order to prevent such issues from going to court. Obeah, family land, the village lawyer, the peace-maker or the revivalist priesthood are among the institutions which serve these ends. During slavery, informal courts were held by the slaves under their headmen;[13] after slavery, missionaries and other prominent persons acted as arbitrators in community disputes.[14] Even today court cases involving members of the lowest section only are mainly criminal in character, and usually include some verbal or physical violence. Cases brought by members of the intermediate section against their social inferiors are mainly for misdemeanour or for recovery of debts. The judicial maladministration of inter-sectional issues was especially important in producing the Jamaica 'Rebellion' of 1865.[15] Even today the high cost of legal advice and procedure effectively deprives the lowest section of justice in civil issues against their superiors. Illiteracy and widespread unfamiliarity with the details of the law are equally disadvantageous to them. The dominant section always employs legal aid in its litigation; the lower section can only do so rarely; the middle section may do so half the time.[16] Like almshouses and

---

[13] Mrs. Carmichael, *Domestic Manners and Social Customs of the White, Coloured and Negro Populations of the West Indies* (2 vols.; London: John Murray, 1833).

[14] Philip Curtin, *Two Jamaicas: The Role of Ideas in a Tropical Colony. 1830–1865* (Cambridge: Harvard University Press, 1955), pp. 32–33, 114–16, 163, 169.

[15] M. G. Smith, "Slavery and Emancipation in Two Societies," *Social and Economic Studies*, Vol. 3, Nos. 3, 4 (December 1954), pp. 239–90.

[16] Peter Evans, "Legal Aid to the Poor," *The Daily Gleaner* (Kingston, Jamaica), Nov. 30, 1956, p. 12.

approved schools, prisons are primarily populated by the lowest section and are administered by members of the intermediate section under the supervision of the metropolitan power and its nationals.

Government is the institutional sub-system which expresses the conditions of social stability and change in Jamaica most directly. Historically, all important governmental institutions—law, the judiciary and magistracy, the militia and army, the administration and the legislature, were monopolized by the dominant section at the parochial and island levels, and these rulers were assisted in subordinate executive roles by members of the intermediate section. The lowest section remained outside the pale of political life until 1944. Until then they were denied the chance to develop their own political institutions or to imitate any other models. After emancipation, restrictive property franchises maintained the disenfranchisement of the ex-slave section; and with this was associated control of administration and law by the other two sections. Under this system the dominant section directed policy and the intermediate section executed it, while control of the lowest section was both the object and condition of many policy decisions.

In the historical development of Jamaican society the majority of its members have had no active role or status formally assigned to them in any phase of its political or legal systems. Under and since slavery, this massive subordinate section has only been able to express itself politically by riots, rebellions and the like. The 'disturbances' of 1937–8 which produced Bustamante's charismatic leadership and hothouse unionism were the inevitable result of this political order and socio-cultural pluralism. These social eruptions led to the introduction of adult suffrage, and this has since been followed by the establishment of the ministerial form of responsible government in the colony. However, the revocation of the British Guianese constitution in 1953 repeats the pattern of constitutional abrogation so familiar in Caribbean history, and shows that the formal transfer of power is hedged about by many reservations and can be reversed by force if necessary.

One most interesting reservation held that economic independence is prerequisite for political autonomy, and argues that since only a Federation of the British Caribbean colonies may develop this economic self-sufficiency, it is a *sine qua non* of Caribbean self-government. Within Jamaica, sectional sentiment has contributed greatly to acceptance of the federal idea, notwithstanding its contradiction of nationalism and certain other obvious disadvantages. From the popular point of view, perhaps the most far-reaching disadvantage is that the federal association will reduce the political power of the lowest section within Jamaica. This follows because the island government will now operate under surveillance of the federal legislature and administration, within limits set by federal policy, and under a federal constitution which places conservative political forces and values in a stronger position than they have recently occupied in Jamaica.

The question has been asked how the colonial élite can still maintain control of policy and their dominant status in the face of strong desires for rapid change among the newly enfranchised section. The answers to this question are many and various; they may do so, firstly, by capitalizing on their indispensability for the performance of certain élite functions, notably, of course, those of economic development and administration; secondly, by constitutional revisions of the type which promote the values of conservatism rather than popular movements; thirdly, by federation, which involves simultaneous limitation of local power and the transfer of control from popular leaders to a federal executive which substantially represents the interests of élite sections throughout the Caribbean; fourthly, by prolonging their dependence on the metropolitan power for economic aid, and therewith the colonial status; or by stressing the need for imperial or federal forces to guarantee the current social structure to encourage oversea investors; or finally, by the technique of buying out the popular leaders, which is not unknown in Jamaica. The point to notice in all this is that the introduction of liberal franchises and constitutions has been followed by an extension of political action to a federal field, and that these federal developments tend to restore control to those two social sections which formerly monopolized it. Thus the abrupt reversal of the political order of 1937 may yet prove to be pure illusion; and an effective restoration of this order may now be under way, with federation as its basis. In such a case, the federal association would simply replace the metropolitan link.

So far we have discussed only those social forms which provide the institutional core of the society, namely, the systems of kinship and marriage, religion, government, law and economy, education and occupational differentiation. There are also important differences between Jamaica's social sections in language, material culture, sport, associational patterns and value systems. In Jamaica a complete linguistic dichotomy does not obtain; but it has been found that middle- and 'upper-class' natives do not know the meaning of 30 per cent of the words current in the Anglicized folk dialect.[17] It would also be surprising if those Jamaicans who habitually speak this folk dialect should know more than 70 per cent of the words commonly used by those who do not. Bilingualism in such societies is a characteristic of cultural hybridism, and such hybrid cultural adjustment is most typical of the intermediate section. Thus, while the small top section speaks and understands English, but not dialect, and while the large bottom section only speaks and understands dialect fully, the intermediate section tends to employ either linguistic form according to the occasion.

Recreational patterns also distinguish the three social sections. To begin with, recreation is typically an intrasectional activity, and has different organizational and activity forms in each section, cricket being the outstanding exception to this rule. Clubs taking part in a variety of sport competitions, and organized therefor, are typical of

[17] R. B. Le Page, personal communication.

the intermediate section and rare among the lowest, whose usual sport association is the single-purpose cricket club organized on a community basis in rural areas among populations which are not institutionally differentiated. Competition between clubs of the upper section is not usual, and those which provide sport facilities normally hold open-entry individual tournaments in games such as golf or tennis, occasionally inviting foreign professionals to participate. Proprietary clubs organized for gambling, dancing and drinking are typical of the lowest section, while members' clubs are the typical forms of the upper two sections. Exclusive top-section clubs also offer facilities for the accommodation of members and guests, sometimes on a reciprocal exchange basis with certain of the London clubs. Club life among the top two sections is heterosexual and may include family units, but in the lowest section only men are members.

In their recreational activities the three sections differ even more strikingly than in their organization. Golf, polo, water-skiing and certain other aquatic sports such as yachting are clearly limited to members of the top section, who do not take as active a part in athletics, football or cricket as do the other two, especially the intermediate group. Tennis is commonly played among the upper and middle sections, together with billiards, bridge and certain other indoor games which do not, however, include dominoes or those gambling games typical of the lower section. Boxing, cricket, athletics, bicycling, and to a lesser extent football, are the main outdoor games of the lower section. Such heterosexual activities as dancing and swimming are common to all groups, though the sex and age participation patterns, the forms of the activity and the typical situations in which they occur also vary. It is almost a rule that intersectional participation in such activities as dancing, swimming and the like should not take place. This restrictive sectional barrier has a considerable effect on the membership patterns of clubs in all sections.

Informal associations vary similarly among these social sections. Economic and political associations have already been mentioned. Excluding these, the clique is the typical form of association among the intermediate group, and is multi-functional in relation to occupation, mating, kinship, business and recreation. Among the small dominant group, relations are both more specific and more widely distributed, the cocktail party attended by near-strangers and acquaintances being the stock alternative to the intimate dinner party. Among the lower section, cliques and parties are far less significant than are neighbourhood, kinship, age-peer and workmate relationships.

To an outsider, the most striking differences between these sections are those of the material culture. The material culture of the lowest section is symbolized by a chattel-house, few but gaudy clothes and the cutlass for a tool. That of the intermediate section may be symbolized by the concrete bungalow, gadgets such as washing-machines and refrigerators, and the motor-car or the type-writer for a tool. The upper section is characterized by 'the Great House', of which modern versions are still being built, though in different style, the team of servants, and the cheque-book or telephone for a tool. Although the intermediate and higher sections have many elements of material culture in common, they also differ significantly, and the differences between the material culture of these two sections and that of the third are even more striking. Technological aims and differences also correspond with these differences of material culture.

The study of value-systems presupposes an adequate semantic analysis and an adequate body of data. Neither of these exists for Jamaica; but values, beliefs, ideas, goals and norms are of such fundamental moment in social and cultural organization that even in the absence of these investigations, one may tentatively indicate the principal value-foci which differentiate the several sections of Jamaican society. It has already been shown that these sections differ in the modes of action, explanation and proof which they employ. It can also be said that materialism provides the formative principle or reference point in the value-system of the upper section, while social status dominates the value-system of the intermediate section, and values of immediate physical gratification are central among the third section, spiritual as well as secular values reflecting these principles. This tentative differentiation of the sectional value-systems by their foci has two important implications. Firstly, the moral axioms of one section are not the axioms of another, so that the same events or patterns are generally interpreted and evaluated differently by each of the three Jamaican social sections. Thus, the values and implications of colour are peculiar to the intermediate section, in the same way that the notions and values of spirit possession and manipulation are peculiar to the lowest section. Secondly, the co-existence of these divergent value-systems within a single society involves continuous ideological conflict. The need to express these differences of value and morality governs and reflects inter-sectional relations, and this insistence on the incompatibility of the sectional moralities is incessantly activated by the differing sectional reactions to common events, especially of course those which involve inter-sectional relations.

It is not merely that the same event has different meanings or value for the different sections; these differing interpretations compete continuously, and their competition is inherent in their co-existence, and in the corresponding cultural and social plurality which they express and represent. It follows that interpretations of events by reference to one or other of these competing moral systems is the principal mode of thought which characterizes Jamaican society, and also that such sectional moralizations normally seek to define a negative, extra-sectional and disvalued pole in contrast to a positive, intra-sectional and esteemed one. Thus Jamaicans moralize incessantly about one another's actions in order to assert their cultural and social identity by expressing the appropriate sectional morality. For such self-identification, negation is far more essential and effective than is its opposite; hence the characteristic appeal of negativism within this society, and its prevalence.

This summary describes a society divided into three sections, each of which practises a different system of institutions. The integration of these three sections within the larger society has never been very high; and for cohesion Jamaica has depended mainly on those forms of social control implicit in the economic system and explicit in government. Even so, patterns of inter-personal relations do not always correspond with these cultural divisions; and in every cultural section there are some persons who habitually associate with others who carry a different cultural tradition more regularly than with those of their own cultural community. The fewness of these marginal individuals is no adequate guide to their importance.

It may be argued that this account only delineates two institutionally differentiated sections, and that the white and brown strata described above are really two social classes which form a common section, because they have a number of institutions in common. Clearly, the greatest cultural gulf within this society lies between the two upper sections and the large lower one; but although these two upper sections do share certain institutions, each also practises a number of institutions which are quite specific to itself, and since these sectional systems of institutions each tend to be integrated separately, I have regarded them as quite distinct.

12.

The sociocultural complexity of the Caribbean region is reviewed by an American geographer in terms of the concepts of pluralism sketched in the preceding selection. This article provides a comparative view of the range and variety of societal types. The author examines some of the principal approaches to the social scientific study of these diverse territories and indicates the range of difference in such variables as territorial and demographic size, metropolitan connection, political status, national identity, racial composition, and language. This survey of societal variation in the Caribbean will help place in perspective the case studies which follow in this section.

DAVID LOWENTHAL was Fulbright Research Fellow at the University College of the West Indies in 1956–57 and has done field work in many parts of the Caribbean. The concepts presented here are amplified in his *West Indian Societies*. He was Research Associate at the American Geographical Society, and is presently Professor of Geography at University College, London.

The Range and Variation of Caribbean Societies
David Lowenthal

Pluralistic circumstances affect Caribbean societies in a
variety of ways. No society is altogether plural or even
heterogeneous; if it were, it would not be a society at all,
but only an assemblage of functionally unrelated communities. No society entirely lacks institutional diversity; if it
did, it would be so homogeneous that it could not survive
in any environment. Between these theoretical extremes,
however, there is a continuum of possible sociocultural
configurations. Some societies exhibit more, or different,
evidences of pluralism than others. Aspects and combina-
tions of pluralism vary from place to place in intensity, in
structure and interrelatedness, in degree of formal institutionalization, in the extent to which they are locally ap-
prehended, in historical stability, and in functional import.
In any particular society, for example, one or more determinants of social stratification, such as color, descent,
wealth, occupation, age, or sex, may inhibit freedom of
choice or expression more or less completely in various
realms of activity.

Elsewhere in this monograph† Smith has set a theoretical

Social and Cultural Pluralism in the Caribbean, edited by
Vera Rubin, *Annals of the New York Academy of Sciences*,
Vol. 83, pp. 786–95. Copyright, The New York Academy of
Sciences, 1960; reprinted by permission of the Academy and the
author.

† [The author refers to M. G. Smith's article "Social and Cultural Pluralism" in *Social and Cultural Pluralism in the Caribbean*, pp. 763–77.]

framework; I shall consider how to assess the varieties of sociocultural diversity that actually do occur within West Indian societies. I limit myself to the islands because I know them best, and because their insularity suggests a manageable scheme for analysis. I use the word "diversity" rather than "pluralism" advisedly. The distinction Smith makes between heterogeneous and plural is a valid one, but it is difficult to use. At just what point do differences in ways of life become so incompatible as to make a minority a separate cultural section? How does one decide whether stylistic similarities conceal fundamental diversities? Are the basic institutions the same in one society as in another, and have they always the same relative importance? How much social mobility, actual or perceived, makes a plural society merely heterogeneous? How large must an institutionally distinctive minority be to qualify the whole society as plural rather than merely pluralistic, and does the size of the group effectively measure its significance?[1] It appears to me that nonplural societies grade imperceptibly into plural ones. In any case, diversity is a necessary element of pluralism. This paper concerns both concepts.

To compare societies, one must first decide what one means by a society. No functional hierarchy of social groups properly fits circumstances throughout the West Indies. The role of the family, the estate, the parish, the society, the empire, or indeed of any social or territorial unit, is here crucial, there trivial; its scope or size here extensive, there narrow. Smith's definition of societies as "territorially distinct units having their own governmental institutions" establishes sufficient and perhaps necessary criteria, but does not actually identify them; how potent or inclusive need governmental institutions be to qualify a social unit as a society? I shall instead experiment with an arbitrary geographical measure.

To my mind, the most apposite realm for societies in the

---

[1] A. I. Hallowell, "The Impact of the American Indian on American Culture," *American Anthropologist*, Vol. 59, No. 2 (April 1957), 201–17.

West Indies is the island. There are obvious exceptions: Hispaniola and St. Martin, for example, both divided by sovereignty. However, the island does less violence to social reality, involves less Procrustean chopping and stretching than any other topographic category, because insularity is a basic fact of life. An island is a world, to use Selvon's title.[2] The network of social relations seldom survives the sea. Polynesians and Melanesians, more at home with the ocean, make it a highway instead of a barrier; but for West Indians (save, perhaps, in French Martinique and Guadeloupe) the island is in most contexts the most compelling areal symbol. A man who says, "I am a Jamaican," or "I am a Barbadian," is very likely expressing the broadest allegiance he knows.[3]

Each of the smaller islands also has special characteristics, a unique self-image, and a particular view of all the others. What is more, large and small islands are equally conscious of their individuality. Jamaican and Montserratian parochialisms are much alike, although one country has 1,700,000 people and the other only 14,000. Physical insularity intensifies a sense of belonging within each island, whatever its size. To be sure, Jamaicans who live in the Blue Mountains are unlike inhabitants of the Cockpit Country, and those who dwell in Kingston have little in common with people on Frome sugar estate at the western end of the island. However, these differences do not divide Jamaica into one hundred separate Montserrats; indeed, not even into two or three.

Communities do exist, of course, along with neighborhood self-consciousness, but these microcosms are hard to identify; self-sufficient in no respect, they are socially and culturally integrated with island society as a whole.[4] West

[2] S. Selvon, *An Island Is a World* (London: MacGibbon & Kee, 1955).

[3] D. Lowenthal, "The West Indies Chooses a Capital," *Geographical Review*, Vol. 48, No. 3 (1958), pp. 336–64.

[4] M. G. Smith, "Community Organization in Rural Jamaica," *Social and Economic Studies*, Vol. 5, No. 3 (September 1956), pp. 295–312; R. T. Smith, *The Negro Family in British Guiana* (London: Routledge & Kegan Paul, 1956); C. Wagley, "Recent

Indian communities cannot be understood as worlds in themselves. To be sure, community organization and sub-regional ties are more important in some islands than in others, though not necessarily in the largest or most populous of them. Barbados, with 230,000 people, is practically one geographical community, despite fairly rigid class barriers, owing to its excellent road network and its historic cultural homogeneity. Dominica, on the other hand, with only 65,000 people, has considerable village and local self-consciousness because population centers are isolated by difficult topography and poor communications and, in part, because of the collapse of the plantation economy that once supported island-wide social institutions. In Jamaica and in Trinidad, physical and social distance notwithstanding, island feeling prevails over local and sectional interests, partly because island radio and newspapers, island government and politics, are omnipresent. However, these unifying forces are weaker in an island such as St. Vincent and practically nonexistent on Bequia, in the Grenadines. One can walk around Bequia in a day, but its 4000 inhabitants include 3 mutually exclusive communities. On the other hand, the web of kinship brings the 8000 people in nearby Carriacou into a close network of associations.

The administrative status of these and other tiny islands is no gauge to the local state of mind. Many constituent parts of The West Indies federation are themselves island groups: Trinidad includes Tobago, St. Kitts includes Nevis and Anguilla, Antigua has Barbuda, St. Vincent and Grenada share the Grenadines, and both Jamaica and the federation are involved with the Cayman Islands and the Turks and Caicos Islands. Long association or political expediency might promote unit solidarity, but most of these unions are fortuitous or recent; a man from Tobago is apt to think of himself as a Tobagonian, not as a Trinidadian. The primary geographical identification is that with the island, no matter how small or dependent it may be. St.

Studies of Caribbean Local Societies," in A. C. Wilgus, ed., *The Caribbean: Natural Resources* (Gainesville, Florida: University of Florida Press, 1959).

Kitts and Nevis are only 2 miles apart and are economically interdependent (Nevis grows food for Kittician sugar plantations), but the inhabitants of each island seldom have a good word to say for the other, and both snub Anguillans, who are 60 miles away and a different kind of folk entirely, in their own view and in reality. Grenada and its dependency, Carriacou, likewise have little in common; the difference between the hierarchical social structure of the former and the egalitarianism of the latter is just one of many vital contrasts.[5] At the same time, Carriacou and its own tiny dependency, Petit Martinique, are quite dissimilar; the Petit Martiniquaise would seldom call himself a Carriacouan any more than he would a Grenadian. Only the smallest islands and those used as resorts by the "mainlanders" lack this overriding sense of individuality. One scholar termed Lesser Antillean feeling "a case of insular psychology gone mad."[6]

A sense of individuality does not, of itself, suffice to make an island a society. West Indian islands are not discrete social organisms; they are both more and less than this. There are inter-island family and economic ties throughout the eastern Caribbean. Many small-island elite live elsewhere: Martiniquaise own Guadeloupe *sucreries,* important Tobagonians reside in Trinidad, and Petit Martinique is governed by a Grenadian District Officer who visits once a week from Carriacou. However, the social institutions of Jamaica (not just its government) are similarly truncated with respect to Port of Spain and London. Similar qualifications limit most societies. Only the largest nations are entirely self-governing, and even these have myriad links with other peoples: property owned abroad, social, economic, and religious enclaves and exclaves.

The choice of islands as social units is statistically as well as methodologically convenient. There are 51 Carib-

[5] M. G. Smith, *Kinship and Community in Carriacou* (New Haven: Yale University Press, 1962).
[6] R. H. Whitbeck, "The Lesser Antilles—Past and Present," *Annals of the Association of American Geographers,* Vol. 23 (1933), p. 25.

bean islands of whose essential social integrity I am reasonably certain: each of them is an "enduring, cooperating social group so functioning as to maintain and perpetuate itself."[7] The units range in population from Cuba, with 6,500,000 people, to Mayreau, one of the St. Vincent Grenadines, with 250. Almost nine tenths of the 18,700,000 West Indians live in societies larger than 1,000,000 people. Eight per cent inhabit societies ranging from 100,000 to 1,000,000, 4 per cent in societies smaller than 100,000. The picture is quite different when one takes social units as the measure. Only 5 societies (one tenth of the total) have more than 1,000,000 people; 5 others have between 100,000 and 1,000,000 each, while 41 societies are smaller than 100,000. Most of these (53 per cent of all the social units in the West Indies) have fewer than 10,000 people each, even though together these small-islanders comprise less than 0.5 per cent of the Caribbean population. Of the islands having populations of less than 10,000, two thirds have less than 2500 inhabitants apiece. In other words, more than one half of all West Indians live in a society larger than 3,000,000 (Cuba or Haiti); but the mean population per society is 366,000 (one half again as many as Barbados), while the mode is a society of only 7000 persons (about the size of Anguilla).

The small size of most West Indian societies has a significant bearing on individual heterogeneity and pluralism. Unless they are completely cut off from the modern world, social groups with fewer than 100,000 people face many special problems: a "colonial" relationship with some larger territory or, in the case of The West Indies federation, with a federal government; a dearth of trained men and of leaders for external as well as for local governmental positions; a lack of cultural focus; and a narrow, conservative outlook and sometimes pathological sensitivity to criticism, exacerbated by small-island feuds and a claustrophobic absence of privacy. Common metropolitan bonds, like economic interests, and analogous social cleav-

[7] Webster's New Collegiate Dictionary, "Society," def. no. 7 (Springfield, Mass.: Merriam, 1947).

ages result in superficial but trivial similarities. Jealousies, rivalries, fears, and, above all, mutual ignorance, tend to make each small island a museum in which archaic distinctions are carefully preserved. It is precisely because so many of the West Indian islands are isolated and miniscule that they exhibit pluralistic features. Geographical and sociocultural heterogeneity reinforce each other.

Colonial status, a frequent feature of pluralism, is likewise linked both with insularity and with small size. It is no accident that, of the 51 West Indian societies, only the 3 most populous are politically independent: that is, ruled by their own elites, not by outsiders. The next largest one, Puerto Rico, is semi-autonomous. The remainder are in effect colonial, whatever their formal status. A high proportion of the smallest territories (those with populations under 40,000) endure double colonialism as dependencies of dependencies. Indeed, some of the Grenadines are dependencies of dependencies of dependencies. However, neither government nor size is an infallible indicator of sociocultural heterogeneity, much less of pluralism.

There are, however, several more direct approaches to an appraisal of the range of West Indian societies. One method, inherent in Smith's paper,† is holistic and functional: to assess the general condition of each society and rank it according to intensity of pluralism, that is, the degree of incompatibility or antagonism between the different cultural sections. This approach demands analysis not of institutional differentiation but rather of the strains to which it leads: the extent to which government is maintained by force rather than by consent; the degree to which the activities and aims of each cultural section offset or negate those of other sections. What is crucial is the relationship between the cultural sections.

Not every disagreement or difference is evidence of pluralism, however, nor is discord an infallible yardstick. Horizontal plural societies, in which cultural sections are not hierarchically arranged, display little strain if there is

† [M. G. Smith, "Social and Cultural Pluralism"; see earlier note.]

little contact between the sections. On the other hand, apparent agreement on goals and values in stratified societies is not necessarily an indication that pluralism, much less tension, is absent. The fact that each cultural section in British West Indian societies parades loyalty to the Crown, avoids manual labor when possible, admires white skin, and fancies Christian marriage as an ideal does not indicate that they share a basic way of life or common institutional systems, but rather that each strives to advance by emulating the perceived behavior of the ruling section and by discrediting its own circumstances and ways of life. Cultural unity may mask institutional diversity. What is more, horizontal and vertical pluralism have disparate origins, careers, and terminations. When differences between nonstratified sections become intolerable, partition, as in Israel and to some extent in Canada, is a likely result, while stratified societies, such as that of Haiti, are more apt to suffer revolution.

When one considers that some West Indian societies (notably Trinidad, British Guiana, Surinam, and St. Croix) contain important horizontal as well as vertical sections, and that the character and role of each is constantly shifting, the difficulty of judging the intensity of pluralism becomes evident.[8] A pragmatic, comparative assessment of the incompatibility of sociocultural sections demands prophecy as well as omniscience.

A second approach involves a holistic but synthetic type of analysis. This is to ascertain the extent of sociocultural heterogeneity in each society and then compare the societies with each other, starting, perhaps, with pairs of approximately equal size: Barbados and Guadeloupe, Aruba and Antigua, St. Croix and Montserrat, Bonaire and Bequia, St. Barthélemy and Providencia, Union and Saba. This method raises several questions. For one, heterogeneity is not pluralism; cultural diversity often coexists with institutional unity. Nevertheless, without heterogeneity there

[8] H. C. Brookfield, "Pluralism and Geography in Mauritius," *Geographical Studies,* Vol. 5 (1958), pp. 3–19.

can hardly be pluralism; they are correlated. To rank societies according to their degree of internal diversity is certainly relevant to a study of pluralism.

A more serious difficulty is that no one has devised a formula for adding up different sorts of diversity. How many points does one allot to this or that amount of ethnic heterogeneity, how many points to various differences in rural and urban living patterns, how many to property and kinship systems? Social and cultural elements can hardly be combined quantitatively for any society, let alone for more than one. Any general comparison must be essentially impressionistic, as much a work of art as a product of science. This is probably why it is seldom undertaken in the Caribbean, or elsewhere, except by travelers, novelists, and poets. Social scientists usually find the task temperamentally disagreeable. Nevertheless, we need more such studies by competent observers, especially studies comparing British, French, and Dutch dependencies.

The third approach is particularistic and synthetic. This method is to examine specific aspects of society and culture and to study the range and variation of each throughout the West Indies. This approach yields no generalizations about any particular society as a whole, but it has its uses, nonetheless, and it has the advantage of being possible. It has been tried, for various traits, at various levels of sophistication, and with various degrees of success by Proudfoot[9] for the British and American dependencies; by Kruijer[10] for St. Eustatius, St. Maarten, and St. Thomas; by the Keurs[11] for the Netherlands Windward Islands; by M. G. Smith[12] for Grenada and Carriacou;

[9] M. Proudfoot, *Britain and the United States in the Caribbean: A Comparative Study in Methods of Development* (London: Faber & Faber, 1954).

[10] G. J. Kruijer, "Saint Martin and Saint Eustatius Negroes as Compared with Those of Saint Thomas: A Study of Personality and Culture," *West-Indische Gids,* Vol. 24, No. 4 (1953), pp. 225–37.

[11] J. Keur and D. Keur, *Windward Children* (Assen, Netherlands: Van Gorcum, 1960).

[12] Smith, *Kinship and Community in Carriacou.*

and by Cumper[13] for the British Caribbean generally. Two kinds of study are needed: detailed comparisons of all facets of life in a few societies, and broad surveys of particular traits and institutional sub-systems for the whole area. Class and color configurations; the roles of minor ethnic groups; metropolitan policies, influences, and images; ecological and economic patterns; religious, legal, and educational systems; mating and kinship; and other aspects of culture and society should be separately scrutinized for each and compared for all West Indian societies.

Let us consider color-class stratification. The classic white-colored-black system of status ranking,[14] significant in many West Indian societies, is unimportant in others. In Cuba, the Dominican Republic, and Puerto Rico, where Negroes are a fairly small minority, the elite is hardly distinguishable, in terms of color, from most of the lower class. Many of the smallest West Indian societies are virtually homogeneous with respect to race and color: Carriacou, San Andrés, St. Eustatius, Barbuda, and Mayreau being almost entirely Negro communities, and St. Barthélemy being almost entirely white.

Elsewhere the pattern and the significance of color heterogeneity vary profoundly. Warner views status systems based on color as the most inclusive and rigid form of social stratification, one in which the position of the individual is fixed and determined by birth.[15] In few Carib-

[13] G. Cumper, *Social Structure of the British Caribbean (Excluding Jamaica)* (Parts 1, 2, 3), (Mona, Jamaica: University College of the West Indies, Extra-Mural Department, 1949).

[14] M. G. Smith, *A Framework for Caribbean Studies* (Mona, Jamaica: University College of the West Indies, 1955), pp. 47–50; M. G. Smith, "Ethnic and Cultural Pluralism in the British Caribbean," International Institute of Differing Civilizations, Lisbon, 1957; L. Braithwaite, "Social Stratification in Trinidad," *Social and Economic Studies,* Vol. 2, Nos. 2–3 (October 1953), pp. 5–175.

[15] W. L. Warner, "The study of social stratification," in J. B. Gittler, ed., *Review of Sociology: Analysis of a Decade* (New York: Wiley, 1957), pp. 234–35.

bean societies, however, do color-class differences retain these castelike attributes; all have some measure of mobility and assimilation. The white *békés* of Guadeloupe and Martinique, an endogamous and genealogically self-conscious group, form a closed elite (closed to metropolitan and other Antillean whites as well as to *gens de couleur*) at the summit of an otherwise open class structure. Until recently the mulatto elite in Haiti occupied a similar position. In many of the smaller islands, such as Saba, Bequia, and La Désirade, black, colored and, when present, white groups tend to form separate communities rather than ranked sections within the same community; despite some status difference, each group is essentially classless.[16] In still other societies (St. Croix, St. Thomas, Aruba) special economic circumstances such as tourism or oil refining, together with continual in- and out-migration and skewed age and sex distributions, obscure the color-class pattern and diminish its functional significance.

Even where color-class hierarchies clearly operate, it is difficult to estimate how important they are. Barbados is most self-conscious about color-class distinctions, but other British Caribbean social hierarchies may well be more rigid. Too little is known of the different character and varying roles of the elite in, for example, Barbados, where many whites are not members of it; in Trinidad, where it is deeply divided by nationality; and in Grenada and Dominica, where it is becoming predominantly light-colored. We need comparative studies of the elites of each society in terms of their ethnic and social origins, numbers, proportions to the total population, residential patterns, occupational and economic roles, uniformity or diversity of circumstances, internal solidarity, extent of identification with the whole society (greater in Barbados, for example, than in Trinidad and St. Vincent), affluence relative to others, control of political, educational, and religious institutions,

---

[16] G. Lasserre, "La Désirade, petite isle guadeloupéenne," *Cahiers d'Outre-Mer,* Vol. 10, No. 40 (1957), pp. 325–66.

and stereotypes and self-images of the rest of the population.

We also need comparative studies of peoples partly or wholly outside the stratified social order. The extent to which East Indians in Trinidad, British Guiana, and Surinam have been Creolized is debated in this monograph,† as it probably will be perennially, but few will deny that these East Indians constitute a separate cultural section. This is not true of East Indians in other West Indian societies, who are generally assimilated to, sometimes integrated with, the Creole lower class.[17] Is it because these East Indians are much smaller minorities (7 per cent in Guadeloupe, less everywhere else)? East Indian minorities (predominantly urban, to be sure) in other parts of the world maintain separate social organizations.

The same is substantially true of other ethnic minorities in the West Indies. The Chinese, Portuguese, and Syrian communities together do not account for 3 per cent of the population of any West Indian territory, but in many of them they play significant roles.[18] Their virtual monopoly of retail trade in some societies represents, for the Creole majority, a social truncation as serious, perhaps, as the truncation of political functions involved in colonial relationships. On the other hand, the presence of certain minorities may serve to ease other status relationships. If Syrian merchants, for example, are accepted to any extent by the elite, the middle class is also apt to find areas of acceptance; on the other hand, rejection of these "foreign" elements

† [Author refers to *Social and Cultural Pluralism in the Caribbean;* see earlier notes. The debate is between Daniel J. Crowley and Morton Klass, however, and both articles, "Cultural Assimilation in a Multiracial Society" and "East and West Indian: Cultural Complexity in Trinidad," are included in this book on pages 277 and 287, respectively.]

[17] G. Lasserre, "Les 'Indiens' de Guadeloupe," *Cahiers d'Outre-Mer,* Vol. 6, No. 22 (1953), pp. 128–58.

[18] M. H. Fried, "The Chinese in the British Caribbean" in M. H. Fried, ed., *Colloquium on Overseas Chinese* (New York: International Secretariat, Institute of Pacific Relations, 1958), pp. 49–58.

may promote an awareness of common outlook among Europeans and Creoles.[19]

It is interesting that all these West Indian minorities have achieved a measure of economic success; however much or little they fit into the general social order, they are not at the bottom of it. There are no West Indian counterparts to the Negroes and Puerto Ricans in northern cities of the United States, the eta in Japan, or the Albanians in Belgrade, who perform certain menial tasks that are virtually badges of caste. Until recently the few Javanese in Paramaribo, Surinam, were the only garbage collectors and sewer cleaners, but today they abjure such occupations. Convicts used to perform similar services in French Guiana until the termination of the penal establishment there.

Data are needed from each West Indian society about all of these minorities and about their relative and absolute numbers, their economic roles, and the extent to which they remain aloof from, or merge into, the general social order.

The extent of linguistic differentiation within West Indian societies similarly illustrates their diversity. Language is both a symbol of and an adjunct to status. What proportion in each society speaks the "standard" tongue, and on what occasions? How different is the Creolese variant in pronunciation, vocabulary, and grammar? How do various sections of the population feel and act about the use of patois? There are several fundamentally different situations.[20] In most societies the patois is a dialect of the language of the educated, but in Dominica, St. Lucia, Curaçao, and Surinam the local patois has no relation whatever to the official prestige tongue; the two are mutually unintelligible. Linguistic differentiation is thus formalized, and the gulf between social classes is greater than in

[19] I am indebted to Rhoda Métraux, Institute for Intercultural Studies, New York, N.Y., for this suggestion.
[20] R. B. Le Page, "The Language Problem in the British Caribbean," *Caribbean Quarterly,* Vol. 4, No. 1 (1955), pp. 40–49; E. Efron, "French and Creole Patois in Haiti," *Caribbean Quarterly,* Vol. 3, No. 4 (1954), pp. 199–213.

societies where the patois is a variant of the metropolitan language. The opposite is true where the lingua franca derives from a European language that is more widely spoken in the region than the local official language. In the English-speaking Netherlands Windward Islands and, to some extent, in San Andrés and Providencia, linguistic differentiation tends to break down rather than to reinforce social stratification, because the values associated with the language of the majority outweigh the prestige associated with metropolitan Dutch or Spanish.

To describe the range and diversity of social institutions and cultural forms is not enough, however; one must also account for them. How is it that pluralism affects one society more than another? How can one explain heterogeneity in one place and homogeneity in another? Why are certain traits diverse in this place and uniform in that one? Answers to such questions require comparative analysis, to avoid oversimplified or excessively functional explanations.

Let me illustrate with data on the European Guianas.[21] Here, I think, comparisons have special validity because these territories are contiguous, because their inhabited areas are remarkably alike physically, and because their settlement for a long time followed similar models, particularly in Surinam and British Guiana, which were drained and diked for plantation agriculture along the same lines until the late eighteenth century.

Ethnic heterogeneity characterizes both British Guiana and Surinam, principally because many indentured laborers were brought in after the emancipation of the slaves. One half the population of each territory today is of Asian origin, virtually all Indian in British Guiana, while three tenths is Indian and two tenths Javanese in Surinam. However, Surinamese society is generally less integrated. In British Guiana, East Indian ways of life have become more and more similar to those of other rural or urban folk, while in Surinam the Creoles, Hin-

[21] D. Lowenthal, "Population Contrasts in the Guianas," *Geographical Review*, Vol. 50 (1960), pp. 41–59.

dustanis, and Javanese for the most part have their own villages, languages, and even customary garb. British Guianese East Indians refer to their compatriots in Surinam as "good" Indians, that is, closer adherents of old-country fashion and ritual (personal communication from C. Jayawardena). Unlike British Guianese, Surinamers do not hesitate to assert their separate ethnic interests; political parties are avowedly divided along racial and religious lines; there is scarcely any sense of a general Surinam society. Occupational and rural-urban ethnic differentiation are also more pronounced in Surinam. Three fourths of the Creole population is urban, compared with less than one half in British Guiana, and most of Surinam's rural Creoles are concentrated within a few districts.

Several factors help to account for these differences. For one, slavery lasted twenty-five years longer in Surinam than in British Guiana. In the interim many slaves fled the country and, when emancipation finally came, in 1863, the Negroes still left on Surinam estates were not willing to wait out an additional decade of indenture. In British Guiana, many former slaves pooled their savings to buy up estates and turned to subsistence agriculture; in Surinam, most of them moved off the land.

The delay of emancipation also retarded the introduction of indentured workers. East Indians began to enter British Guiana as early as 1841, but did not reach Surinam until after 1873, and the Javanese came there still later, between 1891 and 1939. Neither group in Surinam has had as long to become assimilated as have the East Indians of British Guiana. Moreover, the East Indians of Surinam (known there as Hindustanis) have found acculturation more difficult for lack of a continuing tie with certain British institutions and aspects of culture. Besides, there is little in common between the Hindustanis and the Javanese. Many of the latter are still first-generation immigrants, for the most part content with their alien status as Indonesian citizens, and are regarded as clannish and unenterprising by Europeans, Creoles, and Hindustanis alike.

Dutch colonial policy is partly responsible for the fact

that Surinam's rural villages are, by and large, more homogeneous racially than those of British Guiana. Until after the Second World War the Surinam government promoted residential segregation by leasing abandoned estates to ethnic groups. This practice is now disavowed, but efforts to promote integration have had little success, perhaps because many people still believe, at heart, that the different races simply will not work or live well together.

The linguistic situation displays similar segmentation. In British Guiana English is both the vernacular and the prestige language of the educated, but in Surinam the common Creole tongue (*Taki-Taki,* an amalgam of African, English, and other elements) is utterly unlike the official, upper-class Dutch. Dutch is unimportant elsewhere in America, and *Taki-Taki* is incomprehensible outside Surinam, so it is little wonder that Javanese and Hindustanis prefer to retain their own, more widely spoken, languages. Even the Creoles are divided, some preferring Dutch, others promoting *Taki-Taki* as their "own" tongue, that is, as an appurtenance of nationalism. Lacking a viable common language, Surinam is unlikely to reach a level of social or cultural integration comparable to that in British Guiana, even should Surinamers desire it.

These features represent, of course, only one aspect of social organization in the Guianas. Analogous contrasts can be drawn with respect to the varieties of stratification within the Creole groups and the roles of the European and other minorities. Whatever point of departure one selects, society and culture can be understood best, as Furnivall remarked of colonial practice, when studied both comparatively and historically.[22]

[22] J. S. Furnivall, *Colonial Policy and Practice: A Comparative Study of Burma and Netherlands India* (Cambridge: Cambridge University Press, 1948), pp. 9–10.

13.

This selection, which is part of a longer monograph "Social Stratification in Trinidad," sketches the complex status ranking and other relationships of communities and ethnic groups as they were in 1953. The author, himself a Trinidadian, also analyzes the opportunities available for social mobility and status acquisition. Whereas M. G. Smith focuses on disparities of institutional forms in analyzing Jamaican society, Braithwaite emphasizes the factors, real and symbolic, which support the general acceptance of Trinidad's stratification system, the prospects for individual movement within the system, and the linkages between that system and the metropole. Careful comparison of M. G. Smith and Lloyd Braithwaite reveals some of the theoretical and methodological differences between the pluralist and the consensualist approaches to the understanding of West Indian society.

LLOYD BRAITHWAITE, a Trinidad-born sociologist trained in England, has long been connected with the University of the West Indies, having served as Director of the Institute of Social and Economic Research, Head of the Department of Sociology, and Dean of the Faculty of Social Science in Jamaica. He is currently Pro-Vice-Chancellor of the University of the West Indies, Trinidad.

Stratification in Trinidad*
Lloyd Braithwaite

THE SYSTEM OF SOCIAL STRATIFICATION IN TRINIDAD

In order to understand the structure of the island as a whole it is necessary to pay special attention to the system of social stratification. This is a more complex problem than appears at first sight, because there are various systems of stratification within the society. Some of these are systems of stratification of particular communities within the island, but others are generally accepted for the island, although they do not necessarily coincide with the stratifications of any other particular community. The divergence of class judgements as between communities has not received the attention that it deserves. In the past most field-work studies have been related to the social stratification of one particular community and have generalized from the local evaluations about the system of social stratification in the national society. Of particular significance in this respect is the work of the Warner group[1]

Social and Economic Studies, Vol. 2, Nos. 2–3, October 1953, pp. 38–60 (excerpts). Reprinted by permission of the Institute of Social and Economic Research, University of the West Indies, and the author.

* [Editors' title]

[1] William Lloyd Warner, ed., *Yankee City Series* (New Haven: Yale University Press, 1941–47): Paul S. Lunt, *The Social Life of a Modern Community* (1941) and *The Status System of a Modern Community* (1942); Leo Srole, *The Social System of American Ethnic Groups* (1945); J. O. Low, *The*

and other work which it has inspired. In the Introduction to "Democracy in Jonesville", Warner writes: "The life of the community reflects and symbolizes the significant principles on which the American social system rests . . . . we can say that Jonesville is in all Americans and all Americans are in Jonesville, for he that dwelleth in America dwelleth in Jonesville and Jonesville in him", and "By such a study (of Jonesville) we could see and understand the larger design of American life".[2]

Even when Lloyd Warner is dealing not with the specific local community but with the whole of the American scene, he makes similar assertions. Thus in his "Structure of American Life", he writes: "In my research the local community was made to serve as a microcosmic whole representing the total community", and "careful examination of the evidence elicited from local studies, when related to what is known about our economic life, gives great insight and social knowledge about the processes of work throughout the system".[3]

However, other sociologists have become increasingly concerned with the divergence between the national stratification and the various systems of stratification in the local community, and the way they are all articulated into a coherent system. The late Paul K. Hatt was one such sociologist. More recently Charles Wagley and his group[4] in their studies of "Race and Class in Rural Brazil"[5]

Social System of the Modern Factory (1947); W. Lloyd Warner, *Democracy in Jonesville* (New Haven: Yale University Press, 1949); Allison Davis, et al., *Deep South* (Chicago: University of Chicago Press, 1941); A. B. Hollingshead, *Elmtown's Youth: The Impact of Social Classes on Adolescents* (New York: Wiley, 1949); John Dollard, *Caste and Class in a Southern Town* (New Haven: Yale University Press, 1937).

[2] Warner, *Democracy in Jonesville*, p. 15.

[3] Warner, *Structure of American Life* (Edinburgh: Edinburgh University Press, 1952), p. 33.

[4] Charles Wagley, ed., *Race and Class in Rural Brazil* (New York: International Documents Service, Columbia University Press for UNESCO, 1952).

[5] *Ibid.*; see, in particular, the section "From Caste to Class in North Brazil," p. 142, *et seq.*

have clearly recognized the difference posed by the national and local systems of stratification.

While it is true that the social structure of any small community within the larger national society reflects in some degree the structure of the larger society, this method of looking at social stratification tends to ignore the problem of the integration of communities, of the fact that in terms of the national society all communities do not rank as equal. The problem is not solved by selecting a typical community for study because the very fact of typicality tends to ignore the most important problem of all, that is, the stratification between communities and the way in which it becomes linked up into a nation-wide system of stratification. In this linkage the dominance of certain metropolitan and political areas (the political capital) appears to be of crucial importance although in terms of typicality these areas would have to be ignored.

In the island society of Trinidad there appears the same phenomenon of the ranking of districts, localities and communities. Port of Spain, the capital city, would immediately be placed first. Even the inhabitants of the second largest town, San Fernando, often speak of going to Port of Spain as going to "town", thus giving themselves inferior "country" status. In terms of the smaller places like Blanchisseuse, we shall see that although Blanchisseuse has subordinates, its place in rank order of importance from the stratification point of view would be low down on the list.

The hypothetical ranking of communities in Trinidad is as follows:

1. Port of Spain
2. San Fernando
3. St. Augustine
4. Arima
5. Sangre Grande
6. Blanchisseuse
7. Brasso Seco.

We can be sure that the gaps between these are not equidistant and the ordering most generally shared by the population could be represented not unfairly in the accompanying diagram (Fig. 1).

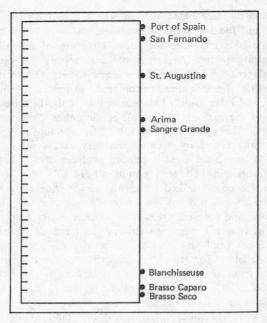

Fig. 1 Ranking of communities in Trinidad

Here, as in the phenomenon of ranking individuals and classifying them according to some scale of superiority and inferiority, there is room for divergence of opinion. Local patriotism, limitations of contact, ignorance, divergence in the scale of values upon which the judgements are based—all these may lead to some diversity of outlook. In terms of the island society of Trinidad this divergence is not great. This is probably due to the small size of the island, and the fact that there are few difficulties in communication. This has led to nearly all communities accepting the dominance of Port of Spain. However, even here, there is a challenge from San Fernando. Arising from the fact that these two major communities dominate several minor ones there is a tendency to divide the island into two sections—North and South—between which there is a certain amount of rivalry. This is reflected in the institutionalization of North-South competitions in athletics, football and cricket. This is merely a minor reflection of a division in the social structure which could possibly have greater significance. This is shown in the political field in the sharp divergence between the support obtained by the radical political leader Uriah Butler, and the marches and demonstrations that he was able to organize from the South into the North.

In this connection the single, most important thing is that no matter what divergences of judgement there are people must accept in some form or fashion the national stratification system, primarily through the acceptance of the upper class and the symbolism associated with it. The manner in which the separate individuals and groups may come to accept the nation-wide stratification system, may either be direct or indirect. That is, the individual may either himself accept the upper class as an upper class, or he may merely, in terms of a smaller community, of a partial segment of the society, accept the superiority of another social group which is itself thoroughly imbued with the values which make for the acceptance of the national upper class. This linkage may be many chains removed and varies in strength.

In terms of Trinidad society this acceptance of a common upper class and its symbolism is made more complicated by the fact that a large proportion of the upper class of Trinidad society is not Trinidad-born and does not have its roots in Trinidad life. Many of these individuals are oriented to a social system other than the island society. If all the "Britishers" were concentrated in one region, Port of Spain, the problem of linkage of communities would not be so difficult. The fact, however, that there are relatively self-contained groups of Britishers in St. Augustine, Pointe a Pierre, and Port of Spain, makes the acceptance, directly or indirectly, of the values of this external or super-ordinate social system a matter of cardinal concern. Again, the close interlinking of the political and

social class system which results from the fact that the
island society is a colony, and part of the larger structure
of the British Empire, makes the acceptance of the su
periority of the super-ordinate system by all the member
of the society of increased importance. In other words
although we are concerned with the analysis of the social
structure of Trinidad and not with that of the British
Empire as a whole, we have to take account of the way in
which the British social system and its representatives im
pinge upon the social stratification system. The relationship
between the communities can perhaps be illustrated by a
diagram (Fig. 2).

We are not dealing here with the social structure of the
British Empire, the way in which the British social system
links up the diverse communities within the Empire and
Commonwealth. However, in so far as the manner in
which the linkage between the British social system and the
island society is characteristic, it should throw revealing
light on that problem. Similarly, the study of the social
structure on the village level of Blanchisseuse is not merely
a study of the social structure of the village, but also of a
characteristic form of linkage by which subordinate com
munities become integrated into the larger society.[6]

If the ranking of communities in Trinidad was a clear
cut one which served as an absolute guide to status, so
that a person of middle-class status, say in the village of
Blanchisseuse, automatically assumed a similar status on
moving into Port of Spain, Arima or San Fernando, the
problem of the relationship of social stratification on the
national level to the social stratification of communities
would be easy. The function of the ranking of communi-

---

[6] From a theoretical point of view the similarity of the problems would appear in a different light on different levels. It is
also clear that the discrepancies of judgement between the subordinate members of the Colonial Empire with regard to their
relative importance will be quite great, and the need for insulat-
ing mechanisms, which keep the relationship with the British social system paramount as compared with a spontaneous ordering
of relationships between communities, becomes of paramount
importance.

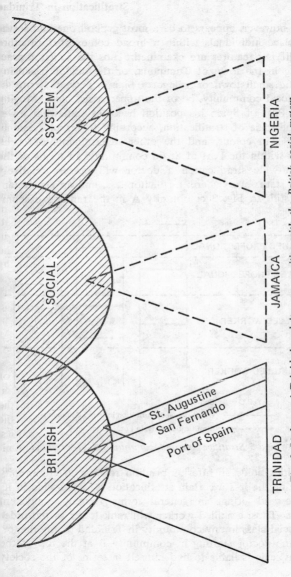

Fig. 2 Linkage of Trinidad and its communities with the British social system

ties, however, appears to be a most general one and serve:
to place individuals within a broad context before othe:
qualifying features are examined. Thus the solicitor prac
tising in the town of Tunapuna, or the doctor practisin;
in the small town or village of Siparia may, in terms o
the local community, be of the upper social class. Movin;
into Port of Spain his position becomes somewhat lowe:
in the scale of stratification, according to his professiona
skill, skin colour, and the other determinants of socia
class within the Port of Spain community. In terms of th
island-wide stratification a doctor will possess relativel;
high status everywhere; a solicitor less, and an accountan:
less still. In Fig. 3 community A in the ranking of com

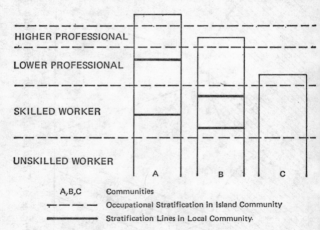

Fig. 3 Stratification and communities in Trinidad

munities holds an inferior position relative to community
B; none the less a certain stratification is island-wide in its
scope and brings in general terms roughly equivalen:
status. Thus, a skilled worker will rank lower in the orde:
of social class in any community in Trinidad to any doctor,
but the doctor starting in community B at the top of the
social scale is liable to find himself in terms of the society

of Port of Spain on a somewhat lower level. Again, the labourer or lower-class person will find himself at the bottom of the stratification scale in any community.

Conversely, the movement out of community B may have the opposite results. Thus, a doctor in the upper class of community B will certainly enjoy upper-class status in community A, but a doctor in the middle class of community B is also sure of enjoying upper-class status in community A. Further, the smaller communities frequently do not possess a large enough population for such a rich differentiation of social classes as in Port of Spain. It has been commonly observed in studies of social class that the members of the upper class are not aware of the differentiations which members of the lower class make among themselves, and which the middle class, likewise, make of the lower class. Similarly, the members of the lower classes tend to group all those above them at a certain remove as members of the "upper class", ignoring the differentiations which others more highly placed make. These phenomena are likewise to be observed in the communities of Trinidad. There also appears to be a difference in communities in this regard. Some communities are large enough for the distinctions to become extremely important because of the distance between the upper and the lower social groups.

On the other hand in the really small community such as the village of Blanchisseuse, its remoteness from the larger communities tends to result in the amalgamation of heterogeneous elements (from the standpoint of Port of Spain or San Fernando) into the common category of the upper class.

SOCIAL STRATIFICATION AND ETHNIC STRATIFICATION

The problem of analysing the social stratification in Trinidad becomes more acute when we realize that together with the ranking of communities we have also to consider the ranking of the various ethnic groups in the island.

The existence of a large variety of ethnic groups has led, not to the development of an eclectic cosmopolitanism, but to a certain separateness of the groups and to a ranking of them in terms of superiority and inferiority, as groups. The main reason for this appears to be that these various ethnic groups entered a society which was already stratified very largely on racial lines; and one in which the biological division of skin colour played an important part in the differentiation of social class, even within the broad bounds determined by race. Thus during the 19th century and early in the 20th century we had a social stratification of the island as depicted in Fig. 4. In the upper group there was a differentiation on a social class basis; but, as between the white group and the coloured group, the condition resembled much more of a caste situation than one of class. The barriers to rising were almost completely prohibitive and in many respects that situation still obtains. The middle class consisted predominantly of coloured people, that is of light-skinned and brown-skinned people, while the lower class consisted predominantly of black.

Just as whiteness tended to put the individual automatically at the top of the social class scale, so blackness of skin colour automatically put the individual at the bottom end of the social scale. At the same time there was a limited mobility from the lowest end of the scale from among the blacks and the browns into the middle class. Unlike the barriers between the whites and non-whites the "caste" barrier could be circumvented by marriage. For the most part, the coloured person could only procure a white wife by going outside the society and seeking a mate who did not subscribe to the particularistic scale of values of Trinidad society. Even this did not, however, serve to make possible the crossing of class lines. On the other hand within the middle-class group there was a differentiation based on skin-colour, but there was no impassable barrier as regards marriage between a light-skinned person and a dark-skinned person. The light-skinned person, all other things being equal, was at the top of the middle-class

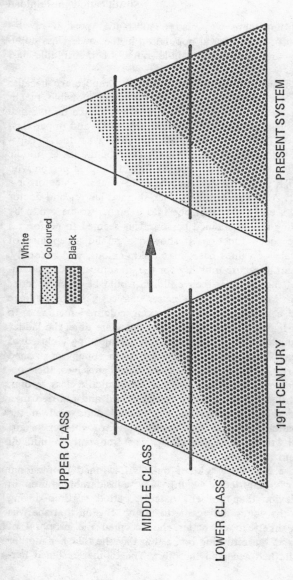

Fig. 4 Stratification in 19th century and change to present system in Trinidad

UPPER CLASS

MIDDLE CLASS

LOWER CLASS

19TH CENTURY

PRESENT SYSTEM

White
Coloured
Black

group but there was also a substantial portion of this
section of the coloured population in the lower-class population, and within the whole range of the middle-class
group.

This form of mobility was of great importance because
it became closely linked with the other possible means
which the social structure permitted within the middle and
lower-class groups and between the middle and upper-class
groups. This other form of mobility was the occupational ladder. Thus a light-skinned girl of the lower middle
class would be keen to marry a darker-skinned person who
was high up on the professional scale—that is, a doctor or a
lawyer. At the same time a dark-skinned lawyer and doctor
would seek to obtain entree into a higher status group by
marrying a light-skinned person. This seemed to perform a
double social function. It showed a public acceptance of
the scale of values based upon skin-colour, and secondly,
it sought to secure mobility for the kinship unit. Consideration of the fact that their children would be given a better
start in life, would have "better chances", seems to have
played a prominent part in making coloured men seek to
marry lighter-skinned women. At the same time, the ladder
of occupational mobility was for the most part closed to
women. While, therefore, most women sought or wished
to marry lighter-skinned persons than themselves, their dependent status, particularly in the middle-class group,
meant that they frequently compromised and married men
darker than themselves, but who had done well in the
occupational world. The decision as to whether a girl
should "trade caste for class" was frequently a difficult
problem to decide.

There is a story told of one dark-skinned professional
man who courted a young lady considerably fairer in
complexion than himself. After a period of time during
which the young lady came to the conclusion that she was
hardly likely to do better she accepted the proposal of
marriage. On returning home that day she told her mother
that she had accepted the offer. The mother resigned her-

f to the situation, saying that although she had hoped
at her daughter would do better than that, there was
me consolation in the fact that she had got a profes-
onal man. On her other daughter returning home and
earing the news that her sister was proposing to marry a
ack man she fell into a fit. She became so distraught that
er mother became convinced of the enormity of the crime
at her daughter proposed to commit. Faced with the
orrow of her other daughter, she realized the true social
gnificance of the act. Reproachfully, she accused the
uilty daughter of wishing to bring sorrow upon the house,
nd the engagement was consequently broken off.

The social structure was clearly founded on an
scriptive-particularistic basis. It was based on the one
and on the positive evaluation of the white group and,
n the other, on a negative evaluation of the black group.
he other groups which entered the system, therefore,
ought to differentiate themselves from the black group as
much as possible, even if acceptance by the white group
appeared to some of these groups as an impossibility, or a
very distant possibility. In other words, the fact that the
social order was based on ascriptive values did not escape
the other groups. Ethnic affiliation and ethnic purity were
the values upon which the social stratification system was
erected and, therefore, this served as a positive encouragement to non-Negro groups to try to retain their ethnic
identity. Of course, there were other important reasons
for this as well based on cultural differences, e.g., the
nationalism of the immigrant. But a contributing force it
was, none the less.

To a certain extent these immigrant groups remained
outside the social system. They were considered for the
most part by the rest of the population to be on the lowest social scale. The Portuguese were identified as dirty
shopkeepers who spoke "rash-potash" and could not speak
English. The Indians coming in as indentured labourers
were despised and thought of as "coolies". Both in official
circles and in popular language the term "coolie" for long

remained the means of identifying this particular ethni
group.[7]

The Syrians came in for the most part as peddlers o
dry goods moving from house to house, granting credit i
return for small monthly payments. Their exorbitant price
and their closeness to the local population, linked to thei
foreign culture, and the humble nature of their work
caused them, too, to be considered as almost outside th
system.

Precisely because they did not share the same scale o
values, they were able to accumulate wealth with greate
ease than the local population who were committed to th
"standards of living" and the symbolism of their respec
tive classes. For these and other reasons there emerged i
time a middle-class among these ethnic groups who i
terms of the values of the society could not be considere
outside the social system. However, for various reason
they continued to retain their ethnic identity although th
attempt to shed some of their ethnic characteristics be
came more marked as they became more assimilated. I
fact, the general movement seems to be in the direction o
shedding the greater part of their cultural heritage whil
seeking to retain their ethnic identity by prohibiting inter
marriage—except with the dominant white group.

The diagram (Fig. 5) seeks to illustrate how individual
of the various ethnic groups who were considered "out
side the system" moved (in some measure at least b
methods which were lowly valued by those inside the sys
tem) into positions higher up on the social ladder. Thi
movement tends to produce a certain amount of ambiva
lence on the part of the society as a whole towards thes
groups. Because of the previous association of these group

[7] The term "coolie" as a racial term was naturally resente
by the Indian middle class. Although it has disappeared fron
use in public it is still in use as a derogatory term in private
As late as the 1940's the term was still so much taken fo
granted, that a locally educated professional man was heard t
remark on reading the news item that "Chinese coolies wer
rebuilding the Burma Road", that "they seem to have a grea
deal of racial intermixture there"!

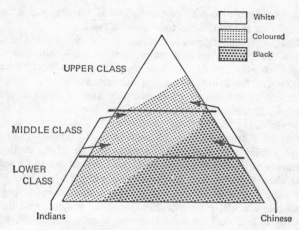

Fig. 5 *Mobility of ethnic groups in Trinidad*

with the lowest social status, and because of their own ambivalence implicit in their commitment to the status-striving in the social system, the (coloured) middle-class and lower-class groups tend to be very resentful of the progress of the other ethnic groups.

The hostility tends to express itself in judgements of the ethnic group based on the lower-class affiliations of the majority of its members. They would rank the ethnic groups in order of superiority and inferiority in an order such as this:

1. White
2. Coloured
3. Black
4. Indian
5. Portuguese
6. Syrian

or would seek to rank the last group as being outside the system, as being "not really Trinidadian".

On the other hand the members of the upper social group tend to look upon the upward mobile individual belonging to an ethnic group in terms of his ethnic similarity or dissimilarity to the white group, viewing the mass of the ethnic group as exceptions. The possibility of mobility of these groups into the white society is equivalent in large measure to that of the lighter skinned group who are able to infiltrate into the upper classes.

Thus individuals from the Chinese, the Syrian and the Indian groups are, in that order, breaking into the lower fringes of white society. In this connection it is interesting to note that the criteria which apparently are used in making a racial judgement of individuals and of groups are common throughout the society. They are the factors of high visibility, "skin colour" and "hair". The Chinese and the Syrians are light-skinned and have "good" hair and hence appear to be more acceptable to the white group. Certainly of all the ethnic groups, the Chinese are the ones who have first "broken into" white society.

To the extent that these groups retain their culture they constitute a social system within the social system; and the way in which these interlock poses a somewhat difficult problem in the integration of the social structure. If we plot the highest point reached in the various island communities by individuals of the Indian ethnic group, we shall get a dotted line similar to the given one in the diagram (Fig. 6). However, the lines which ensure recognition and esteem and high social status within the ethnic group, do not necessarily serve to bring esteem within the larger group (although the possibility of exploiting such prestige for this purpose undoubtedly exists). Similarly, low esteem and status within the ethnic group may be associated with high status within the larger society. Specifically, the ascriptive status given by birth into a particular caste, may result in a "Maharaj" or "Brahmin" possessing high status within the ethnic group, while through his occupational position as a postman he has low status in the larger society. Conversely, a Chamar or lower caste person at the foot of the social scale in the ethnic community might be a doctor enjoying the upper middle class status in the larger society where his particular caste origin would be of no concern.

In the field of ethnic stratification we see the same phenomenon of discrepancy of judgements between individuals as we get in the ranking of communities, and in the

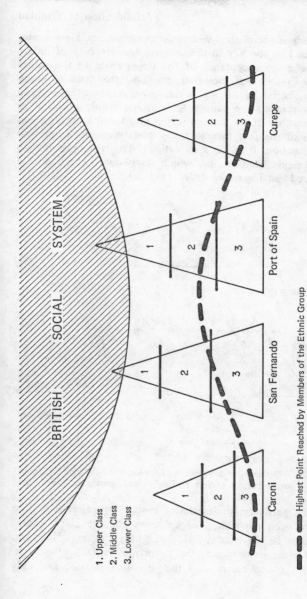

1. Upper Class
2. Middle Class
3. Lower Class

▬ ▬ ▬ Highest Point Reached by Members of the Ethnic Group

Fig. 6 Indian ethnic group and social stratification in various communities in Trinidad

ranking of social class within the communities. Here again, we see that the key to the unity in the diversity of judgements is the acceptance of the upper class as the upper class. In this case, however, we have the main common value shared by all the social groups in the society. In many respects we cannot look at the ethnic criterion as just another of the factors which go to make up class because of the fact that so many caste elements enter into the situation. It is, on a superficial view, the most important single element by which individuals come to be "placed" in the social order (Fig. 7).

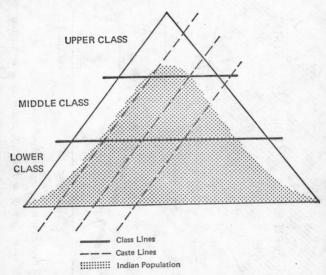

UPPER CLASS

MIDDLE CLASS

LOWER CLASS

———— Class Lines
– – – – Caste Lines
::::::::: Indian Population

Fig. 7 Differences between national system of stratification and stratification within Indian ethnic group in Trinidad

The particularistic-ascriptive basis of social stratification as between the white, the coloured and the black groups became finally established during the period of slavery. Under the slave regime the identity of racial and occupational groups meant that this stratification had not only a social but a legal sanction. The emancipation of the slaves in 1838, was followed by an increasing emphasis on achievement values. The social order was being transformed in the United Kingdom itself and while under an autocratic regime these values effected only slow infiltration into the coloured society, they did, none the less, infiltrate. It is particularly interesting in reading the official documents of the 19th century to see how the changing climate of opinion in the "mother country" influenced the views of administrators and Englishmen resident in the colonies. This orientation towards the United Kingdom scale of values was marked because of the impact of governmental policy in the United Kingdom upon the West Indies. In the case of Trinidad, there had been the model legislation of the Crown Colony preceding the emancipation of the slaves; there had been the general question of the emancipation of the slaves; the compensation to be given to the planters therefor; and the problem of apprenticeship. Following this, there was the question of the control of indentured labour, which had to be viewed in Imperial perspective. This factor dominated the island's history during the 19th century and was intimately linked with the crisis in the sugar industry. The state of the sugar industry was the cause of various commissions of enquiry during the century. This concern flowed not only from the normal commitment to improve the conditions of the inhabitants of the territory, but from the fact that sugar was an export crop, and the fate of the industry depended so very much on the economic policy of the Imperial Government.

Moreover, the mere existence of the Englishman with his particular scale of social values meant that these values would tend to spread to the lower elements in the society. It may be true, as one critic has remarked, that the British have given as culture to the colonial people "the cheapest side of commercial cinema and just so much education as to ensure a cheap supply of clerical labour on the spot." Certainly, in the case of the West Indies there was never any attempt to establish, as in some of the Spanish areas, any institutions of higher learning. But education on the lower levels, even if it was to ensure cheap clerical labour on the spot, was supplied. In fact in some respects it can be claimed that educational policy was more progressive in Trinidad than it was in the United Kingdom. For instance Lord Harris, Governor in the middle of the 19th century sought to establish a school in each governmental Ward, the schools to be free but supported by local taxes. In any case, formal education even on the lowest levels seems to be almost intrinsically linked with a universalistic scale of values. Moreover, while it may be possible to a large extent to control the reading of a society by controlling its publishing, and its external contacts with other societies, it is certainly more difficult to control the reading of one segment of a society, particularly where there are no language barriers to communication.

Many of the 19th century educators in Trinidad were intellectually committed to the idea of equal opportunity for all and the boast was made by one that the humblest citizen of Trinidad could get a post in the Civil Service of India by making his way through competitive examination. In the progressive establishment of education there were several different elements involved—not all absolutely "universalistic-achievement" centred. Thus the provision of secondary education at first appears to have been started as a means of meeting the needs of the white residents of the colony. Similarly, the provision of scholarships for professional study at universities in the United Kingdom sprang from a desire to give opportunity to children of deserving whites in the colonies. Even where coloured people were admitted to schools, the stringency with which class lines were drawn in the society is indicated by the fact that when scholarships were first granted for the elementary schools of the colony to the secondary schools, one of the leading newspapers of the island warned of the undesirability and danger of having lower-class children mixing with children of the middle and the upper classes.

Once the institution of island scholarships for study

abroad and of secondary education had been established out of public funds, and continued to exist out of public subsidies, it became impossible to deny the right of competition in the particular context of island society. The colonial Government was committed to looking after the welfare of the inhabitants. Indeed, that was the justification for its rule; and hence public funds spent on awards based upon competitive examination could not be used in such a way as to imply overt discrimination. It was the ladder thus established by the educational system that became one of the most important methods by which members of the middle and lower classes could improve their position on the occupational scale and come to play an important role in public affairs.

The initiative of the Government in the sphere of education had other important consequences. The fees charged in the Government secondary schools were necessarily low and as the climate of public opinion veered towards an increasing concern with public provision of educational facilities, it became difficult for the Government to raise the fees in the secondary schools. Government was forced by its position to run a school of a standard that would face up to public criticism both in the colony and in the United Kingdom. This meant that the standard of teaching had to be high. Salaries had to be paid on a scale that would attract good teachers (chiefly from the U.K.). The pattern of low school fees and high standards set by the Government institutions had to be taken over by the voluntary bodies running secondary schools if they were to receive public funds.

The impetus to education in the post-emancipation period, as at present, did not come from the Government only. There was acute religious concern for the "morals and welfare" of the inhabitants and in the case of the Roman Catholics there was the well-established Catholic doctrine, that education was in the main an affair of the family and the Church, and only indirectly an affair of the State. Hence, schools run by the various religious denominations became common and the system of "dual control" was eventually established after stubborn resistance on the part of religious bodies (the Roman Catholics in particular) to the establishment of a State system of education in the 1870's.[8] The other field in which there were to be established on a large scale the values of universalistic achievement was in the public service. Once educational ability was recognized by Government as being worthy of encouragement it seemed incumbent upon the Government to provide opportunities for those for whom they had provided the education. Here again, in the public service the expenditure of public money could not be made on caste lines. Appointments had to be made, formally at least, on the basis of ability. The definition of the qualities necessary for making good civil servants was notoriously lacking. Intelligence was obviously important, but other factors of personality and character were admittedly of great relevance. It was through this factor that the discrimination against the dark-skinned coloured person was, until yesterday, maintained, since these were matters for the most part incapable of objective test. Judgement in this respect had to rest on the subjective evaluation of individuals in authority, and of committees. However, just as the white creole was able to wrest the right to appointment to certain posts in the Civil Service on the grounds of his ability, so was the light-skinned coloured person able in his turn to lay his claim, on the basis of ability. In time the dark-skinned person has made his claim to consideration; and the public service in so far as it has been opened to local control is organized, in principle at any rate, on the objective bases of ability and, in the lower ranks, seniority. The way in which the individuals with a particularistic scale of values emotionally attached to one ethnic group and antagonistic to others came to meet the discipline of the achievement-centred and universalistically oriented public service would make an interesting field

[8] For an account of this crisis in education see L. A. G. de Verteuil, *Trinidad: Its Geography, Natural Resources, Administration, Present Conditions and Future Prospects* (2nd ed.; London: Cassell, 1884).

study. The fact of the interplay of the two factors of "favouritism" and ability has had far-reaching consequences. Where abilities have been equal the particularistic values became dominant and because of the acceptance by the mass of the people of the ascriptive scale of values based on skin colour, the struggle for the open ladder has not been an easy one within the Civil Service, or in the granting of scholarships and awards. One result of this was the widespread belief, still alive, that it is necessary to have a patron (a "godfather" in local terminology) in order to advance within the Civil Service. Belief in the integrity of the Civil Service has always been asserted. If we neglect the plundering of public funds which occasionally takes place and is regarded in a somewhat different light by the general public from the appropriation of private funds, we can accept the assertion that the standards of integrity with regard to financial matters (the absence of bribery, etc.) have followed, in the main, the traditions of the British public service. But in respect to "nepotism", the use of an intrinsically irrelevant scale of values in the conferring of appointments and in determining promotions, the problem assumed great proportions because the particularistic values tended to reinforce one another. Not only skin colour was used as a criterion, but class origin as well. In view of the historical background and the relative lack of mobility, skin colour tended to be closely identified with social class. Into the judgements of social class went certain other personality characteristics which had a greater relevance to effectiveness of performance. It was therefore easy for an individual so inclined to rationalize his prejudice (based on racial or skin colour grounds) by asserting that a dark-skinned person, say, was uncouth or undesirable on other grounds. Partiality was thus difficult to attack until achievement values became so general in the society that the possibility of "racial" prejudice hiding under social class discrimination could not find a sympathetic response. In this respect the spread of democratic ideas and of political reform were of crucial importance in breaking down the barriers of social class and producing a more achievement-oriented civil service.

The way in which the pressure of opinion influenced political action and in this way helped to democratize attitudes is in no way better illustrated than in the manner constitutional advances have taken place in the colony. The result of the fact that the Secretary of State for the Colonies was responsible for training people for self-government meant that any disturbance of law and order which assumed a general form became his responsibility. In this way his concern was led out from the narrowly political into the more general problems of the welfare of the inhabitants of the area. Hence it was that bad conditions in any area that led to a general upheaval would lead to the establishment of some commission of enquiry. Thus it was that after the strikes and riots of 1937 which originated in the oilfield area, the Foster Commission was sent out. Following the spread of these riots and strikes to other areas the West India Commission was appointed. Again, following the strikes and riots of 1946, an experienced trade unionist, Mr. F. W. Dalley, was sent out to report on the allegations of maltreatment of trade unionists and repressive Government action.

All of these Commissions of enquiry were appointed in response to criticism coming from within the United Kingdom. When a Royal Commission was appointed, individuals of the competence and integrity that is expected of a Royal Commission had to be selected. But an examination of the personnel of these various Commissions seems to show that people had to be appointed who held the confidence of British public opinion. They were acceptable to public opinion in Trinidad because they were people of established reputations and could view the problems from outside since they were not involved in the particular issues. None the less, their orientation was to the larger society, and it was through the crystallization of their criticisms of the social order that the universalistic-achievement scale of values made one of its most important impacts on the island society.

In the face of critical opinion those who had taken upon themselves the burden of training the subject peoples for self-government took various courses of action in order to remedy the situation. The action taken was usually action in Imperial perspective, and the general lines followed the prevailing climate of opinion in the United Kingdom. For various reasons, among which was the fact that the political machinery of government was most easily responsive to administrative control, recommendations for political change were prominent. Hence, under the pressure of public opinion, the most obvious sphere of reform was in constitution changing. These constitutional changes were all in the direction of increasing democracy.

To the extent that adult suffrage and increased responsibility of the elected members were accepted in the island there arose the problem that, if there was to be any real surrender of power the Civil Service would have to be West Indianized. The demand for promotion within the Civil Service had in large measure been met only on the lower levels because of the lack of any schemes for the training of people for the higher positions. However, schemes were "pushed" and financed to a large extent by the new Colonial Development and Welfare Organization set up in the West Indies following the recommendations of the Moyne Commission. Initiative came largely from the Secretary of State for the Colonies. Both programme and performance outstripped any demands made by the articulate section of Trinidad opinion. The process of West Indianization proceeded at such a rapid pace, no doubt, because, due to war conditions and the existence of full employment in Great Britain in the period immediately after World War II, it became increasingly difficult for the Colonial Office to fill senior appointments. However, an important point is, that altogether, in recruiting people within the service for scholarships and in subsequent promotion, discrimination became increasingly difficult. For one thing, the successful candidates had to follow courses attached to the universities, and therefore had to be of sufficient ability to profit from these courses. The assessment of their work on an objective basis by people accustomed to such assessment[9] also ensured the recognition of achievement. Even where, as in some cases, the training received was not attached to the university (such as the training involved in secondment for work at the Colonial Office) the candidates came under the scrutiny of people from outside the island society, who frequently had no experience of colonial society and its particular set of prejudices.

The overall effect of this achievement in the field of administration was reinforced by the general change in climate of opinion that took place in the island society as a whole. The idea that elections should be held on the basis of adult suffrage had been current in radical political circles in Trinidad for quite a while. The championship of the "barefooted man" by Captain Cipriani and the Trinidad Labour Party in the period immediately after the First World War, meant that in any reform less attention would have to be paid to property qualifications. The general mass support achieved by the Labour Party and its leader indicated that the old 19th century conception of property qualifications was outmoded. In the terms of the development of the island the future belonged, like the 20th century, to the common man or, in terms of the island society, to the barefoot man. The grant of adult suffrage also ensured for the Colonial Office a breathing spell from hostile criticism, since it gave a great deal of the external appearance of democracy while the positions of real administra-

---

[9] The problem involved in such assessment should not, however, be overlooked. On the one hand where the training was merely the admission of colonial candidates to a course of training previously directed to U.K. Colonial Officers, there tended to be carried over something of the imperial tradition into the training. More important was the fact that frequently university professors, only vaguely aware of the limitations of colonial students, and with hazy notions of the capacity of students of different racial origin, tended to be over-generous in their estimation of West Indian students' abilities. Furthermore, the study of West Indian conditions had been more or less neglected.

ive authority remained in effective control.[10] The symbolic significance as well as the practical importance of the vote was not lost. It meant a real gain to the black lower lass.

This movement towards increased democracy helped to spread even further the general ideas of equality then present. It is interesting to note that the House elected on adult suffrage went on record, in principle, as being in favour of free secondary education for all, and that the number of scholarships or free entry places to the secondary schools was incidentally increased from fifty-two to one hundred.[11] The long-vexed question of teachers' salaries for the first time approached something in the nature of a satisfactory settlement and the number of open island scholarships was increased from three to five.

In the more subtle spheres of social life the political democratization also had its effects. Here we are only concerned to point out its effects on the achievement values of the society and in producing within the Civil Service a career open to talent.

[10] This is, of course, an interpretation based on the fact that his policy was only one of a number of possible alternatives. On the merits of the case there could be some justification for advocating a course of development radically different from the one adopted. The explanation cannot be made in terms of "rational" grounds alone.

[11] "The large increase in free exhibitions and bursaries to secondary schools meets a long overdue need. The provision of maintenance allowances opens the door for the first time to the est brains from any corner of the colony" (Trinidad, Department of Education Report, 1948).

14.

The present situation of West Indian whites—always a crucially important segment of the Antillean social order—is virtually unknown. This lacuna is partly a consequence of the fact that social scientists have tended to shun the study of elites and dominant minorities. The following selection provides an insight into the most entrenched and socially viable white population in the non-Hispanic Caribbean, the *békés* of Martinique. These hitherto unpublished pages detail the organization of, and internal distinctions among, this long-resident elite. The white position in Jamaican and Trinidadian society, touched on previously in this section by M. G. Smith and Lloyd Braithwaite, should be compared with this vivid analysis of whites in Martinique.

EDITH KOVATS-BEAUDOUX, a resident of France, was born in Hungary, received her undergraduate degree from the University of Montreal, and did her Martiniquan field work under the auspices of the Department of Anthropology of the University of Montreal. Her doctorate is from the Faculty of Letters and Human Sciences at the Université de Paris.

A Dominant Minority: The White Creoles of Martinique
Edith Kovats-Beaudoux

DEFINITION AND CLASSIFICATION OF THE GROUP

White Creoles are individuals born in Martinique, of the Caucasian race, whose families have lived on the island for many generations. This is the standard definition given by the group itself, whose individual members might place more or less emphasis on how long the family has been established on the island. In principle, one is a Creole if he is Caucasian and born on the island, although some families in Martinique for two or three generations are still considered "newcomers." Almost completely French in origin, the Creoles nevertheless also include a few families originally from other European countries such as Germany or Portugal. In the preceding chapter [of Kovats' thesis], it was seen that the peopling of the island came about gradually and that certain families emigrated at different periods. Moreover, entire families were destroyed in the catastrophe of 1902 [the eruption of Mont Pelée]. In numerous genealogies, therefore, we find family names that are no longer represented in Martinique. In addition, other family names have become practically extinct, for they are borne today only by females.

We have counted 150 Creole family names on the is-

Une minorité dominante: les blancs créoles de la Martinique, Doctoral thesis, University of Paris, 1969, excerpts, pp. 67–148. Translated by Marquita Riel and Penelope M. Collins. Copyright © 1973 Lambros Comitas and David Lowenthal. Printed with permission of the author.

land, but since each line furnishes a varying number of branches, this number has little significance. Thus we find some family names (or patronyms) represented by only one or two nuclear families, whereas others are carried by more than 100 individuals, split into many branches of different social standing. We have observed, for example, that sixteen patronymic families account for 50 percent of the Creole population of the island. Of these 150 patronymic families, twenty-eight arrived before 1713 and represent 39 percent of the total Creole population; thirty-seven arrived between 1713 and 1784 and make up 22 percent of the population. The families that arrived during the nineteenth century are 35 percent of the population; first or second generation families make up 4 percent.

According to our figures, the Creole population of the island (including students temporarily resident in France or abroad) totals 2,339, distributed as follows:

Under 25   1,212 (643 boys, 569 girls)
25–50   758 (396 men, 362 women)
Over 50   369 (173 men, 196 women).

By residence, this population is distributed as follows:

Fort-de-France   1,309
Rural counties   913
Students in France   117.

At the same time, in every generation, many Creoles emigrate, mainly to France and Guadeloupe but also to French Guiana, Puerto Rico, the United States, and Canada. The approximate number of emigrants from the present generation (parents and grandparents) is 1,560, to which might be added an equal number of children. But in this study, we are considering only those Creoles who live in Martinique.

We have divided the working population into occupational categories, a task complicated by the fact that an individual may be active in more than one sector at the same time. Therefore our figures can be only approximations:

Primary sector	142	(agriculture)
Secondary sector	73	(industry)
Tertiary sector	374	(service)
Professions, religious orders, retired, and not defined	47.	

From the point of view of social rank, the figures are as follows:

Employers and proprietors	153
Senior and junior executives	217
Employees	88.

It is noteworthy that white informants who were asked to estimate the number of individuals in their own group gave widely differing answers, ranging from 2,000 to 5,000, with the figure most frequently submitted being 3,500. Thus Creoles noticeably overestimate their numerical importance, thereby revealing their sense of their own worth and of their role in society.

Their definition of themselves and their very slow acceptance of new immigrants, which contrasts with processes observed in other countries of the New World,[1] are perhaps a result of their insular position. Confined for generations to a tiny island, often quite cut off from the external world, even from France, living in virtual isolation, fighting the economic demands of France and the power of its representatives, and observing suspiciously the rise of the colored bourgeoisie, the white Creoles have, in effect, found it easy to develop an autarchic way of life as well as a strong feeling of identification with their own group. The small size of the island fosters close contacts between individuals and facilitates strong social control; isolation checks rapid progress and makes the preservation of traditional values easier. These are ecological fac-

---

[1] Exceptions must be noted, however. Hence in Brazil, where mixed marriages are numerous, there is a similar structure: families that go back 400 years, even if they are bankrupt, constitute the social elite of the country; they tend toward endogamy and avoid foreign whites' mixing with them through marriage.

tors of prime importance to the life of the group, and their influence can be seen at all levels. Creoles view themselves, with some ethnocentricity, as the descendants of slave-holding planters and rank themselves above others on the ground that these ancestors were masters and soldiers of fortune. They have a sense of belonging to an exclusive caste that has always had economic control of the island: "It is we who have created this country, who have made it what it is. Even now, it is we who make the wheels of industry turn, who cultivate the land, even if it is often not very profitable. The Blacks do not want land, they only think about being officials. If we were to leave the island, there would be anarchy, and from an economic point of view, a half-century setback." This feeling, manifested despite the heterogeneous social origins of the *Békés* [white Creoles], determines certain attitudes, to be discussed later, toward other social groups.

The Creoles' view of themselves as occupying a place apart from others is illustrated by the way they describe the Martiniquan social structure. All our informants' answers on this point have been almost identical. The principal criterion of social differentiation is race, which divides this society in two: on the one hand, there are the whites; on the other, the mulattoes and blacks. These are two very distinct groups that do not mix except in business relationships or sometimes in relationships of camaraderie, among men only. These categories are further subdivided by criteria of wealth. The society can thus be divided into the following classes; first, the Creoles; second, a colored "aristocracy," composed of wealthy and/or educated mulattoes who socialize only among themselves; third, a lower middle class in comfortable circumstances; and last, the mass of the population, urban and agricultural laborers. Most informants stress the fact that while Creoles still constitute a group apart, this distinction was still more rigorously maintained ten or twenty years ago. They say that nowadays *Grands Mulâtres* [the colored aristocracy] frequently socialize with Creole families and are even invited to their funerals.[2] Very few of those queried thought to mention the Metropolitans [residents born in mainland France], numbering several thousand. The Creoles are generally little interested in them, but it was called to our attention that high ranking Metropolitan dignitaries readily socialize with the Creole elite of the island. The foreigner arriving in Martinique is immediately struck by the almost impenetrable unity of the Creole group and also by the fact that one can either remain indefinitely and completely outside of it or, on the other hand, become completely enmeshed in it. A Metropolitan woman, the wife of a Creole, told us: "It is quite clear, they always say, 'We *Békés*'; they are as one."

However, this group is far from being homogeneous, except in terms of race, which is the essential criterion for belonging to it. An internal hierarchy has existed since the start of colonization. . . . Three principal subgroups are generally distinguished, together with a fourth marginal subgroup.

* * * *

The Grands Békés. The upper class consists of those families whose members are commonly called *Gros Békés* and who as a rule possess both wealth and name. They are masters of the island, being descendants, for the most part, of old established families who generation after generation have been able not only to maintain their wealth but even to increase it. Numerically this class is now quite small, constituting only about 10 percent of the Creole population. According to our informants, it consists of about fifteen families; but if the two criteria of wealth and name were followed rigorously, it would apply to ten families at the most. These families pass for a homogeneous group, a closed society, and socialize only among themselves. In fact, for a number of reasons, the reality is more complex.

[2] In this regard, one mulatto commented: "Yes, we are sometimes invited to funerals, but never to baptisms or to weddings."

Some of these families are numerically among the largest, and they therefore include various branches which, bearing the same patronym, should all be able to consider themselves members of the upper or ruling class. But although wealth is hard to evaluate precisely, it is clear that different branches of the same family are often in different financial circumstances. The "poor" branches, while enjoying the prestige of the patronym and the general respect accorded it, are not admitted to the ruling class but are relegated to a lower rank. Their members are received in the usual fashion by the rest of the family but, since they are not really on an equal footing, a certain uneasiness persists. And if the difference in wealth is too great, they are at times even excluded. Other families of the ruling class—those not bearing the same patronym—have little to do with them. Different financial circumstances thus create barriers between members of the same extended family; some belong entirely to high society while others are relegated to the middle class. Since the prestige of a nuclear family is closely linked with the frequency and manner of its entertaining, as well as with its general life style, the members of the poorer branches cannot keep up with their more fortunate cousins.

Therefore, despite the enduring luster attached to a patronym, inequalities of wealth separate families bearing the same name, however prestigious it may be. Thus a subgroup is not a homogeneous entity but rather a framework for classifying together a number of families while ignoring the differences among them. This method of categorization is tantamount to saying: "The Godards are a great family, they bear one of the best names, they own a factory and many hectares of land"; but not including in this statement the nuclear family of Lionel Godard, which would be considered a "minor branch."

Within the ruling class in the strict sense of the term there is a remnant of the old rivalry between city and country dwellers. The former, big merchants and exporters, especially those who live in the residential section of Didier [the most exclusive suburb of Fort-de-France, the capital], tend to form an exclusive community. Conscious of their progressive role as the island's economic leaders, they consider themselves more sophisticated and dynamic. It is noteworthy that our informants, when asked to describe the internal structure of the Creole group, always placed urban dwellers before landowners in the elite class, affirming that the landowners had lost importance. Landowners and factory owners, when questioned, maintained the opposite, claiming for themselves a kind of privilege of nobility or seniority based on their occupations. But can we, therefore, really speak of a rift between urban and rural? Given the present socioeconomic conditions this distinction seems quite arbitrary, for if there are feelings of rivalry or superiority, they are based on rather superficial points of form and prestige. Urban dwellers reproach country dwellers for living in isolation, for being at times a bit uncouth, but the latter cite in their own favor the nobility of the land. In fact, the large landowners enjoy great prestige because they represent tradition, a bygone way of life, reflected in their manner of entertaining. But this tradition is now breaking down, especially since the difficult period that the sugar industry has undergone. Notwithstanding the differences noted, there is no great distinction between urban and rural, at least as far as the upper class is concerned. Moreover, from an economic point of view, agricultural and commercial activities are closely related and interdependent; while at the same time, we find hardly any families, except at the lower level, which can be considered either entirely urban or entirely rural. Rather the family will have some members occupying key administrative positions on the land, others in the city managing their diverse commercial undertakings, and even, in certain cases, some representatives in France. In any case, town and country elements remain in constant contact.

There are two other categories of upper-class families, occupying a lower rank because they do not possess both name and wealth. Some are of very good name, often descending from old, illustrious, and formerly important and wealthy families; but having grown progressively poorer, they now possess only average means. Among our list of patronyms, eighteen can be placed in this category, although, here again, some branches are wealthier than others. With regard to these families, the same phenomenon is occurring in Martinique as in France, where an old family, although relatively impoverished, still remains esteemed; socially if not economically, its members still belong to the upper class. Conscious of their past, and also sometimes of the fact that they live on their capital, they tend to think that they represent and must defend traditional values; hence the rigidity of their moral and racial attitudes. On the other hand, there are families—we have counted eight—who, although not bearing a "great" name, are classified among the elite mainly because of their wealth. Without going so far as to use the term *nouveaux riches,* our informants nevertheless pointed out that the wealth of these families was relatively recent and was acquired primarily in commerce and in the banana industry. For some time perceptibly excluded, these families have now been accepted into high social circles, owing to the increased importance of economic criteria. By the same token, the prestige of their names has been enhanced.

It is obviously within this subgroup [*Grands Békés*] that one finds the leaders of Creole society and, at least from an economic point of view, of Martinique. Some individuals still hold several offices simultaneously—for example, key posts in agriculture, commerce, and banking—although they were more numerous and powerful in the past. For instance, the most important member of a family rather recently established, which has become very wealthy in two generations, simultaneously owns and rents estates specializing in banana cultivation, sugarcane, and stock farming; he is also an importer and a wholesale merchant of fertilizers and chemicals, an exporter of bananas, president of the administrative council of a local bank, vice-president of SICABAM [the banana producers' association], and vice-president of the organization of rum exporters. These men also travel the most; they go to France or elsewhere many times a year, primarily on business trips. Finally, this upper class, although not homogeneous, is for many reasons highly conscious of its status, quite exclusive, and distrustful of anyone—Creole or foreigner— who tries to enter its ranks.

Békés Moyens. The second large subgroup is that of the *Békés Moyens,* composed of the less wealthy branches of families of the preceding subgroup and of respectable families whose name and wealth do not, however, have the prestige of the *Grands Békés.* Of our list of patronyms, about thirty have been classified in this category. But here again, the situation is not uniform, some families being slightly superior to others either in name or in wealth. Incomes are middling, ranging from about 1,800 to 3,600 francs per month, although the group includes better-off families with incomes up to 5,000 francs per month.

This subgroup manifests no distinction between city and country. Some of the urban dwellers own businesses and are self-employed, but most of them constitute the administrative cadres in the enterprises owned by the *Grands Békés.* Many in this subgroup are landowners, but they possess neither large estates nor factories. Some cultivate cane or bananas, practice stock farming, or operate small distilleries. Others have managerial positions in the factories or on the plantations of *Grands Békés,* living on the estates with their families. In the past, administrative posts were much sought by those who were not themselves landowners, for the administrator actually managed the estate and kept a good part of the profits, the owner often being absorbed in the management of another estate. The most beautiful houses to be seen in Martinique were in many cases those of estate administrators. This situation has since changed; the owner now runs his own estate and employs members of his family, his heirs, in the administrative positions.

This large subgroup is the one to which the fewest stereotypes are attached. Intermediate between the *Grands* and *Petits Békés,* it nonetheless sharply keeps its distance from the *Petits.* Those interviewed also held a markedly dualistic view of Creole society, distinguishing the *Petits* on the one hand and lumping together all the rest on the other. Although the *Békés Moyens* recognize the existence of a ruling minority, they emphasize the fact that it is only wealth that separates them from it, since they share the same value system. Some are a little bitter about the exclusivity of high society and about the meager extent of their contact with it. They are aware that they are related to these privileged families but complain that these ties are worthless: "We see them, so to speak, only at weddings, funerals, and of course, at election meetings since we are all of the same party."

This subgroup thus occupies a middle position and, like all middle classes, it is the most difficult to delineate because it is the most fluid, the least defined in its origins, and has the most permeable boundaries. Its members are the most apt to change levels in the hierarchy, given an opportunity for social mobility. There is no doubt about the existence of the class itself, but the identity of its individual members is subject to frequent change.

Petits Blancs. The third subgroup is known as the *Petits Blancs.* It is composed of about thirty families of modest name and small income but, here again, financial differences appear. Some urban families lead meager lives, either running small businesses or, more often, living on small salaries from enterprises belonging to other Creoles. But the true *Petits Blancs,* the most numerous and the poorest, are usually to be found in the country. This type of family, referred to in English as "poor white," occurs in every plantation society of the Western Hemisphere. These people, with families usually exceeding four children, often live in less than moderate circumstances, but they do not give the impression of misery or of physical degradation, as, for example, do some whites on the islands of St. Barthélemy or Réunion.

In Martinique, the *Petits Blancs* are called *Békés en*

bas feuille and those of the countryside, *Békés Goyaves* or *Bitacos*. The latter sometimes own a few hectares of land, and they manage to increase their means of subsistence by growing vegetables and raising a few animals for domestic consumption. Most are employed by other whites, sometimes as managers, but more often as foremen, mechanics, cashiers, and the like. Generally paid from 800 to 1,200 francs a month, they are housed by their employers. Lacking the means to become independent or, in most cases, to gain an education, they are soon engrossed by the need to earn a living. Thus, in many families, the job of foreman is handed down from father to son. In short, their situation is unfortunate; lacking the power to assert their rights, they are often exploited. They participate in no trade union activities, and when they venture to do so, they are to all purposes rejected by the white community. They probably suffer more as a consequence of their social position than the colored foremen or managers, since they are highly conscious of their status: they feel at the same time excluded from the circle of higher-level Creoles and despised by the colored who have achieved a better economic position. Their pride wounded, most of them direct their bitterness toward other Creoles: "We are white like them, yet they never invite us, our young people never mix with their children. When we meet in the street, they barely say 'Good day.' What blights everything here is the question of money; because they have more, they think that they are superior to us and no longer recognize us; often they even pretend not to know about the family ties that exist between us." The poorer, who feel more isolated, mix a great deal with the Metropolitans, for example, with the policemen who live in town, and the men are in frequent contact with the blacks. However, interracial relationships are forbidden to white women, who are very "protected." Above all they value their white status, since at their social level they lack economic superiority. Consequently, they prefer to be closely dependent on their employers, whose prestige they hope will reflect on them. Obligated to the wealthiest whites and asserting their membership in the Creole group, they are thus the real allies of their employers, whose interests they defend and whose political tendencies they espouse in order to safeguard their own status as Creoles within the larger society.

How do the members of other subgroups view the *Petits Blancs*? First, they define the *Bitacos* as poor rural families distinguished by their "rustic" traits. In the past, when from time to time they came to town, they were conspicuous in dress, somewhat old-fashioned and uncouth. Nowadays, differences in attire tend to disappear, but since the *Petits Blancs* always live among themselves in the countryside, they are "ill-bred," they lack "style." In addition, they are accused of vulgarity in manner of expression and style of life, of being dull and clumsy, and of speaking Creole more often than French. At this point of the inventory, our informant generally adds that, to be sure, there are *Bitacos* among the rich families of the countryside but "it is not the same," because the latter are "saved by their name," and even though their appearance and language are somewhat loutish, they are not, for all that, *Petits Békés Goyaves*. The latter have indeed an attitude all their own: they have an inferiority complex vis-à-vis other Creoles because they are poor and cannot entertain them. This is why they prefer not to associate with them at all but to live among themselves. Furthermore, they are not educated—but, at this point, our informant notes that, of course, as long as there were no scholarships for whites, they could not afford higher education and that this situation is now getting better. It is also mentioned that they do not really have the ambition or the will to improve their condition, that they tend to reason more like employees than like employers. Finally, it is held against them that they mix freely with the blacks, if not by marriage, at least by association, so much so that they might be considered closer to the blacks than to the Creoles and that therefore they have a very limited view of the world.

Stereotypes about this subgroup are thus numerous and

rsistent. Most higher-ranking Creoles acknowledge that
s group includes some very decent white families which
nnot be held responsible for styles of life and ways of
nking that, in the final analysis, depend on lack of fi-
ncial opportunity. Others, however, appear more severe
 their judgments. For example, one of our informants, a
rty-year-old descendant of a *grande famille*, who man-
es various estates in the north of the island, spoke about
 neighboring lower-class family as follows: "They work
 r my father. When their daughter got married, they
vited me; I honored them with my presence, but I do not
ually socialize with them. Besides, I wonder if they are
ite white." This young man may be an extreme case, but
 e fact remains that one does not readily socialize with
tacos, and, if one sees them occasionally, one does not
come intimate with them. Furthermore, it is significant
at informants from other subgroups, questioned about
arriages, could give exhaustive and precise information
 spouses and numbers of children. They could go back
 o or three generations and even calculate the amount
 wealth involved. (This extensive knowledge is under-
ndable, given the small size of the island and the close
 ationships maintained among families.) But whenever
 was a question of *Petits Blancs* families, we were able
 obtain very little information, if any. A frequent reac-
 n was: "He is a White, but I do not know him at all.
 e lives in the neighborhood of Trinité. He must be a
 all businessman and he has many children, but this is
 I know." Others had not even heard of such and such
 family. Another quite typical response concerns a cash-
 r in a factory bearing the same patronym as the in-
 rmant: "Why, I did not even know that fellow existed."
 ch recurrent lacunae in a society where everybody
 ows everybody else—"besides, we are all a bit related"—
 nnot be due solely to chance.

Not Quite White. Finally, the last, highly marginal sub-
 oup comprises some fourteen patronyms belonging to
 milies "miscegenated or not quite white, but who want

to pass for white." This is a rather fine distinction, for th
members of these families are phenotypically exactly lil
the *Békés,* and only a good genealogical knowledge wa
rants assertions of the difference. In effect, miscegenatic
(*mésalliance*), that is, the entrance of a colored elemei
into the family, is often a unique case harking back se
eral generations, leaving no apparent trace. Nevertheles
the distinction endures: they are not white, and althoug
the wealthier among them are tolerated from an economi
point of view, the *Békés* prefer to exclude them socially.

Two comments should be added about these familie
First, is it certain that they are not "quite white"? Creol
themselves do not always hold the same opinion about
given family. When we compiled the list of patronym
some families were considered white by some Creoles bu
not by others. Our count includes as white families recog
nized as such by most Creoles. But we have also include
families who, though not reputed to be white, almost cei
tainly are, according to an informant long interested i
the history of Martinique and the compiler of a collectio
of genealogies. Indeed, some of the recently establishe
families are little known to a majority of Creoles, wh
regard them with some suspicion. All that is needed t
spread rumors about the "purity" of a recently establishe
family is for one member of an old family to express
doubt. Doubt is similarly expressed about the purity of ver
poor families whose members are in occupations consid
ered unworthy. Additionally, this category includes a fam
ily that is actually white but whose ancestors were th
illegitimate children of a parish priest. Are the bearer
of this patronym excluded and not considered white b
most Creoles because of ignorance or because of the in
fringement on traditional morality? Another case came t
our attention in questioning the wife of a Creole belongin
to the first subgroup [*Grands Békés*]. She mentione
that her sister (who is married to her husband's brother
was worried about her son wanting to marry Miss X, givin
the name of a white family related to many other highl
respected families. Our surprise elicited this explanation

"But this family is not quite white, there has been something . . ." It is thus quite difficult to obtain definite information in this regard. Nevertheless it is possible that the isolated nature of Martiniquan life and the close ties among many Creole families have favored a relatively extensive knowledge of genealogy, which can be used to exclude the lesser-known families. It is also possible that rivalries or resentments are the original sources of such disparagements.

The second comment arises out of a discussion we had with a Creole who is also a specialist on the history of the island and of various white families. He has compiled the complete genealogy of his own family (which is part of the *Grands Békés* subgroup) as well as of all related families. Among the latter, he mentioned an ancestor married to a woman "who was not white." Hence this family, of ancient stock and related to numerous Creole families, and unanimously considered white, would not in actuality be "quite" white. But, added our interlocutor, "it is not known and I will not reveal it, because then, their whole system would fall apart." This clearly indicates the frailty of that system and the arbitrary nature of many distinctions.

The white Creole group is thus far from homogeneous, and a considerable distance often separates the various strata. Stereotypes still stronger and more persistent than the actual divergences between subgroups further contribute to fragment the small Creole group. This group is divided in the usual fashion according to economic criteria, but other finer distinctions, perceptible only in the local context, such as name, seniority, and good manners, play an important role in the making of the social hierarchy. The past still continues to weigh heavily on this group.

FAMILY AND HOUSEHOLD

Before examining how this protective structure and its mechanisms are expressed in the choice of a spouse and what collective attitudes that choice reflects, let us analyze briefly the family and household.

Among white Creoles, the family (the patronym) immediately identifies the individual, who unless he becomes a "leader"—quite a rare occurrence—not only depends on his family but is immersed in it to the detriment of his individual identity. . . . Many informants told us that the family formed a kind of clan; the more distinctive ones have their own customs, jokes, indeed, their own language, to such an extent that a stranger in the circle—a new spouse, for example—feels left out and must spend a considerable time adapting to ways of living that could almost be called a subculture. Families willingly ascribe to themselves such flattering traits as intelligence or originality, and this quality will be considered as their general defining trait. The child is first raised in the cult of the name, then in that of the social group to which it belongs.

Family identity is one of the dominant bases of the rigid social mores on which this society depends. The extended family coincides with the circle of friends. When we asked our informants which people they saw most often and with the most pleasure, an overwhelming majority specified relatives from all generations and related branches of the family. Many receptions are given solely for members of the extended family, and holidays as well as vacations are spent together. We have noted the case of a group of related families, one of which possesses a small island off the Martiniquan coast. The island is covered with cottages belonging to these related families, and in the summer, they spend time together there.

Two or three times a year, during holidays, the various branches of a family meet in the home of the eldest member on the paternal side; however, the meeting can take place in the home of a member of the maternal side, if this part of the family is obviously more important or is reputed to be especially hospitable or powerful. At other times, members of the same family often meet in smaller gatherings; men for example go fishing with cousins, women visit an aunt or a sister-in-law during an afternoon.

They frequently invite one another to meals. An interesting case in point is afforded by the Creoles who live in the villages: several of the men go to Fort-de-France a few times a week on business; almost everyone, including wives on shopping tours, makes the trip at least once a week, usually on Thursday. Thus hundreds of rural Creoles are apt to be in town on the same day. Yet at meal time they cannot be found in restaurants; they are all invited to lunch by family members.

The Creole family, as an entity, offers great security to men and women of all ages. The individual is aware that he is surrounded by people who know him, who have affection for him; he has reliable allies and does not feel isolated. The boy who looks for work, the woman who becomes a widow, each knows to whom to turn. Most of our informants, when asked why they like to live in Martinique or if they would consider living elsewhere, emphasized this familial aspect of their lives. At this point, moreover, the term *famille* is extended to apply to the whole Creole group, which is often considered one large family, though this is far from objective truth. In reality, the fact that they bear a well-known name, familiar not only to the whites but also to a good number of colored people, gives the Creole the feeling that, come what may, he will not be alone. Numerous informants, even young ones, asserted that what they would fear most, if they had to settle elsewhere, was solitude—struggling alone to overcome competition and to make their way: "In a big country, there is an attitude of almost automatic, frantic selfishness—a struggle for life that is not to be found in the colonies, where Whites have always helped one another. Here one finds a generosity, a kindness, which does not exist in countries like France." Another facet of this feeling is revealed by a young Creole from a well-known family but who is himself of modest means and without a diploma. He is employed in a garage belonging to an upper-class family: "I would not like to go elsewhere, because with my level of education I could not find the equivalent type of work; and even if I found it, I would be a 'nobody'! I could socialize only with other petty employees, whereas here I will always be a Godard."

Each family takes such pride in its name that even the adoption of children is criticized. We know of a young couple who had adopted two children; the "patriarch," head of the clan, was so displeased that he did not want them to bear his name. Each family is above all concerned with protecting its name and reputation. If a member behaves contrary to the norms, the family will gather together to discuss the situation and take preventive measures. For example, in the case of a boy who mixes too much with colored girls, members of the family will warn him, fearing that he may get attached to one and want to legitimize the liaison; if he persists, he will be sent to the Metropole. Similarly, a girl's brothers will look after her, indeed, supervise her social life, check her companions' identities, and make sure that her behavior in society does not arouse scandal. A somewhat more marginal example is that of a young *Béké* from a *grande famille* who became involved in illicit political activities in France. On learning of this, his family made him return to Martinique, and he thereby avoided prosecution. Familial solidarity thus clearly emerges when a member of the group deviates from the norm or when he needs help. If a person drinks excessively or if he goes bankrupt, he will be kept home or his debts will be paid, because he must not harm the reputation of the family. If a young cousin or a nephew needs a job, one will be found for him—probably in a family enterprise—even if his hiring necessitates the dismissal of a colored employee. But, if the job is sought by a relative from a poor branch of the family, the feeling of solidarity takes on a strong color of necessity and one "resigns oneself" to helping.

Familial solidarity is not absolute, however, since factors that can divide a family do exist. Economic rivalries can provoke permanent estrangements—a topic we will return to later. Moreover, as we have seen, a rich branch of a family practically never socializes with those of very modest rank. Creoles are ashamed of their poor relations, some-

mes to the point of denying any close kinship ties. Fi-
ally, the extreme case is that involving mixed marriage:
Creole who marries a colored person can be repudiated
y his family, which very often will not even know what
ind of work he does or how many children he has.

Insofar as the name or the reputation of a family plays
n important role in determining the social status of its
nembers, they understandably tend to avoid any incidents
hat might damage that reputation. Should the occasion
rise, the ensuing sanctions are approved and implemented
y the whole Creole group. Since the latter is but the sum
otal of a small number of families closely connected by
inship and marriage, the Creole group makes every ef-
ort to safeguard its integrity before the outside world. If,
lespite everything, an individual rejects the principles
vhich have been inculcated in him, his whole subgroup,
f not the entire Creole population, feels attacked and
oetrayed.

* * * *

MARRIAGE AND CHOICE OF SPOUSE

Both the theoretical and practical importance of mariage for such a group as the white Creoles is quite obvious. This institution is the backbone of the group, which
s organized entirely around it, and the choice of a spouse
oecomes a vital operation with weighty consequences for
he collective future. Numerous marriages between *Békés*
and colored people would soon end in the dismantling of
he group as a racial entity. Similarly, frequent unions
vith Metropolitans or foreigners would result, notably
hrough the mechanism of inheritance, in a perceptible
lispersion of wealth toward the outside world and simul-
aneously in an increasing control of *Béké* assets by
foreign elements. Marriage, at the level of the choice of a
pouse, constitutes one of the mechanisms that guards these
wo potential points of disintegration. In our opinion, it is
he most important mechanism, lying at the center of the
lynamics of the group.

Without having carried out an exhaustive statistical analysis, by sex, of the choice of marriage partners, but keeping in mind a number of economic and social criteria, our census allowed us to obtain a satisfactory approximation and to observe some marked regularities. Including all marriages contracted by Creoles of the grandparental and parental generations, we obtain the following results.

Marriages of men with:

Creole women	498
Metropolitan women	81
Foreign women	27
Colored women	21

Marriages of women with:

Creole men	498
Metropolitan men	105
Foreign men	23
Colored men	9

On the other hand, excluding persons who married and live abroad and couples who have emigrated after their marriage, that is, counting only married Creoles living in Martinique, the proportion of foreign spouses is very small: sixty-two men have non-native wives—forty-four from Metropolitan France, eight foreigners (German, American, Canadian, etc.), five Trinidadians, four Guadeloupeans, and one St. Lucian. All ten women from the three Caribbean islands are white descendants of French families long established there. As for Creole women, thirty-one have non-Martiniquan husbands: twenty-six are Metropolitans, two are Guadeloupeans, and three are foreigners. These few observations suffice to draw the following conclusions: first, the Creole group exhibits a strong tendency toward endogamy, especially if we consider only the couples living in Martinique. Moreover, of those who marry nonnatives, many emigrate, particularly the women. Finally, marriages between Creoles and colored people do occur, but their number remains extremely

ow. Interestingly, the Creole men who marry colored
women belong to no particular subgroup, but are distributed among the different social strata. On the other hand,
we have found no case of a Creole woman belonging to a
grande famille who has married a colored man, and to
our knowledge there is only one example of hypergamy,
wherein a woman brought whiteness as a dowry in return
for her colored husband's wealth.

We discussed the choice of a marriage partner with our
informants: first, in order to bring out stereotypes, we
asked them to define a *beau mariage* (a good marriage),
a term often heard in Martinique; then, we asked which
criteria played the greatest role in choosing a spouse; last,
referring to a term often used by Creoles, we asked what
a *mésalliance* is. Our informants gave us almost identical
answers. The expression *beau mariage*, besides evoking
the splendor of the ceremony and reception, has many
meanings: it applies either to a marriage between two
wealthy people or to any marriage with someone from a
very superior socioeconomic level—one might say, "He
(she) has made a *beau mariage*"; it is also used when
both partners belong to esteemed families and appear well
suited, likely to create a harmonious household. As for
the choice of a spouse, many criteria come into play, the
most important being racial, exclusion applying to mulattoes, blacks, "coolies" [East Indians], and also Syrians.
Then account is taken of the social class, standard of
living (wealth), name, and upbringing of the future mate,
be he or she Creole or alien to the island. Nationality and
religion are only secondary factors: parents quite definitely
prefer their child to marry a Creole and a Catholic, but,
should such not be the case, they will not oppose the union, provided that the future mate is white and of acceptable social rank. The term *mésalliance* then applies
to marriages that contravene the group's principal criteria
of selection. In principle, this term is used only in the case
of a Creole marrying a colored person (mixed marriage),
but it is used frequently in a wider sense when an individual marries someone of a much lower social level.

Racial criteria. To view the institution of marriage from the perspective of race seems easy at first. We have already seen that the primary qualification for belonging to the Creole group is to be white. We have also seen how strict the social control and the norms are on that matter, with every legal union of a white and a colored person being penalized, even by expulsion from the group. The child's whole social upbringing tends to reinforce this rule in his mind and to impress upon him the inviolability of the system. As a result, many young people do not even dream of the possibility of marrying a colored person, and others, having thought of it, pronounce categorically against it: "I would never marry a Black girl, and I would not want my sister to marry a Black man," said a young *Béké,* adding, "I know them too well." Creoles of all ages manifest a negative opinion of mixed marriages, although there are individual nuances in the way they express this. An extreme case is represented by a planter who said to us: "In stock rearing, you crossbreed only to obtain animals for the slaughterhouse." On the other hand, a young *Béké* told us: "Of course, I would like to marry a Creole girl, but if I had to envisage another choice, I would rather marry a respectable Mulatto girl from here than the daughter of a French *concierge.*" Many informants asserted that they were opposed to mixed marriages, not because of racism but because such unions are *a priori* doomed to failure; the differences of mental habit between the two spouses is too great to overcome, and the social pressures on such couples eventually crush them: "They will no longer be welcomed socially by either the Whites or the Blacks; they will become embittered." As for the white woman who marries a black man, the comments stress the overbearing and unfaithful character of "the blacks": "A Metropolitan woman might conceivably marry a Black man, because she does not know what she is getting into, but we, who know them, know that they cannot make a White woman happy." It is quite evident that Creoles seek to rationalize their attitude toward mixed marriages, but in finding the motive for their opposition in the social pressure exerted

gainst such couples, they are at one and the same time
ctims of, and active participants in, this social pressure.
Vhen asked if they would entertain at home a friend
arried to a colored woman, they all answered that they
ould certainly not receive the wife and that, on second
ought, they would not receive the friend either, because
it would get around and we would be held in low esteem;
esides, the friend himself would probably prefer not to
ome, because he would feel ill at ease." Thus members of
e group not only feel obliged to dissociate themselves
om the excluded individual for fear of being in turn ex-
uded, but in addition, they project their disapprobation
n him in believing—or pretending to believe—that he on
s part feels shame. A young *Béké*, who has himself
ntracted a *mésalliance,* described at length his family's
pposition, his own stubbornness, the steps taken by his
ther to have his Creole employer fire him: "I have been
arried for five years, but it's only since last year that I've
een seeing my parents again. On the other hand, they
ave never wanted to see either my wife or my children.
nly my sister comes to visit us. All the *Békés,* my friends
d others, have completely rejected me. They pretend
at I am bitter, unhappy, and that this is the reason why
am interested in syndicalism. They do not want to or
annot accept that I love my wife, that I am happy, and
at I am involved with trade unionism because I am aware
f the conditions in which most Blacks are living. For
e Whites, I am a traitor, and I have turned against them."

This obsession against marrying anyone who might have
black blood" is one reason a Creole knows—or claims
 know—the genealogical tree of almost every family; the
ame of the family thus becomes a guarantee of purity.
 many precautions, such clearly defined norms, such
arsh punishments should make mixed marriages rare ex-
eptions. Yet we have found about thirty cases of them
ccurring today on the island, distributed among the three
ain subgroups previously cited, and including some
reole women. Fewer white women than white men are
volved in mixed marriages, partly because the offense is

considered more serious when committed by a woma
Moreover, everything in a white girl's upbringing an
social life keeps her at a distance from the black man an
makes her feel distaste for him, whereas the Creole yout
is in frequent contact with colored women. It should b
emphasized, however, that *mésalliance* cannot be quantifie
—it is above all a qualitative matter. Indeed, the case wi
depend on whether a Creole marries a person of mixe
blood or someone classified only as "not quite white." Th
latter is as discreditable as the former, but the degrada
tion affects only the guilty party and his future descendant
not the rest of his family, which keeps itself in good stand
ing with the clan by repudiating the "misallied" or, if i
continues to see him or her, by refusing to entertain th
spouse. Moreover, if the "misallied" Creole occupies a hig
economic position, he keeps his *Béké* relationships mor
readily than if he is of modest means and thereby at thei
mercy.

Mixed marriage is thus more frequent than Creoles ar
generally willing to admit. It is considered a blemish, an
the parents of the "misallied" will often feel embarrasse
with other *Békés*. Many informants, not wanting to tal
about these mixed marriages, denied that they even existec
Creoles consider the maintenance of the white race and it
purity their sacred duty, and every mixed marriage is con
sidered a stain.

Marriage outside the group. Granted that the choice of
spouse in principle excludes colored elements, to what ex
tent do marriages occur at random among the white popu
lation? Some informants said that there were no rules an
that one could marry anyone, provided, of course, tha
he or she was white. But it must be noted that traditiona
norms excluded *a priori* any element alien to the grour
even though white. We have seen that even today the vas
majority of marriages occur within the Creole group it
self. Few men from metropolitan France have settle
permanently in Martinique after a marriage there. Thos
who do usually look after enterprises owned by their wive

amilies. The children for the most part are well integrated
nto the Creole milieu, although it will be mentioned in
peaking that one of their parents is not a Creole. As for
he alien spouse, he will be accepted to the extent that he
dheres to the values of the group and submits to its social
norms. The acceptance of outsiders, mostly French (young
Metropolitans of both sexes are being invited with greater
requency to parties at Creoles' homes), and the growing
number of young *Békés* studying in France tend to favor
he increase of such marriages. This phenomenon is rela-
ively recent and prompted a Guadeloupean woman to
ay: "The *Békés* have become less racist; they marry
Metropolitans." Still, one does not marry *any* Metropoli-
an: a marriage with a person from the "common people"
s not well thought of and can border on *mésalliance*. But
f the inquiry into the family of the future spouse turns
out satisfactorily, consent will be given.

Marriage within the group. Since most marriages are
endogamous,[3] what then are the criteria of selection
within the group? It is often said of a family that "it is
llied to another, itself allied to a third, which in turn is
llied to the first." In other words, there are marriage
circles, and informants can identify many of them without
ifficulty. Also, there are many cases of marriage between
rst or second cousins. Such cases occur far too fre-
uently for them to be considered coincidental. A woman
rying to explain the relatively large number of marriages
etween cousins told us that until quite recently, girls were
losely supervised and kept busy, alone or among others,
vith reading, embroidering, and the like. They were mar-
ied at a very young age and often to a cousin, for the
ircle of their male friends did not extend beyond the
amily, and they were only rarely allowed to meet strangers.
. . In this context it is noteworthy that our informant's

[3] No study has been made of the rate of consanguinity in
he Creole group; many informants assured us that it does not
xceed that of a small French provincial town. We think that
would probably be higher.

parents, themselves cousins and products of many genera tions of marriages between cousins, warned her agains consanguineal marriage, although the only men she me during her entire girlhood were cousins (moreover, she i still unmarried). Today the circle of friends has extende beyond the family, and the young enjoy more freedom although holidays and vacations are still customarily spen among kin. However, the number of consanguineal mar riages is decreasing, owing to an awareness of the problem they engender as well as to the greater mobility of youn people. Changes in the social ranking of some familie also lengthen the list of possible mates for a young *Béké*.

The marriage circles we have been able to identify, to gether with an inventory of the patronyms in each house hold based on our own census, reveal certain regularities.

4 We have classified each spouse from our census accordin to patronym in one of three subgroups (upper [*grands*], mid dle [*moyens*], lower [*petits*]), and we have calculated th proportion of marriages by sex and by subgroups:

(a) *Men:* First subgroup
 56.7% have married women of their own subgroup
 35.1% have married women of the second subgroup
 8.2% have married women of the third subgroup

 Second subgroup
 38.3% have married women of the first subgroup
 48.2% have married women of their own subgroup
 13.5% have married women of the third subgroup

 Third subgroup
 7.4% have married women of the first subgroup
 24.2% have married women of the second subgroup
 68.4% have married women of their own subgroup

(b) *Women:* First subgroup
 65.6% have married men in their own subgroup
 32.1% have married men in the second subgroup
 2.3% have married men in the third subgroup

 Second subgroup
 43.0% have married men in the first subgroup
 45.1% have married men in their subgroup
 11.9% have married men in the third subgroup

There is an almost total cleavage between the "great families" and the "lesser ones," each marrying mostly among themselves. While the "middle families" also often marry among themselves, they also marry more readily into the other two subgroups. It seems that in the past, a great number of marriages of convenience took place, especially with regard to land-ownership, but unions of this type are now disappearing. Nevertheless, name and wealth, the principal criteria for determining the social status of a person or a family, continue to play predominant roles in the selection of a mate. Thus a family with a prestigious name but with diminished wealth will marry into a *nouveau riche* middle-class family whose name is thereby enhanced. As for the *Petits Blancs,* there is a distinction between those families that one never meets (*ipso facto,* marriage is totally excluded) and those that are judged "visitable" but "not marriageable," even though they may possess moderate wealth, since their name does not carry enough prestige.

Imbalance between mates can also arise from upbringing, but this is a matter of individual circumstance. In this connection, we were told of one husband of a social rank inferior to that of his wife, who was called a "white Negro" because he was interested in football, cockfights, and the like. This marriage was considered a clear *mésalliance;* the wife hardly saw her family any more, and eventually she got a divorce. "You see," we were told, "it is better to marry someone of your own background; then there is a better chance of understanding each other."

Although in recent years the criteria of acceptance have become more flexible, the selection of a spouse is still

---

Third subgroup
15.0% have married men in the first subgroup
22.4% have married men in the second subgroup
62.6% have married men in their own subgroup.

However, it is necessary to recall the numerical disproportions that exist among patronymic families: seven out of ten of the largest families are considered "upper class" (*grandes familles*). . . .

largely confined to the circle of friends, that is to say, to the social subgroup to which one belongs. Theoretically and many examples support this, the criterion of race alone increasingly governs marriages, but the vast majority still occur between persons of the same or adjacent social levels.

Social significance of marriage. We will consider marriage from two points of view: first, its external function, that is, whether or not it links the Creoles with other groups in the society; second, its internal function, that is, its structural role within the *Béké* group.

In so far as marriage reconstitutes and extends the white Creole family in an ideally endless chain, every foreign element is traditionally excluded, and endogamy within the group (and within the subgroup when it is a privileged class) is its preferred form. We know that the rules of marriage have a two-fold aspect: they forbid marriage with some individuals or groups, and they approve it, even prescribe it, with others. Among the *Békés*, we find in the rules of marriage a preference for endogamy, accompanied by negative attitudes—their intensity varies with each group—toward exogamy.

The most peremptory negative view concerns interracial marriages, which are socially prohibited. This attitude is understandable if one takes into account the underlying ideology shared by all Creoles: maintenance of the "purity of the race" is practically considered a sacred duty. Wagley and Harris, in an analysis devoted to minorities in the New World, show how "the relations between minority and majority and the internal structure of these groups correspond in several important respects to the relations and structures which characteristically exist between completely autonomous societies. These features are *ethnocentrism* and *endogamy*."[5] Ethnocentrism manifests itself in the fact that each group tends to value its own charac-

[5] Charles Wagley and Marvin Harris, *Minorities in the New World: Six Case Studies* (New York: Columbia University Press, 1958), p. 258.

teristics from a triple point of view: racial, social, and ideological. Endogamy reflects this ethnocentrism and, as the groups in question occupy different socioeconomic positions, it perpetuates inequalities.[6] These tendencies are all the more prominent in Martinique, since the different groups belong to different races. Ethnocentrism being accentuated by racial prejudice toward the blacks, it is translated into strict social rules whose purpose is to prohibit marriages between whites and non-whites. It is necessary to emphasize, however, that the prohibitions apply only to legal unions, which alone can modify the group from within. Consensual unions, although not encouraged, are commonplace and acceptable (for men of the white race), since they do not constitute a threat to the homogeneity or standing of the group. When legal unions are contracted in violation of the rules, the group systematically eliminates the reluctant households in order to protect and maintain its homogeneity. This extremely rigid racial barrier has led some authors to speak of "caste," since it is impossible for a person with "black blood" to pass into the white group, and, inversely, a *mésalliance* involves an element of stain for the whites. Thus, analyzing the Creole reaction toward the "misallied" individual, Leiris writes: "They are unwilling to accept this marriage and behave as if the white spouse had passed out of the superior caste to which he belonged by birth into the inferior caste of his partner."[7] This person will become a *Béké sauté barrière* or a *Béké dissident*. However, we do not agree that the term "caste" applies here; we think that Leiris uses it in a sense close to the subjective meaning given to it by the *Békés* themselves. Blacks and whites do have some contact; intimate relationships are not prohibited by law, as in South Africa, for example; interracial marriages can be legally contracted. Rather, the case here is that of one racial group protecting itself from another that it considers inferior and dreads at the same time.

[6] *Ibid.*, pp. 258–61.
[7] Michel Leiris, *Contacts de civilisations en Martinique et en Guadeloupe* (Paris: UNESCO, 1955), p. 127.

Creole endogamy fills another important function with regard not only to the colored people but also to any foreign group; this function is essentially economic. Up to now, property has not passed through marriage and inheritance into the hands of colored people; endogamy thus prevents the partitioning of the estates and at the same time fixes the framework of the Martiniquan social structure, in which racial characteristics and socioeconomic positions largely coincide. But it does still more: if the economic aspect of endogamy is useful to Martiniquan Creole society internally, it takes on a wider and deeper significance in the exclusion of other whites, be they Metropolitans or foreigners. Indeed, the Creoles cannot justify their objection to marrying members of other white groups on racial grounds. Surely, such marriages do occur—they have always occurred, especially with Metropolitans—but in limited numbers, and they are always surrounded by a negative social atmosphere. To explain this, one can cite insularity, the relative isolation in which *Békés* have always lived, the fact that the non-Martiniquan is regarded as a foreigner, "the other," who immediately arouses suspicion or feeling of xenophobia. But when "the other" is white and in most cases French, these explanations seem inadequate. Rather, the foreigner is feared as a usurper, who might seize part of the group's wealth, or as a competitor in a small territory where the number of properties, factories, and important businesses is strictly limited. A currently observed fact supports this hypothesis: when Metropolitan interests seek to buy and gain possession of Martiniquan property, Creole families come to each other's assistance and take all possible measures to ward off such a possibility. And if marriage with a Metropolitan is envisaged, the Creole family first ascertains the economic and social position of the future spouse's family.

The preceding considerations do not, however, explain why the *Petits Blancs* families are also endogamous, as much as if not more so than the other white families. The explanation is probably to be found in the poverty and isolation of these rural families, which mitigate against

contacts with outsiders. Most of these families do not have
the means to send their children abroad to study and moreover do not live in permanent contact with urban dwellers
like the Metropolitans.

* * * *

Up to this point, we have emphasized the analysis of
norms, though noting that they were not always obeyed by
all individuals in the group. According to our informants,
however, these norms have themselves been evolving for a
dozen years; they have come to delimit a more extensive
field of socially acceptable relationships. The criteria for
the selection of a spouse have accordingly become less
rigid. We will try briefly to specify what these changes are
and what has caused them.

Our informants emphasized the increasing number of
marriages with white non-Creoles, Metropolitans or others,
and the greater tolerance accorded these marriages. As we
have seen, this phenomenon can be related to the number
of young Creoles who leave to study in France and spend
many years there, thus stepping out of the narrow circle
of relationships to which they were limited on the island.
They consequently fashion a frame of reference that is less
exclusive and less rigid; they marry more easily outside
their own group; in many cases, they also settle down in
the Metropole. The last feature seems to make the evolving
movement closer to emigration than to exogamy strictly
defined. Let us repeat that the number of Metropolitan
spouses living in Martinique remains relatively low, which
explains why *Béké* households living on the island still
exhibit a high rate of endogamy. As for exogamous marriage combined with emigration, the proportion of young
Creole girls who take this path (in this connection, some
say that "girls from here suffocate and want to flee the
island") is higher than that of boys, who spend more
years outside the island and come back more willingly to
marry here. In any case, the young *Béké* man living in
France feels himself to be Martiniquan and *expatrié,* and

tends to socialize with his *compatriotes*. Furthermore, he is never completely cut off from the island, to which he returns every summer, readily resuming his traditional way of life. At the end of each summer there is an outbreak of new engagements. But, among these new young couples the relationships between man and wife tend to be modified, departing from the Creole tradition and drawing closer to Metropolitan models. The young Creole wife will no longer be only the mother of children, but also the companion of her husband. As for the strictly exogamous marriages, there has been no radical change but only the beginning of a noticeable evolution. . . .

A second evolutionary current involves the choice of a spouse within the *Béké* group itself. Here again we witness more marriages between subgroups. This liberalization could be explained by the impoverishment of some *grandes familles* and by the increasing importance of money, which makes it possible to forgive a family for being only middle class. But the root cause seems to be the stronger external pressures now being exerted on the Creoles: demographic pressure by the colored population, social and economic pressures that bring into question the traditional structure in Martinique. These facts force the Creoles into compromise solutions. The group's very survival threatened, it has had to establish a hierarchy of values and of vulnerable points to be defended. Priority seems to have been given to the desire to maintain racial purity, even to the point of disrupting the internal stratification of the group. Thus, a new attitude is emerging with the aim of avoiding marriages with colored people. At a certain level in the scale of choices, it is preferable to marry "anybody" in the *Béké* group, even, if worst comes to worst, a "poor white."

These two new currents are capable of bringing about a complete change in white Creole society. And if external pressures continue to intensify these currents, they may well come to threaten the very existence of the group.

*   *   *   *

IDEOLOGY AND SOCIAL CONTROL

The white Creoles of Martinique have up to now succeeded in overcoming political, social, and economic crises, because they are an organized group. However, that does not mean that the group is homogeneous, as is sometimes too readily assumed. And we have tried to show to what extent it is segmented and which internal tensions threaten its stability. But it never falls into anarchy, because it has understood that survival depends on its solidarity vis-à-vis the outside world. Therefore there is a value system, ethnocentric perforce, which gives the diverse elements of the group a sense of identity sufficient for the survival of the collectivity. The identification is all the stronger for being linked with a feeling of pride in the group's past and in its role in the history of the island. Deep down, the Creole thinks of himself as The White Man, the one who has always been in charge. Even the economically disadvantaged Creole feels he is bound up with the group, not only because his belonging is a personal warranty on which his status depends, but also because he is conscious of the "hereditary" distance that separates him from the rest of the Martiniquan population. Whatever his social status, the Creole, in order to maintain his privileged position or to mark the distance that isolates him from the colored population, sees himself obliged to perpetuate the existence of the group; this becomes his first duty. The interest of the community outweighs and conditions the interest of the individual.

We have tried to specify how this ideology is expressed in social life, how the elements of cohesion—"racial purity," the maintenance of economic structures, and the safeguarding of group unity—prevail over internal tensions. Furthermore, the Creoles are also concerned with preserving the reputation of the group: a Creole never criticizes another Creole in front of a foreigner; on the contrary, he is ready to defend him despite personal rivalries that may divide them.

* * * *

Among the Creole group, rules [of behavior] are not only clearly defined and explicit, they are also very constricting. This rigor is doubtless attributable to the particular character of the group, a minority bent on defending its distinctive but precarious qualities, that is, its very existence. The closer and more intense the relationships among members of a group are, the more rigid the community becomes and the more threatening and treasonable is a person's refusal to obey the norm. He who denies his origins and "goes over to the other side" constitutes a more serious danger than any pressure from the outside. The person who has broken away from his society to integrate into another one will criticize his original background all the more freely, for he is intimate with the value system he is attacking and thinks he can judge its merits. Thus while the group is confident that external pressures can be coped with by the maintenance of cohesion, it fears above all disintegration from within. It is for this reason that a strict social control aims to insure respect for the norms and to penalize the deviants.

The Creole group tolerates very few deviations. One category of persons is somewhat marginal, but as long as they do not overstep the permitted limits, they remain an integral part of the group. This category brings together those whom the *Békés* call "originals," meaning Creoles who take liberties with established forms of thought and action. They are said to have a turn of mind that is more individualistic than social and to have a great desire for freedom. This description can be applied either to a person (a "woman of action," a girl considered a little too independent, a man who socializes too much with colored people) or to an entire family—as for example, "The Godards are all 'originals.'" If the family is wealthy, this behavior will be more easily tolerated. As long as those who stray from the norms do not really pose a threat to the group, they will not be rejected.

But, as we have seen, anyone who negates the values of the group through a public and effectively implemented contestation of the norms (marriage with a colored person, trade union activities, and so forth) or who denies the internal hierarchy of the group is immediately rejected, indeed, excluded. This defense system commends itself to the community as effectual and reassuring, since the expelled individual can no longer do it harm, at least not from within. Anything he says or does will no longer matter to the group nor will it reflect upon it; all will be as if he no longer existed. Since the island is very small and since the Creoles living in France are not isolated either ("everything is known quickly"), social control is rigorous. No member of the group is shielded from the eyes and critical evaluations of others. As best as possible, one will try to put the deviant back on the right path, first by reasoning, then by applying pressures, and finally by taking preventive actions. Many suffer from the strictness of the norms; most nevertheless do submit.

15.

We turn now to another dimension of West Indian society —the position of East Indians and their relations with Creoles. The next three articles deal with the East Indians of Trinidad and Guyana, the two West Indian nations with the largest population concentrations of the descendants of indentured laborers from the Indian subcontinent. Following the emancipation of the slaves in the British Caribbean in 1834, planters fearing labor shortages made concerted efforts to recruit other workers from various parts of the world, most successfully from India. After nearly a century, the East Indians have become a potent social and political force in the Caribbean. Their place in West Indian societies, the extent of their assimilation into Creole culture, and their political power are examined in these selections.

The following article by Crowley cites evidence to show that East Indians have been culturally assimilated into Trinidad's "permissive" Creole society, sharing cultural traits and aspirations with other Trinidadians.

DANIEL J. CROWLEY was born in the United States and received a doctorate in anthropology at Northwestern University. He has had research experience in Trinidad, St. Lucia, and the Bahamas. He is presently Professor of Anthropology at the University of California, Davis.

Cultural Assimilation in a Multiracial Society
Daniel J. Crowley

When numbers of people from one culture move to another, they cannot help but alter their original culture. Even the most prolonged and powerful attempts to preserve intact a racial or cultural group in a new milieu have ended in failure. Since culture is both conservative and ever changing, we preserve bits and pieces of our ancestral cultures, but combine and recombine them with the forms and values of the one or more cultures in which we participate in the course of a lifetime.

Since the time of Columbus, West Indian societies have been both biologically and culturally mixed. European institutions adapted to new local circumstances by provincials were soon being used by Africans and their Creole children, who gave them a content never found in Europe. As other peoples from Asia, Europe, and Africa arrived, old traditions merged and new ones developed, and the Creole cultures of the islands are the result. These are local variants of Western culture, but with considerable retention of non-Western forms, attitudes, and values.

Racial purity is an infinitely more personal concept than cultural integrity, but every West Indian street corner attests to the fact that, for this area at least, it is a thing of

Social and Cultural Pluralism in the Caribbean, edited by Vera Rubin, *Annals of The New York Academy of Sciences*, Vol. 83, pp. 850–54. Copyright, The New York Academy of Sciences, 1960; reprinted by permission of the Academy and the author.

the past. Except for a very few groups, the West Indians who are not yet mixed will be mixed in a few generations. The last handful of pure Caribs are dying, while their daughters "make babies for" Dominican Creoles. Every year a few more Windward Island whites emigrate permanently to Canada or Britain or marry their colored mistresses, so that the once-large local white populations of Dominica, Montserrat, Carriacou, or Grenada are dwindling. Although overlooked by the 1946 Census,[1] the so-called Blacks include a large number of people more precisely described as Coloured, if the presence of at least one known non-African ancestor is the criterion. In the same census, the Chinese in Trinidad were already nearly half mixed, and this figure is undoubtedly far too low for anyone who knows the population of the north coast, where every family is reputed to have "one Chinee chile."

East Indians, too, have more racial mixture than they sometimes care to admit, as well as ancestry from different castes and areas in India, which in traditional terms is almost as objectionable as race mixing. Most, but certainly not all, offspring of Indians and non-Indians in Trinidad are classed with the Creoles. On the other hand, both Creoles and Indians seem uncertain as to how to classify the many unmixed Indians who are leaders in typically Creole activities such as steel bands, acting, dancing, and carnival masquing.

However, cultural assimilation can take place even without race mixture, as in the American melting pot, where all but a few ethnic groups seem to be melting into three lumps based on religious affiliation.

In the United States much of the assimilation has been conscious on the part of emigrating Europeans desirous of adapting as quickly and as completely as possible to their new culture. In the contemporary Caribbean, conscious assimilation can be found among culturally Europeanized upper-class local people who, in the throes of racial or other nationalisms, have decided to cast their lot,

[1] *West Indian Census, 1946:* Part H, Windward Islands (Kingston, Jamaica: Government Printer, 1950), pp. 24–25.

especially politically, with the local lower classes. They learn the local dialect, salt it well with Creolisms, cook local dishes, espouse local beliefs and prejudices, "jump up" in carnival, and play at being "real Creoles."

Unconscious assimilation is a much more subtle process and, like culture itself, not often perceived by its practitioners. Through this process West Indian-born whites are no longer Englishmen or Frenchmen and can never fully belong to their ancestral cultures. The same process works for the Chinese, Syrians, Portuguese, and other groups who preserve some aspects of their ancestral traditions in their homes, but otherwise belong to the local culture more than they realize.

The only group in the West Indies for which a case of cultural isolation can be made is the East Indian, particularly in Trinidad. Elsewhere their numbers are so small that almost complete Creolization has taken place, as in St. Lucia, St. Vincent, and Grenada, or East Indian customs may be preserved only within the family circle, as in Jamaica. In Trinidad, however, the nearly 300,000 East Indians make up one third of the population. Current politics in the island, although complex, is divided more and more sharply between Creole and East Indian. Diet, dress, and especially family patterns and economic attitudes are clearly distinguished by members of the two groups. Unquestionably, both Creoles and East Indians think they are culturally different; neither group intends to assimilate with the other, but what are the facts of their actual relationship?

Like the other groups, the Indians were forced to leave behind much of their culture when they emigrated. Hindu "indentures" broke a basic law of their religion by "crossing water." The great majority of the East Indians were low caste or casteless, poor, uneducated, rural, and drawn from far-flung and culturally diverse areas of the subcontinent. Undoubtedly, some upper-caste Hindus, even Brahmins, came as indentures, and a few of these knew the written language and some of the religious and secular traditions. In spite of half-hearted attempts to keep families and friends together, the barracks and, later, the rural villages were mixed in caste, class, religion, and language, so that East Indian cultural variations became generalized. Although neither group liked it, Creoles and East Indians were compelled to associate with each other in the fields, in the market and shops, and in village life and, because of the scarcity of Indian women, many men took Creole mates. By converting to Christianity, low caste could be left behind and opportunities for mobility increased. Some East Indians soon became wealthy but, instead of reorganizing their lives and surroundings on Indian principles, they seem to have become thoroughly Europeanized, although some did return to India to visit.

The less successful East Indians, or those less interested in adapting to the standards of the rest of the island community, became small landowners or day laborers in the sugar fields. They often work side by side with "small-island" Creoles, speak English or Creole with them, and drink and gamble together. Doubtless there are tensions and divisions between these two racial groups, but until recently these divergences were hardly more serious than cleavages within each group on the basis of religion, class, caste, and color.

According to one estimate (Arthur Niehoff, personal communication) one fifth of the Trinidad East Indians live in St. George County, in and around Port of Spain, while many others live in the string of contiguous villages running east to Arima or in the populous San Fernando area. Even when these people work land they go in and out of town almost daily and, in my opinion, are best considered suburban. Even in the Caroni and Oropouche enclaves, where nearly all the people are East Indian agriculturalists, the amount of daily contact with the towns is tremendous. Schools, libraries, the motion pictures (both Western and Indian), sports such as cricket or the races, newspapers, and the omnipresent radio are all sources of unconscious assimilation. While in town, East Indian men see the newest in clothes, cars, and gadgetry, watch the shipping and tourist activities of the port, and meet the demimonde on Green Corner, the Broadway of Port of Spain. Even in homes where they are relatively secluded, women must go out to market and to shop, to visit relatives, to attend socioreligious events, and to visit the doctor and the dressmaker. The East Indian community has never seriously attempted self-segregation from the Creole world around it, and most East Indians interact daily with their Creole neighbors.

There are East Indians in all social classes. Those at the top are culturally indistinguishable from white, colored, or black urban locals of the same class, except where Hinduism or Islam requires some variations in dietary patterns. These people are more Europeanized than Creole, like their non-Indian compatriots of the same class. Toward the middle of the social scale, urban and suburban Indians again tend to be quite similar to their neighbors. In communities such as Tunapuna, St. James, and San Fernando they share most of each other's popular culture, and have similar attitudes toward government, education, leisure, and the acquisition of wealth. Dietary patterns are frequently interchanged, as people of different origins share each other's foods at homes or at fetes. The Creole kiosk at a bazaar held on Government House lawn in September 1953 served *pelau* as the typically Creole dish, though it is East Indian in both name and origin. The East Indian kiosk served *roti* (wheat pancake) made in the "oil-bake" manner preferred by Creoles, rather than the *sada roti* of traditional Indian homes. Neither example of assimilation was conscious, and doubtless considerable embarrassment, even disbelief, would have resulted had these facts been mentioned.

Since World War II, Trinidad Creole and East Indian intellectuals have been inspired by the success of India, Ghana, and other formerly colonial areas, and have developed greater race pride and political consciousness. The Indians grew concerned over the rapid attenuation of their ancestral culture. Hindi was dying with the last of the indentures, children attended Christian schools, few of the pandits could explain or defend Hinduism against the better-educated and more prestigeful Christian clergy and, most important of all, the younger people began to leave the land and parental domination, especially in choosing marriage partners, for the greater freedom, better pay, and higher prestige of town life. Local Indian nationalism was thus born in reaction to the extreme degree of assimilation that had already taken place. The usual devices of cultural separateness were then introduced: Hindu and Moslem schools where Hindi is taught, a study program in India for young pandits and other promising scholars, bigger and better mosques and shivalas (Siva temples) in more prestigeful locations, and the building up of social pressure against further Creolization and conversion. However, in the words of Kumari Santosh Chopra, the Punjabi headmistress of Gandhi Memorial High School in Penal, "This latter-day 'revival' of Indian culture is not Indian at all." In the typical competitive Creole way, East Indians are using Indian culture and often mythical caste for "making style" and as a club with which to beat contemptuous Creoles.

Except for the recent racially oriented political developments, the Hindu and Moslem schools seem to be the most effective means of creating and/or preserving a Trinidad East Indian subculture. However, it is difficult to find teachers, and they are among the most Europeanized of all Trinidadians. In the Moslem schools, teachers flatly refused to adopt the wearing of the *orhni* (head veil) in spite of the insistence of the religious leaders. Many of these schools are staffed by Christian East Indians and even by Creoles and, of course, the great majority of East Indian children continue to attend Christian denominational schools with their Creole age peers. Conversely, some Creoles attend Hindu and Moslem schools, learn Hindi and, in a few cases, are converted to Hinduism or Islam. Hindi is still a home language for some families and a religious language for a much larger number but, being largely unwritten, it has become virtually unintelligible to a non-Trinidadian Hindi speaker, since it has acquired vocabulary and pronunciation from English, Creole, and

Spanish. A course in Hindi offered by the Extra-Mural Department of the University College of the West Indies had scores of students at the first meeting, but only a handful completed the six-week course. Since practically all of the East Indians already speak English, Hindi seems to have little chance in the future except in rote prayers, sermons, and rituals.

Informed Trinidad East Indians are likely to admit all of these facts and to have little hope for the success of their goals. Students of the Indian community such as M. Klass, M. Freilich, and A. Niehoff also make no claim of a present or future subculture in Trinidad that is like any in India, but both scholars and East Indians seem to feel that in economic and family matters there remains a clear line between Indian and Creole. Indians are said to be willing to save and plan and work toward a distant goal, while Creoles are supposed to spend their money in constant "fête" and not to give a thought to the morrow. Anyone who has met with a carnival band on Ash Wednesday morning to plan next year's masque knows that Creoles can and do plan ahead for distant goals, though their prestige forms may be different from those of some East Indians! The attitude of Creole families toward education and their willingness to make heroic sacrifices for their children can be validated in the lives of most prominent Creoles, although these characteristics may actually be more closely connected with middle-class status or the desire for it than with ethnic origin. Profligate, rum-drinking Indians, or thrifty, abstemious Creoles are definitely not unknown in any Trinidad community but, since they do not serve the stereotype, they tend to be dismissed as atypical. Indians seem to talk more about saving money, even when their actual performance is not unlike that of Creoles of their same class, and the Creoles, traditionally averse to "money-grubbing" business careers, see the growing economic power of upward-mobile Indian businessmen, with its concomitant political power, as a threat to their own social hierarchy, which is based on the Civil Service.

In family structure the ideal pattern for East Indians is an early, family-arranged, monogamous marriage but, like so many ideal patterns both in the Caribbean and elsewhere, it is often honored in the breach. "Under-the-bamboo" Indian marriages are similar in function to Creole consensual unions, and Hindu widows, forbidden by their religion to remarry, merely take a new mate in the Creole manner. Many Indian youths recognize early marriage as an effective means of parental domination, "to keep me in the rice field," and fiercely resist it. Girls, disliking the arranged union, sometimes give their husbands reason to wish for the reintroduction of *purdah* (seclusion). Both sexes show the strain of trying to approximate an ideal Indian value system in a real Creole world by a suicide rate phenomenally high in contrast to that of the Creoles. In the higher classes, where social pressures are more effective, Indian women are more likely to be monogamous, although the men are expected to experiment more widely, often with Creole girls. While more Indian men may be more faithful more often to their wives than some Creole men, their behavior is so similar that the habits of both in this respect are not readily distinguishable.

If the data have been correctly interpreted, both racial and cultural assimilation have proceeded far in Trinidad, although admittedly with a wider range of variations than in some other societies. The somewhat similar institutions of slavery and indenture produced parallel results, so that the East Indians have no more valid claim on an Indian culture in Trinidad than Negroes have on a fully African culture there. Most of Indian culture in Trinidad has been so drastically reinterpreted that even the most nationalistically minded East Indian is culturally a Creole, as he realizes if he has an opportunity to visit India. Real differences exist between the lives of some Indians and some Creoles, but these differences can be explained as readily in terms of class and of rural-urban variations as in terms of ancestral cultures.

Even the most assimilationistic Creoles do not expect the Indians to give up their attempts at racial endogamy and do not want them to abandon Hinduism or Islam, which provide so many popular magic practitioners for the Creole world. East Indians understandably want to better their position in the Trinidadian social structure and are using effective, typically Western techniques of capital accumulation, education, and the espousal of middle-class mores to gain these common goals just as are the upward-mobile Creoles. The permissive Creole culture has already made a place for Indian fêtes, foods, magic practices, and thousands of East Indians. The intelligent self-interest that West Indians of all ethnic origins have displayed in the past may still stave off serious disintegration while the necessary compromises are evolved.

16.

The role of East Indians and of East Indian culture in Trinidad is viewed here in a diametrically opposite fashion. On the basis of field research in a Hindu village in the Caroni area, another American anthropologist argues the essential separateness of East Indians and their lack of integration into, and assimilation with, the Creole Trinidadian setting. This position is more fully expounded in the author's *East Indians in Trinidad: A Study of Cultural Persistence*. These two divergent conclusions about the East Indian place in the sociocultural order reflect local anxieties and conjectures on a subject of critical social and political importance, given the rapid growth of the East Indian population, for the future of Trinidad.

MORTON KLASS received his doctorate in anthropology from Columbia University. Trinidad was the locale of his first extensive field research, later followed by studies in India. He now holds the rank of Professor of Anthropology at Barnard College, Columbia University.

East and West Indian: Cultural Complexity in Trinidad[1]
Morton Klass

No one disputes the fact that the island of Trinidad exhibits a marked degree of ethnic heterogeneity. Confusion and disagreement set in as soon as one attempts to go beyond that statement. What, for example, are the nature and number of significant groups and subgroups to be distinguished? For census purposes the government of Trinidad and Tobago recognizes six racial categories.[2] Braithwaite also lists six groups, but he calls them ethnic, and the two lists are not identical.[3] Crowley proposes thirteen "racial and national groups" for Trinidad.[4]

Social and Cultural Pluralism in the Caribbean, edited by Vera Rubin, *Annals of The New York Academy of Sciences*, Vol. 83, pp. 855–61. Copyright, The New York Academy of Sciences, 1960; reprinted by permission of the Academy and the author.

[1] The data in this paper on present-day East Indian life in Trinidad derive from a one-year study conducted on that island during the period 1957–58. This study was financed by a fellowship from the Social Science Research Council, New York, N.Y., to which I extend my sincere thanks. I am also grateful to the Research Institute for the Study of Man, New York, N.Y., for the fellowship awarded me under its research and training program during the summer of 1957.

[2] Trinidad, Central Statistical Office, *Annual Statistical Digest* (Port of Spain, Trinidad: Government Printing Office, 1956).

[3] L. Braithwaite, "Social Stratification in Trinidad," *Social and Economic Studies*, Vol. 2, Nos. 2–3 (October 1953), p. 50.

[4] D. Crowley, "Plural and Differential Acculturation in Trinidad," *American Anthropologist*, Vol. 59, No. 5 (October 1957), pp. 817–19.

These differences reflect the use of local standards of evaluation and the apparent absence of any consistent set of criteria deriving from current anthropological or sociological theory. How else may one explain the use of a category—call it ethnic, racial, or national—such as "Syrian," under which heading are subsumed both Polish Jews and Lebanese Christians? Furthermore, before any attempt is made at a fine categorization of the island's population, it would certainly seem advisable to explore the nature of Trinidad's sociocultural complexity. In an effort to determine whether Trinidad contains one society with one culture or some form of sociocultural pluralism, primary attention will be given in this paper to social structure, to underlying values, and to the effect of rapid change over a short period.

In 1946 about 61 per cent of the population of Trinidad was composed of individuals of African or partly African ancestry. This entire group will be referred to hereafter as West Indians, although attention will be given when necessary to significantly different subgroups. Again in 1946, over 35 per cent of Trinidad's population was composed of the descendants of immigrants from India. This entire group, which also has its subgroups, will be referred to as East Indians. Little attention will be given here to the remaining elements in the Trinidad population; together they accounted for less than 4 per cent of the 1946 total.

Crowley[5] has used the term "Creole" to designate the culture of Trinidad. The West Indian segment of the population unquestionably participates in this culture, but whether the same thing may be said of the East Indian segment is a matter of dispute. It becomes necessary, therefore, to understand something of the nature of this Creole culture. The following analysis derives from the writings of Braithwaite, Crowley, and others, as well as from my own observations in Trinidad.

In almost all aspects of the Creole culture high value is attached to that which is considered to be of European

[5] *Ibid.,* p. 824 and elsewhere.

or predominantly European derivation, and a correspondingly low value is placed on that which is considered to be of African origin. This phenomenon may be observed most clearly in an examination of standards of physical attractiveness and in the relationship noted between physical appearance and stratification. This does not mean, however, that a simple value continuum exists, with "pure" European at one end and "pure" African at the other. There is a developing feeling, affecting all aspects of West Indian life, that the highest value should be given to that which is essentially European but exhibits also some additional quality that is West Indian or Creole or Trinidadian. Braithwaite writes:

By "good hair" is not meant the aesthetically pleasing; or rather the aesthetically pleasing is identified as the "straight hair" of the European, and only something which approximates to this can be classified as good. Similarly European features and the absence of thick lips are considered good. And the judgment of "good-looking for a black man" expresses both the sentiment that the black man cannot in general be good-looking and that even within the category of black men there is a necessary differentiation between those who possess and those who do not possess European-like features.[6]

One may observe, however, that the white European is in the process of being replaced as the symbol of physical attractiveness by the light-colored, West Indian-born Creole. It is no longer assumed by the majority of the island's population, for example, that the annual beauty contest winner, the Carnival Queen, need necessarily be white. However, it is likely to be a long time before she is black. That which is African is still undesirable.

According to Braithwaite, social stratification in Trinidad in the postslavery nineteenth century exhibited certain castelike qualities. In recent years this "caste idea" for the most part has been replaced by the elements of the full open-class system; that is, individual social and eco-

[6] Braithwaite, *op. cit.,* p. 97.

nomic mobility is much easier today than in former years, and there is much more interpersonal association and even intermarriage between members of the three subgroups of West Indian society. The castelike appearance of Trinidad society derived from the presence of a color-class hierarchy and, although modified, this is still very much in evidence. The upper class is still predominantly white, the middle class predominantly colored, and the lower class predominantly black.[7]

This prestige continuum from high-value European to low-value African, with a special value placed on that which is Creole, is reflected in other aspects of West Indian life. Thus, Roman Catholicism and Anglicanism enjoy the highest prestige, while religious sects considered to have large African elements in their composition find their following only within the lowest socioeconomic section of the population.[8] It is interesting that Carnival, the festival observed by many Roman Catholics in the period immediately preceding Lent, became associated with the lower class in the late nineteenth century, but recently has become respectable once more. Powrie writes: "The middle class are at last inclined to take pride in something which is Trinidadian."[9]

In recent years considerable attention has been given to the prevalence of nonlegal or "keeper" unions among the West Indian lower class. There is a pattern of free choice of mates and a tacitly permitted premarital sexual experimentation that often results in the birth of a child to a girl still living with her parents. It must be emphasized that this is not a pattern of promiscuity. After a period of experimentation, a choice is made, and a couple will set up house together. The emphasis in the literature on illegitimacy and on matrifocality or mother-dominated fami-

---

[7] *Ibid.*, pp. 46–48, 60–63, and elsewhere.

[8] *Ibid.*, pp. 130–31.

[9] B. E. Powrie, "The Changing Attitude of the Coloured Middle Class toward Carnival," *Caribbean Quarterly*, Vol. 4, Nos. 3–4 (March–June 1956), pp. 224–34. See also A. Pearse, "Carnival in Nineteenth Century Trinidad," *loc. cit.*, p. 192.

ies tends to obscure the fact that such unions are reasonably stable and about as unlikely to break up as are any
other forms of marital union. It would appear, simply,
that in the West Indian lower class, family formation is
not necessarily regarded as a major life crisis. Whatever
the reasons, be they historical, social, and/or economic,
the setting up of a marital union in this group does not
require the ceremonial *rite de passage* of a marriage ceremony. In the rural West Indian community, death is the
most important life crisis, involving community participation in an extended ceremony requiring financial assistance.[10]

The common-law union, according to Braithwaite, is
rarely encountered in the Trinidad middle class, for it is
"a direct violation of the middle-class code."[11] However,
while church marriage is the approved form of mating
for upper- and middle-class West Indians and for socially
mobile members of the lower class, there are indications
of a developing admiration for what is considered to be
a peculiarly West Indian propensity for the *affaire
d'amour*. This was the subject of a recent paper by Crowley,[12] and Braithwaite devotes attention to the sharp
change in middle-class attitudes toward sex and marriage.[13]

To sum up, the West Indian Creole culture is a variant
of European culture, and prestige is accorded to that which
is considered to be of European origin. Highest prestige,
however, is of late given to traits that are primarily of
European origin but exhibit a West Indian quality and
may therefore be termed Creole. This appears to reflect
an emergent West Indian nationalism, and it might be
argued that commercial and political interests consciously
foster some of these tendencies. Nevertheless, it is signifi-

[10] M. J. Herskovits and F. S. Herskovits, *Trinidad Village*
(New York: Knopf, 1947), pp. 134–66.

[11] Braithwaite, *op. cit.*, p. 108.

[12] D. Crowley, "Polygyny and Class in the West Indies,"
paper read at the Annual Meeting of the American Anthropological Association, Washington, D.C., 1958.

[13] Braithwaite, *op. cit.*, pp. 109–11.

cant that the majority of West Indians respond eagerly t
the suggestion that a Creole society (that is, an integrate
and assimilated one) with a Creole culture (that is, a We
Indian variant of European) is developing in Trinida
A very high value is placed on assimilation. The favorit
description of Trinidad is a cosmopolitan melting po
within which many ethnic strains are blending, contribu
ing the best elements of their various heritages to wha
might be termed the culture-trait pool shared by the tot
society, which is expected to remain distinctively We
Indian and Trinidadian.[14]

This consummation is so devoutly desired by West I
dians that they frequently appear unaware of differe
attitudes among other elements of the population. Thi
should not be taken to mean that all who are not We
Indians oppose assimilation, but it should be obvious tha
such different groups as foreign-born whites, Trinidad-bor
whites, Chinese, and Portuguese must all respond very di
ferently to the pressure for Creolization.

Within the East Indian group there are individuals wh
accept the values, and consider themselves part, of th
West Indian society and its culture. Such Creolized Eas
Indians are usually Christians, although the group doe
contain a few Moslems and a very few Hindus.[15] Neve
theless, as Crowley notes, barely 15 per cent of the Eas
Indian population may be considered Christian.[16] Furthe
more,[17] the greatest amount of acculturation has take
place among the urbanized East Indians, but from th
census reports we may see that the overwhelming majorit
of Moslem and Hindu East Indians resided outside of th
urban and even suburban areas.[18] My own field work,[1]

---

[14] D. Crowley, "Plural and Differential Acculturation in Trin
idad," pp. 823–24.

[15] *Ibid.*, p. 819.

[16] *Ibid.*, p. 817.

[17] *Ibid.*, pp. 818–19.

[18] Trinidad, *Statistical Digest*, p. 13.

[19] M. Klass, *Cultural Persistence in a Trinidad East In
dian Community,* Ph.D. dissertation, Columbia University, Nev
York, 1959.

from which the following statements derive, was done in a village in County Caroni, populated almost exclusively by Hindu East Indian cane laborers.

Among rural Hindu East Indians the Creolized individual is rare to the point of nonexistence; traits and values deriving from India take precedence over those deriving from the non-Indian environment. It is necessary to note, however, that these people are for the most part East Indians of the West Indies; few still live who were born in India. Knowledge of what is Indian, therefore, does not derive from first-hand experience. Second, acculturation has taken place, and there is a value attached to being "modern"; however, to an East Indian, being modern does not always mean being West Indian.

Skin color plays almost no part in the East Indian group as internal stratification. The primary determinant of status among rural Hindus is caste membership. Education, occupation, and wealth are also important, but they all tend to cluster along with high-caste membership. Fairness of skin is one element in individual physical attractiveness, but a dark-skinned Brahman is socially superior to, and maritally more desirable than, a light-skinned Chamar, all else being equal. Individuals of low-caste origin who acquire wealth will often pretend to membership in one of the higher castes. The widespread East Indian tendency to deprecate caste obscures but does not change the fact of its importance in social stratification. In the rural village, leadership, wealth, and high-caste membership go hand in hand, and an examination of the caste affiliations of Hindu members, of whatever party, of the Trinidad Legislative Council reveals that almost all are of the two highest castes, Brahman and Kshatriya.

The rural East Indian might travel to Port of Spain to observe the Carnival festivities, but he would rarely participate in them. His own religious activities occupy much of his time, for the Trinidad Hindu is involved in a yearly cycle of public festivals and private prayers. The average West Indian knows nothing of this, and is rarely even aware that, every year, tens of thousands of Trinidad

Hindus journey to the beaches of the island for a day of ceremonial bathing and picnicking. In Trinidad Hinduism, certain religious practices are rated as superior or inferior. Among the criteria are the caste of the officiating priest, the use of alcohol, the question of animal sacrifice, and certain other points of ritual. The problem of European versus African origins is, of course, completely irrelevant here. Ceremonies rated as superior are almost invariably sponsored by high-caste families (or socially mobile ones), with Brahman priests officiating.

While "modern" East Indian young people insist upon "free choice" in marriage, this means something very different from Trinidad West Indian free choice. The overwhelming majority of rural East Indian marriages are arranged by the respective fathers while the boy and girl are in their teens. The fathers make sure that the marriage is kin-and-village exogamous and caste endogamous. At some point in the proceedings, however, the two young people are allowed to meet each other, if only for a short while, and on the basis of this interview either may veto the match.

Marriage is the most important life crisis for the East Indians. It involves community participation and often requires financial assistance. The East Indian bride must begin her married life as an alien in her husband's father's household and village, for marriages are normally virilocal as well as village exogamous. Her experiences, obviously, will be very different from those of her West Indian counterpart. Indeed, in family structure and life cycle there are few points of similarity between East and West Indian.

To sum up, Indian forms and values underlie Trinidad East Indian culture. Modifications have occurred, but they do not necessarily make the East Indian any more of a West Indian. The West Indian may be said to be striving to become more European, or at least more Creole, and less African. The East Indian might like his circumstances to be bettered, but he has no desire to be anything else and least of all a West Indian.

Since Trinidad unquestionably exhibits only one socioeconomic system, within which both groups participate, it may be said to have most of the important characteristics of a plural society as they are given by Furnivall. Here, as in his examples, "different sections of the community [are] living side by side, but separately, within the same political unit."[20] However, Trinidad society exhibits at least one additional characteristic not provided for in Furnivall's scheme. It would seem likely, from Furnivall's description,[21] that members of the culturally distinct groups making up the populations of Burma or Java are aware of, and appear to accept, the pluralistic nature of their respective societies. In Trinidad, on the other hand, this would be true only of the East Indian. From the Trinidad West Indian point of view, the island contains an essentially homogeneous society; if it did not it should and soon would.

Crowley writes: "A Trinidadian feels no inconsistency in being a British citizen, a Negro in appearance, a Spaniard in name, a Roman Catholic at church, an obeah (magic) practitioner in private, a Hindu at lunch, a Chinese at dinner, a Portuguese at work, and a Colored at the polls."[22]

To the West Indian, moreover, this process of assimilation and integration, what Crowley has termed plural acculturation, is worthy of unquestioned approbation. The merger of different ethnic strains and the emergence of one Creole physical type are also viewed as highly desirable. Braithwaite notes: "people will proudly proclaim that they have 'English', 'Spanish', 'French', blood in their veins. They can even be heard boasting that they are a 'mix-up.' "[23]

It is the universal Trinidad West Indian contention that within twenty to fifty years the East Indian ethnic group

[20] J. S. Furnivall, *Colonial Policy and Practice* (Cambridge: Cambridge University Press, 1948), p. 304.

[21] *Ibid.*, pp. 303–12.

[22] D. Crowley, "Plural and Differential Acculturation in Trinidad," p. 823.

[23] Braithwaite, *op. cit.*, p. 102.

will have merged indistinguishably into the West Indian Creole society.

This view is subscribed to by only a very small segment of the East Indian population; for the most part only by those who have become Creolized to the extent of having married out of their ethnic group. Even for most Moslem and Christian East Indians the idea of the East Indian group losing its ethnic identity and disappearing into the West Indian population is not acceptable. An East Indian who changes his religion is still considered an East Indian by the members of his ethnic group. Among the Hindus, a child of parents of two different castes will be accepted as a member of his father's caste, but a child of an East Indian and any non-Indian is called a *doogla* (bastard) and is considered to have no caste at all.

Thus integration and assimilation, whether cultural or biological, are processes the East Indian tends both to fear and to resist. Although it is customary for East Indians to deny the importance of caste in their social structure, it is very much present, and the values underlying the Indian caste system may well affect present East Indian attitudes toward assimilation. It might even be said that, from the East Indian point of view, Trinidad appears to be composed of permanently separate endogamous groups. These may be ranked relative to one another, and the East Indian's abiding interest in the rise of his entire ethnic group well may be compared with attitudes in India toward caste mobility.[24]

The conflict in attitude and viewpoint between the East and West Indians of Trinidad has recently found expression in politics. Two parties dominate the Trinidad political scene. Although both deny racial orientation, one is for all practical purposes a West Indian party and the other an East Indian party. West Indians, unable to ignore this manifestation of the conflict, frequently are heard to

[24] B. S. Cohn, "The Changing Status of a Depressed Caste," in M. Marriott, ed., *Village India: Studies in the Little Community*, American Anthropological Association Memoir No. 83, 1955, pp. 53–77.

complain that the conflict between the two ethnic groups came into existence with the arrival of party politics. They see the development as a highly unfortunate one, but hope that the emergence of an East Indian party is a temporary phenomenon and that, when East Indians have become West Indians, in time and through education ethnically oriented parties will have no reason to exist. East Indians, on the other hand, appear to see the emergence of such parties as natural and inevitable. They believe that in time they will elect their own leaders to office, and the primary concern of any political leader, many of them seem to feel, is the well-being of his particular ethnic group.

A partial explanation for the divergent views as to the nature of present Trinidadian society may be found in an examination of the rapid changes that have taken place over a comparatively short period of time. From the first arrival of indentured laborers from India in 1845 until fifteen to twenty years ago, the East Indians constituted a cultural enclave[25] within the Trinidad socioeconomic system. The group had clustered within the lowest economic stratum of the society, that of the rural agricultural laborer. Even the limited amount of education available to the group could be had only in schools run by Presbyterian missionaries. Social and economic advancement was possible for an individual only if he were willing to leave his ethnic group and accept the conditions of life in the Christian West Indian society. Despite these circumstances, while there was considerable acculturation, the majority of East Indians resisted significant Creolization.

Today, there is a Hindu East Indian middle class and even an upper class. There are wealthy East Indian businessmen, educated professionals, and powerful politicians.

---

[25] The term "cultural enclave" is used here to contrast the phenomenon described in this paper with that of subculture. By "subculture" I understand an offshoot of a parent culture that is distinct but not separate from it, although it may become so. Using the terms in this manner, New Englanders exhibit a subculture of the total culture of the United States, but the Navajo represent a cultural enclave.

An East Indian youth today may acquire an education and rise both socially and economically without ever venturing outside his ethnic group or questioning its values. The recent independence of India and Pakistan has affected both Hindu and Moslem East Indians. There is both a pride in origin that was lacking before and a strong religiocultural revival.

If East Indians have successfully resisted Creolization thus far, is it likely to occur now that the ethnic group has changed from a cultural enclave to what is effectively a parallel sociocultural system within the total Trinidadian society? Moreover, it is well known among Trinidadian East Indians that within about twenty years they will form the largest single ethnic group on the island. What will happen then if there is at that time no change in either the East Indian desire for a separate and equal status within the Trinidad society, or in the West Indian desire for complete integration?

17.

This selection deals with structural aspects of the East Indian–Creole issue within a "plural society" framework. We are given a view of the ordering as well as of the dynamics of the Guyanese social order on the eve of national independence. Drawing from the literature on pluralism, the author conceptually distinguishes the local and national institutions that facilitate the functioning of the social system. The identification of "minimal," "maximal," and "broker" institutions makes possible the examination of processes of change and political maneuvering in a plural setting. In addition to its intrinsic theoretical importance, this selection provides an overview of the only Commonwealth Caribbean society with an East Indian majority.

LEO A. DESPRES, an American, received his doctorate in anthropology from Ohio State University and is currently Professor of Anthropology at Case Western Reserve University.

Cultural Pluralism and Nationalist Politics in British Guiana
Leo A. Despres

THE STRUCTURAL DIMENSIONS OF PLURALISM

In developing an analytical framework for the analysis of social and cultural pluralism, it has been suggested that the definition of the plural society must take into account two related sets of facts. First, it must take into account the extent to which particular groups display different systems of culture as evidenced by the activities their members engage in. Second, it must also take into account the level at which social activities serve to maintain cultural differentiation as the basis for sociocultural integration. The criteria used to determine the degree of cultural differentiation between groups are structural. It has been assumed that the institutional structures which serve to regulate the activities of individuals in groups are expressive of the cultural values characteristic of the groups in question. From this assumption, it follows that different institutional structures serve to distinguish different cultures and social units.[1]

In extending this analytical framework further, a dis-

Cultural Pluralism and Nationalist Politics in British Guiana, copyright © 1967 by Rand McNally & Company, Chicago, pp. 270–85. Reprinted by permission of the publisher and the author.

[1] This conceptualization is implicit in Parsons' discussion of institutional structures. See Talcott Parsons, "The Position of Sociological Theory," *American Sociological Review,* Vol. 13 (1948), pp. 155–64, particularly pp. 159–60.

tinction was drawn between two general types of institutional structures: (1) those that function with respect to the organization of social activities within local communities (*local institutions*); and (2) those that function to link the activities of individuals and groups to the wider sphere of societal activity (*broker institutions*). Local and broker institutional structures provide the coordinates for determining the degree of cultural differentiation between groups as well as the level of sociocultural integration that exists among groups which participate in a common cultural tradition.

To the extent that local institutional structures are valid only for particular groups, the groups in question participate in different cultural systems. Such groups constitute *minimal* or local cultural sections. On the other hand, when broker institutional structures serve to integrate nationally local groups which are culturally similar, such groups constitute *maximal* or national cultural sections. The plural society has been defined as one that contains *maximal* or national cultural sections.

As defined, the plural model establishes an order of logical priority. In other words, maximal cultural sections presuppose the existence of minimal cultural sections. If minimal cultural sections are not found to exist in an empirical setting, then the plural model has little heuristic value for the analysis of the society under investigation. Thus, this analysis of Guianese society began with a comparative study of local institutional activities among Africans and East Indians, the largest and most politically significant groups in the population.

To recapitulate, it was found that Africans and East Indians form separate and comparatively different kinds of social communities. Even though many of them may live together in disproportionate numbers in particular villages or on plantations, their social worlds remain relatively autonomous. Their kinship networks are not homologous, and this, among other considerations, makes intermarriage somewhat difficult. They do not participate in the same religious traditions. They recreate separately or in competition with one another. Generally speaking, they do not form voluntary groups with one another unless pressured to do so by external governmental agencies. In the village, Africans and Indians attend the same school, but the school is usually Christian, and Indians resent this imposition. More importantly, Africans and Indians value local economic resources differently. They display different patterns of economic and social mobility. And they have markedly different orientations toward authority. In short, at the communal level of sociocultural integration, there are no social structures which serve to bring Africans and East Indians together in the expression of a common system of cultural values.

To follow the order of logical priority set forth in the definition of the plural model, the second phase of the analysis concerned itself with a comparative study of broker institutional activities. With respect to these institutional structures, the analysis revealed that the forces of unification and acculturation are at work in Guianese society. Educational institutions are one case in point. The organization of educational institutions is partially controlled by the government and relatively uniform in terms of educational content. However, the content of Guianese education is distinctly British in origin, and Christian denominational bodies exercise considerable control over the vast majority of the schools. As a consequence, educational institutions have been able to modify East Indian values and thereby mediate the relationships between Africans and East Indians, particularly in certain intellectual circles. Nevertheless, because of the system of dual control of the schools, educational institutions have not been able to generate a new national culture equally acceptable to both groups.

Commercial and industrial organizations represent another important source of unification. Almost all of the large commercial and industrial firms in Guiana employ East Indians as well as Africans. Thus, these organizations represent integrated pluralities. However, when one considers the corporate structures of most of these organizations, it is evident that East Indians and Africans tend to be allocated to different occupational statuses on the basis of ascriptive criteria. These practices are also changing, but the changes that are taking place are too recent to have generated new values capable of integrating the groups in question.

Market institutions represent still another important source of unification in Guianese society. The price mechanism, for example, is a common structural denominator for the expression of economic values. Obviously, this facilitates certain kinds of transactions between the members of different cultural groups. At the same time, however, it should be noted that the price mechanism is also a means by which the cultural values of different groups can be expressed as well as reinforced. In addition, the colonial character of Guiana's market economy imparts to it certain multicentric features. The agricultural and industrial sectors of the economy comprise relatively independent spheres of market activity, and East Indians are significantly more interested in and dependent upon the agricultural sector than are the Africans. Thus, market institutions may mediate certain types of relationships between the two groups, but they have not, as yet, contributed significantly to their unification.

Apart from these tendencies toward unification, Africans and East Indians continue to form separate and relatively well-integrated maximal cultural sections. The broker institutional structures that function to maintain cultural differentiation as the basis for social integration include the communications media, trade unions and labor organizations, agencies of the public service, religious and ethnic associations, and political parties. The communications media are owned primarily by European interests, but they are staffed mostly by Africans. While Africans and Indians belong to trade unions in overwhelming numbers, they belong to different unions operating in different sectors of the economy. Also, until very recently, the public services have displayed a racial imbalance strongly in favor of the Africans.[2] Religious and ethnic associations are exclusive in their memberships and contribute significantly to the integration of similar minimal cultural sections. And, finally, since the Burnham-Jagan split, political parties have catered primarily to the interests of cultural sections.

In conclusion, the patterns of sociocultural integration that exist among the different segments of the Guianese population correspond almost completely with the structural dimensions of the plural model as defined in this book. This correspondence applies to structural forms as well as to the cultural values which these forms express. Thus, Africans comprise minimal cultural sections. The relationships that exist within these local groups in terms of family and kinship networks, children's property, religious practices, associational ties, and the like, extend outward to include relationships between individuals from similar groups. These external ties are supported and reinforced by institutional structures that bind Africans together in terms of their race, religion, education, occupational interests, mobility patterns, and organizational memberships. Such institutional structures not only integrate Africans as a national community, but they also function to express the values that provide this community with a sense of cultural identity.

A similar pattern of sociocultural integration exists with respect to the East Indians. The kinship group lies at the center of Indian sociocultural integration. Its stability is reinforced by religious beliefs, traditional marriage forms, economic functions and, to a degree, vestiges of caste. Relatives are bound together in ever widening circles of diminishing strength. The practice of village exogamy creates affinal ties between one Indian community and another. These circles of relationship are further extended by ceremonial responsibilities and friendship ties. At the periphery of these circles, broker institutions serve to relate Indians to one another in terms of religious and ethnic

[2] B. A. N. Collins, "Racial Imbalance in Public Services and Security Forces," *Race*, Vol. 3 (1966), pp. 235–53.

associations, trade union membership, economic interests, and the like. Ultimately, this pattern of sociocultural integration involves a value system which provides East Indians with a cultural identity as a national community.

PLURALISM AND SOCIOCULTURAL CHANGE

As has been shown, British Guiana is a plural society. From the point of view of system analysis, the interdependent units of Guianese society tend to comprise culturally differentiated groups rather than socially differentiated persons. The integration of the system results primarily from the complementary participation of these groups in a unitary political economy. The institutional structures that make up the political economy were created and maintained by British colonial power. Until recent times, these structures have persisted with a minimum of change. In view of these considerations, what are the structural implications of pluralism for the process of sociocultural change? Two points need to be emphasized with respect to this question. One has to do with the functional autonomy of cultural sections. The other has to do with the structure of intersectional relations which results from functional autonomy.

Cultural sections display the characteristics of isomeric systems. That is to say, they are composed of similar organizational elements, but these elements differ in their properties because they are structured differently. Consider, for example, the differences in social stratification between village Indians and Africans.

Within the Indian village, the allocation of status and prestige is heavily weighted in favor of rice millers or large landowners; then shopkeepers; followed by pandits; certain types of salaried persons such as teachers, small shopkeepers and landowners; agricultural workers and fishermen; artisans; and unskilled workers. The prestige attached to these statuses, including the prestige attached to the status of pandit, is primarily a function of the economic differentials that obtain between them. Thus, a teacher has more prestige and influence than a small landowner or a small shopkeeper because he has a larger and more reliable source of income. A teacher who also owns land has more prestige than a teacher without land. For the same reason, a teacher has less prestige and influence than a rice miller, a large landowner, or a successful shopkeeper.

By way of contrast, among Africans, the emphasis is placed on educational differentials, age and experience, and personality traits such as a willingness to render service to others. Thus, in the African village, the allocation of status and prestige favors head teachers; older heads who are friendly, reliable, and willing to help others; younger teachers; church workers; civil servants; and good providers, regardless of how they may earn their incomes. The status of teacher is an organizational element in both the Indian and African village, but the properties attached to the status differ because it is structured differently in the stratification system of each village. This difference in structure, in turn, reflects the cultural values of each group.[3]

In summary, the functional autonomy of minimal cultural sections derives from their isomeric character. There are at least three ways in which this is evident. First, the cultural sections to which Africans and Indians belong do not reticulate, i.e., the structures that are functional in the African section do not interpenetrate those which are functional in the Indian section. Second, individual Africans or East Indians cannot easily move from one cultural section to another unless (a) the individual changes his cultural values, or (b) the cultural section into which the individual moves undergoes structural change. For example, an East Indian rice farmer cannot enhance his status among Africans by opening a shop in an African village. Similarly, an African teacher cannot enhance his status by being reassigned to a school in an Indian community. Third, different cultural sections can (and usually

[3] For an extremely systematic treatment of stratification in a plural society, see M. G. Smith, *Stratification in Grenada* (Los Angeles: University of California Press, 1965).

do) respond differently and independently to the pressures for change. For example, Indians and Africans have responded differently to the pressures for change generated by the cooperative movement.

From a structural point of view, the difference between the minimal and the maximal cultural section is primarily a difference in scale. Thus, maximal cultural sections also tend to display the characteristics of isomeric systems. This is particularly evident with respect to the differential adaptation of Africans and East Indians to Guiana's colonial economy.

For example, as rice farmers and sugar workers, East Indians comprise a rural proletarian class. Africans who live in rural areas do not belong to this class in large numbers, because they are either part of the urban unemployed or they are elderly persons engaged in subsistence agriculture. Indians do not move out of the rural areas in large numbers. When they do move into the urban sectors, however, it is usually as shopkeepers and businessmen. Those who become teachers generally remain in rural schools. Africans, on the other hand, move out of the rural areas in large numbers, but they rarely move out as businessmen and shopkeepers. For the most part, Africans who move to urban areas do so as mine workers, civil servants, teachers, clerks, artisans, dock workers, or domestics. Thus, Africans make up the vast majority of the urban proletariat.

To continue this analysis further, until very recent times, the sources of power in Guianese society have been lodged in the colonial establishment and those groups which implement the decisions of the establishment. As a group, the rural proletariat is more removed from these sources of power than the urban proletariat. It follows from this that Africans tend to occupy a higher position in the power structure of colonial society than Indians. In addition, the traditional patterns of social mobility characteristic of these cultural sections tend to reinforce the status differential existing between them. Thus, similar social positions within different cultural sections are not functionally equivalent, and the position that one occupies within his cultural section does not correspond to the position that one occupies in the society as a whole. The position that one occupies in the society as a whole is, at least in part, a function of the position his cultural section occupies in the power structure of the society.

In view of these considerations, what is the effect of functional autonomy on the structure of intersectional relations? Let us first examine its effect on intersectional relations in the case of minimal cultural sections.

The functional autonomy of minimal cultural sections has a direct effect upon the structure of intersectional relations within the local community. Specifically, functional autonomy tends to confine interpersonal relations between Africans and Indians to role patterns which are relatively segmental, nonaffective, and instrumental. Since competitive advantage is an important feature of such utilitarian role patterns, interpersonal relations tend to be structured in an order of superordination and subordination. Accordingly, the dimension of power is crucial to almost all intersectional relations. Thus, changes within minimal cultural sections which may affect the structure of intersectional relations invariably raise issues of power between Africans and East Indians within local settings.

By way of illustrating the above point, consider the construction of a new health center by the government. Will the government locate the facility in a predominantly African village such as Ann's Grove, or will it be constructed a short distance away in the Indian village of Clonbrook? Who will be placed in charge of the facility, an African or an East Indian? Similarly, where will the new school be located? Or, who is to be made chairman of the regional development committee? Who will process applications for loans at the district office of the cooperative savings and loan society? Ultimately, these decisions affect the competitive advantage that individuals have with respect to intersectional relations. Although the government may not consider these decisions to be political, they are political from the point of view of the Africans and Indians who are affected by them. As a result, in Guianese society, any change promulgated by an agency of the government which affects intersectional relations between minimal cultural sections will have political consequences within the local setting. What, then, is the situation with respect to maximal cultural sections?

It has been shown that the functional autonomy of maximal cultural sections largely derives from the differential status that Africans and Indians have as a result of their adaptation to the institutions of colonial society. Because of this differential status, the prestige and influence attached to the social position that an individual occupies are, in part, a function of the status attached to the cultural section with which the individual is identified. Thus, it is extremely difficult for individual Indians or Africans to improve their life chances without changing their cultural identities or, alternatively, without seeking to improve the status and power of their respective cultural sections. The structural implications of this fact may be viewed more concretely in terms of a few illustrations.

For example, in spite of their prestige and influence within their cultural section, large Indian landowners, rice millers, and businessmen have not been able to exercise as much direct control over the Guianese economy as a few very high-level public servants of African descent. Similarly, in spite of their growing numbers, Indian schoolteachers have not been able to exercise as much influence over educational institutions as African schoolteachers. Also, educated Indians have had considerably less access than educated Africans to those departments of the public service in which Africans exercise a controlling influence. Or, to cite still another example, Indian-dominated labor unions have not been able to command wages for their members comparable to the wages that have been achieved for African workers by many African-dominated labor unions. In other words, the opportunities available to individual Indians and Africans reflect the differential status which their respective cultural groups occupy in the power structure of Guianese society.

In view of these considerations, three points need to be emphasized with respect to intersectional relations between maximal cultural sections. First, at the national level, intersectional relations tend to involve transactions between organized groups rather than individuals. A case in point would be the transactions between Indian- and African-dominated labor unions within the British Guiana Trades Union Council. Second, the functional autonomy of maximal cultural sections tends to confine these intergroup transactions to a struggle for competitive advantage in the national power structure. This is most clearly evident in terms of the competition for power between such groups as the East Indian Association and the League of Coloured Peoples. And, third, any sociocultural change that can affect the structure of intersectional relations between maximal cultural sections will raise issues of national power between Africans and East Indians. The instances of this are almost too numerous to recount but, to cite one example, all of Guiana's economic development programs have raised issues of national power between Africans and East Indians.

To conclude, both minimal and maximal cultural sections display the characteristics of isomeric systems. They are composed of similar organizational elements, but these elements differ in their properties because they are structured according to different cultural values. As a consequence of these differences, cultural sections tend to comprise functionally autonomous units in the overall structure of Guianese society. The functional autonomy of these units, in turn, has certain implications for the structure of intersectional relations both nationally and within local communities.

At the level of local communities, the functional autonomy of cultural sections reduces interpersonal relations between Africans and Indians to the dimension of power. Similarly, at the national level, the functional autonomy of cultural sections tends to confine intergroup relations between Africans and Indians to a competition for national power. It follows from the structure of interpersonal re-

lations that any sociocultural changes capable of altering
the order of subordination and superordination between
individual Africans and Indians will have political consequences within the local settings in which the changes occur. It follows from the structure of intergroup relations
that any sociocultural changes capable of altering the position of Africans and Indians in the national power structure will have consequences for the political order of
Guianese society. In other words, the conditions of pluralism in Guianese society are such that the process of sociocultural change is intrinsically a political process at all
levels of the social order.

PLURALISM AND NATIONALIST POLITICS

It has been shown how the integration of Guianese society is based upon a system of social relations between
cultural units of unequal status and power. This system
derives its traditional force from the differential adaptation
of Africans and East Indians to the institutions of British
colonialism. The core structure of this system is essentially
political. Intersectional relations not only reflect the power
structure of the political order under which they are subsumed, but they also serve to express the maintenance or
change of that political order.

Herein lies the source of instability which the forces of
nationalism are capable of aggravating. The cultural units
that make up the Guianese social system enjoy a relatively
high degree of functional autonomy. In order for these
units to maintain their respective patterns of sociocultural
integration, it is necessary that the social system continue
to provide for their functional autonomy. Under present
circumstances, the functional autonomy of these units is
maintained by the differential status they occupy in the
power structure of the society. This power structure, in
turn, is reinforced by the political order under which it is
subsumed. It is precisely the political order of Guianese
society that the forces of nationalism seek to change. Thus,
in seeking to implement changes in the political order, the

forces of nationalism must inevitably pose a threat to the functional autonomy of cultural sections and create a problem of tension management between the groups that these sections represent.[4] A question to which this study has addressed itself is whether or not the nationalist movement can prevent these tensions from culminating in conflict and disrupting the social order. The findings with respect to this question may be summarized as follows.

First, in its early stages of development, the nationalist movement successfully integrated African and East Indian intellectuals as members of a new nationalist elite. The leadership which the members of this elite enjoyed was largely sectional. Moreover; they differed among themselves on issues of political ideology. However, they shared a commitment to the goal of national independence. They also shared a commitment to the politico-cultural integration of Guianese society. In view of these commitments, therefore, ideological issues and the conditions of pluralism did not present an obstacle to the movement's further development.

Nevertheless, the nationalist movement could not help generating tensions between cultural sections during this early period. These tensions became increasingly apparent after 1950, when the Peoples Progressive Party was organized in preparation for constitutional change. They were most apparent in the case of the Portuguese and other Europeans who opposed the movement in favor of the status quo. They were evident also with respect to certain groups of Africans and East Indians who favored independence but who were fearful that sectional interests might be compromised in the process of achieving it.

The tensions existing between Africans and Indians during this early phase of the movement's development did not present the new nationalist elite with an insurmountable

[4] For a discussion of functional autonomy and tension management in social systems, see Alvin W. Gouldner, "Reciprocity and Autonomy in Functional Theory," in Llewellyn Gross, ed., *Symposium on Sociological Theory* (Evanston, Ill.: Row, Peterson, 1959), pp. 241–70.

problem. As a group, it was comprehensive in its membership. It also was sufficiently committed to independence and national politico-cultural integration to meet the thrust of such sectional organizations as the League of Coloured Peoples and the East Indian Association. Thus, the new nationalist elite succeeded in achieving adequate political integration between Africans and Indians to provide the P.P.P. with a relatively impressive victory in the 1953 elections. Obviously, this display of unity did not remove all or even most of the tensions existing between cultural sections as a result of the impending changes in the Guianese political order. However, it did demonstrate the ability on the part of nationalist leaders to manage these tensions organizationally during the process of change.

Second, the disintegration of Guiana's comprehensive nationalist movement cannot be attributed exclusively to the particularistic forces of pluralism. Since this conclusion follows as much from the logic of the analysis as it does from the data presented, it needs to be elaborated upon in some detail.

As has been shown, the structure of Guianese society is such that the process of sociocultural change is intrinsically a political process at all levels of the social order. It follows from this that any change capable of altering the structure of the society carries with it the potential of stimulating the forces of pluralism, thereby creating a problem of tension management. Whether or not a particular change will create a serious problem of tension management depends upon (1) the degree to which it poses a threat to the functional autonomy of cultural sections and (2) the extent to which organizational control is exercised with respect to its introduction in order to minimize the tension it generates. In any event, these conditions are inherent in the structure of Guianese society, and they created organizational problems for the nationalist movement. However, the existence of these conditions does not explain why the movement failed to solve the organizational problems related to them.

The analytical situation, then, is as follows: Given the

fact that Guiana's nationalist leaders both recognized and made a concerted organizational effort to cope with the forces of pluralism which the movement had stimulated, how is it that these forces prevailed? In other words, why did the movement disintegrate? To answer this question, one cannot invoke a constant (e.g., the plural structure of Guianese society) to explain a variable (e.g., the success or failure of the nationalist movement to solve the organizational problems that confronted it).

As we have seen, disintegration resulted from a critical conjuncture of several factors, all of which made it increasingly difficult for nationalist leaders to control organizationally the forces of pluralism. These factors included the ideological factionalism that erupted to the surface within the Peoples Progressive Party, the organization of a conservative opposition to the movement, and the internal pressures that were generated by external international developments.

It is difficult, if not impossible, to weigh these factors and to assign the decisive role of precipitant to any particular one of them. We know what happened to Guiana's nationalist movement, but we can only speculate on what might have happened had one thing or another been different. However, the fact that numerous conditions were equally necessary for disintegration to occur is, as MacIver might suggest, no ground for denying the distinctive role of the precipitant.[5] Therefore, to speculate on the conjunction of these crucial ingredients, it would appear that, more than any other complex of factors, international developments precipitated the disintegration of Guiana's comprehensive nationalist movement.

In other words, between 1952 and 1955, Guiana's comprehensive nationalist movement fell victim to the cold war. The ideological factionalism which ultimately resulted in the Burnham-Jagan split was directly stimulated by the efforts that were made, chiefly by the United States and the American labor movement, to alienate from hemispheric

[5] R. M. MacIver, *Social Causation* (Boston: Ginn, 1942), pp. 172–84.

nationalist movements those nationalists who displayed a propensity for Marxist-Leninist thinking. These efforts were not made openly, and they were not carried out by American governmental intervention or through the usual channels of international diplomacy. Rather, they were made covertly and carried out by the exercise of American power and influence within the context of the international labor movement. This influence and power were so pervasive that some local unions, the British Guiana Mine Workers for example, could hardly negotiate a contract without first seeking the advice of American labor diplomats.

The splits in the Caribbean labor movement that resulted from the struggles of the cold war may not have altered the political climate in Jamaica, Trinidad, or Barbados to any significant degree, but the opposite was the case in Guiana. In Guiana, the position that the Marxists occupied within the nationalist movement was largely a function of a balance of power that existed between them and the non-Marxists. This balance of power, in turn, was based upon the relationships which members of both groups enjoyed with respect to cultural sections, Guianese labor unions, and political allies in the Caribbean. As long as this balance of power was maintained, the nationalist movement existed in a state of dynamic equilibrium. However, the divisions in the Caribbean labor movement altered this balance of political forces.

Specifically, the splits which occurred in the Caribbean labor movement made ideological issues much more critical to Guianese nationalists than organizational questions relating to political tensions between Africans and Indians or such other matters as economic development and constitutional advancement. This provided the conservative opposition with its major source of political leverage, the issue of Communism. Subsequently, these splits served to alienate the Jaganites, an important faction of the nationalist elite, from the Guianese labor movement. In addition, they interjected into Guianese politics the West Indian Federation issue with all of its racial overtones. Ultimately, these developments provoked the disagreements that culminated in the Jagan-Burnham split. In effect, this fragmented the movement's comprehensive leadership and severely impaired its organizational capacity to deal with the forces of pluralism.

Finally, the destructive forces of pluralism in Guianese society were not unleashed by the nationalist movement itself but by the competition for leadership that erupted when the movement fragmented into political factions. Once this internal power struggle emerged, its subsequent course of development was largely predetermined. For example, as long as the colonial establishment retained ultimate power for itself, even though it gave evidence of only marking time, the competition for leadership between nationalist elites had to proceed according to the constitutional and other rules which the establishment imposed. As a result, the only effective organizational adjustments that these elites could make were neocolonial in type.[6] That is to say, in order to mobilize mass support successfully, they would have to employ organizational strategies which accommodated themselves to the realities of the existing structure of colonial power.

As has been pointed out, Guiana's colonial power structure was based upon a system of social relations between cultural sections of unequal status. It follows from the nature of such a system that the major sources of power available to nationalist leaders for organizational purposes are the culturally differentiated groups of which the system is comprised. In the event of any internal power struggle which precludes revolutionary change, and therefore the destruction of the existing power structure, it is inevitable that cultural sections will become organizationally aligned in competitive opposition. This fact was fully recog-

[6] I refer to this as a typical neocolonial adjustment because it is predicated upon the proposition, largely imposed by colonial power, that the status quo contains numerous elements worth preserving. Important among these elements are the existing structure of power, economic institutions, and a "rich" diversity of cultures. See Kwame Nkrumah, *Neo-Colonialism: The Last Stage of Imperialism* (New York: International Publishers, 1965).

nized by Jagan, Burnham, and other Guianese nationalists. In what has been suggested as a type of neocolonial adjustment, these leaders adopted organizational strategies designed to make existing sociocultural patterns functional with respect to the internal struggle for constitutional power. Given a neocolonial setting in which cultural sections are politically juxtaposed in a struggle for national power, is violent conflict probable? In general, the answer is yes.

Any change resulting from a direct power struggle between cultural sections will not only reinforce their functional autonomy, but it will also tend to alter their respective positions in the power structure. Therefore, it needs to be emphasized that the political opposition of such units will increase the problem of tension management directly in proportion to the rate and degree of sociocultural change. If such changes are extensive and occur so rapidly that compensatory mechanisms cannot be put into motion, the tensions generated between cultural sections are likely to increase to the point of explosion. However, whether or not these tensions will eventuate in violent conflict, particularly violent conflict of an organized nature, will depend largely upon the decisions that nationalist leaders take with respect to them. If nationalist leaders believe that their particular objectives can be furthered by exploiting these tensions, violent conflict will develop.

The above points may be illustrated in the case of British Guiana. When the nationalist movement disintegrated, both Jagan and Burnham were more or less compelled to accept a neocolonial adjustment to the process of sociocultural change. The political organization of cultural sections followed upon these developments. However, the subsequent election of a Jagan government in 1957, and again in 1961, brought about a relatively rapid change in the status of Indians in the power structure of Guianese society. This change not only contributed to the political integration of Africans, but it also generated explosive tensions between Africans and Indians at all levels of the social order.

It was these tensions that were organizationally exploited in 1962, when the opposition made an effort to force the resignation of the Jagan government by promoting a general strike among government workers. Conflict resulted, and it was primarily confined to outbreaks of violence between East Indians and Africans. A very similar situation developed in 1963, and again in 1964, when Jagan made the organizational decision to promote strikes on the sugar estates following his rebuff at the constitutional talks. In this instance, the decision on the part of the Colonial Office to impose a system of proportional representation not only threatened the Jagan government but also threatened the gains which East Indians felt they had achieved under the Jagan government.

Following the election of the Burnham government in 1964, the tensions existing between East Indians and Africans were hastily reduced, or at least temporarily controlled, by the use of certain compensatory mechanisms. For one thing, British troops were kept on the scene for the purpose of maintaining law and order. In addition, several influential members of the Peoples Progressive Party continued to be detained and prevented from engaging in political activities. Also, Burnham made overtures to East Indians by such devices as implementing a study ostensibly designed to correct racial imbalances in the public services. And, finally, the United States and Great Britain provided Guiana with a massive injection of funds to help Burnham restore the economy and placate East Indians by undertaking various kinds of development projects in rural areas.

Whether or not these and similar compensatory mechanisms can reduce the tensions existing between cultural sections to a level below which they are no longer explosive cannot be known for certain. However, to summarize, we can be certain of several things. First, we can be sure that, as long as Guianese society remains plural, sociocultural changes will generate tensions between cultural sections. Second, we can be sure that, as long as these cultural sections are politically juxtaposed, the tensions existing between them will be extremely difficult to manage. Third, violent conflict will result from the political juxtaposition of cultural sections whenever nationalist leaders see fit to exploit the tensions existing between them. And, finally, we can be relatively certain that these generalizations will obtain as long as Guianese nationalist elites accommodate themselves to vestiges of the colonial power structure.

SELECTED READINGS

GENERAL REFERENCES

BENNETT, J. HARRY, JR., *Bondsmen and Bishops: Slavery and Apprenticeship on the Codrington Plantations of Barbados, 1710–1838* (University of California Publications in History, Vol. 62), Berkeley, University of California Press, 1958.

BRATHWAITE, EDWARD, *The Development of Creole Society in Jamaica*, London, Oxford University Press, 1971.

BURN, W. L., *Emancipation and Apprenticeship in the British West Indies*, London, Jonathan Cape, 1937.

BURNS, ALAN, *History of the British West Indies*, London, Allen and Unwin, 1954; New York, Barnes and Noble, 2nd. ed. rev., 1965.

CLEMENTI, CECIL, *The Chinese in British Guiana*, British Guiana, Argosy Press, 1915.

COMITAS, LAMBROS, *Caribbeana 1900–1965: A Topical Bibliography*, Seattle, University of Washington Press for the Research Institute for the Study of Man, 1968.

CRANE, JULIA G., *Educated to Emigrate: The Social Organization of Saba*, Assen, Netherlands, Van Gorcum, 1971.

CURTIN, PHILIP D., *The Atlantic Slave Trade: A Census*, Madison, University of Wisconsin Press, 1969.

——, *Two Jamaicas: The Role of Ideas in a Tropical Colony, 1830–1865*, Cambridge, Harvard University Press, 1955.

DESPRES, LEO A., *Cultural Pluralism and Nationalist Politics in British Guiana*, Chicago, Rand McNally, 1967.

EQUIANO, OLAUDAH, *Equiano's Travels* [1789], London, Heinemann, 1967.

FROUDE, JAMES ANTHONY, *The English in the West Indies: or, The Bow of Ulysses*, London, Longmans, 1888.

GASTON-MARTIN, *Histoire de l'esclavage dans les colonies françaises*, Paris, Presses Universitaires de France, 1948.

GISLER, ANTOINE, *L'esclavage aux Antilles françaises (XVIIᵉ–XIXᵉ siècle): contribution au problème de l'esclavage*, Fribourg, Éditions Universitaires, 1965.

GOSLINGA, CORNELIS CH., *The Dutch in the Caribbean and on the Wild Coast, 1580–1680*, Gainesville, University of Florida Press, 1971.

GOVEIA, ELSA V., *Slave Society in the British Leeward Islands at the End of the Eighteenth Century*, New Haven, Yale University Press, 1965.

——, *A Study on the Historiography of the British West Indies to the End of the Nineteenth Century*, Mexico, D.F., Pan-American Institute of Geography and History, 1956.

——, *The West Indian Slave Laws of the 18th Century* (in *Chapters in Caribbean History, No. 2*), Barbados, Caribbean Universities Press, 1970.

HALL, DOUGLAS, *Five of the Leewards 1834–1870: The Major Problems of the Post-Emancipation Period in Antigua, Barbuda, Montserrat, Nevis and St. Kitts*, Barbados, Caribbean Universities Press; London, Ginn, 1971.

——, *Free Jamaica 1838–1865: An Economic History*, New Haven, Yale University Press, 1959.

HERSKOVITS, MELVILLE J., *The Myth of the Negro Past* [1941], Boston, Beacon Press, 1958.

HISS, PHILIP HANSON, *Netherlands America: The Dutch Territories in the West*, London, Robert Hale, 1943.

HOETINK, HARMANNUS, *Het patroon van de oude Curaçaose samenleving: een sociologische studie*, Assen, Van Gorcum, 1958.

——, *The Two Variants in Caribbean Race Relations*, London, Oxford University Press for the Institute of Race Relations, 1967.

HOETINK, HARMANNUS, editor, *Encyclopedie van de Nederlandse Antillen*, Amsterdam, Elsevier, 1969.

JAMES, C. L. R., *The Black Jacobins: Toussaint L'Ouverture and the San Domingo Revolution* [1938], New York, Random House, Vintage Books, 1963.

KARNER, FRANCES P., *The Sephardics of Curaçao: A Study of Socio-Cultural Patterns in Flux*, Assen, Netherlands, Van Gorcum, 1969; New York, Humanities Press, 1971.

KLASS, MORTON, *East Indians in Trinidad: A Study of Cultural Persistence*, New York, Columbia University Press, 1961.

KLERK, J. C. M. DE, *De Immigratie der Hindostanen in Suriname*, Amsterdam, Urbi et Orbi, 1953.

LASSERRE, GUY, *La Guadeloupe: étude géographique*, Bordeaux, Union Française d'Impression, 1961.

LEWIS, GORDON K., *The Growth of the Modern West Indies*, New York, Monthly Review Press, 1968.

LEWIS, M. G., *Journal of a West India Proprietor, 1815–17*, Boston, Houghton Mifflin, 1929.

LEYBURN, JAMES G., *The Haitian People*, rev. ed., New Haven, Yale University Press, 1966.

LIER, R. A. J. VAN, *Samenleving in een grensgebied: een sociaalhistorische studie van de maatschappij in Suriname*, The Hague, M. Nijhoff, 1949.

LIGON, RICHARD, *A True and Exact History of the Island of Barbadoes . . .* [1657, 1673] (Cass Library of West Indian Studies, No. 11), London, Frank Cass, 1970.

LONG, EDWARD, *History of Jamaica, or, General Survey of the Ancient and Modern State of That Island* [1774] 3 vols. (Cass Library of West Indian Studies, No. 12), London, Frank Cass, 1970; Portland, Ore., International Scholarly Book Service, 1970.

LOWENTHAL, DAVID, *West Indian Societies*, London and New York, Oxford University Press, for the Institute of Race Relations and the American Geographical Society, 1972.

MALEFIJT, ANNEMARIE DE WAAL, *The Javanese of Surinam: Segment of a Plural Society*, Assen, Netherlands, Van Gorcum, 1963.

MALIK, YOGENDRA K., *East Indians in Trinidad: A Study in Minority Politics*, London, Oxford University Press for the Institute of Race Relations, 1971.

MATHIESON, WILLIAM LAW, *British Slave Emancipation, 1838–1849* [1932], New York, Octagon Books, 1967.

MERRILL, GORDON C., *The Historical Geography of St. Kitts and Nevis, the West Indies*, Mexico, D.F., Pan-American Institute of Geography and History, 1958.

METCALF, GEORGE, *Royal Government and Political Conflict in Jamaica, 1729–1783,* London, Longmans for the Royal Commonwealth Society, 1965.

MITCHELL, HAROLD PATON, *Caribbean Patterns: A Political and Economic Study of the Contemporary Caribbean,* Edinburgh, Chambers, 1967.

MOREAU DE SAINT-MÉRY, MÉDÉRIC-LOUIS-ÉLIE, *Description topographique, physique, civile, politique et historique de la partie française de l'Isle Saint-Domingue* [1797], 3 vols., Paris, Société de l'Histoire des Colonies Françaises et Librairie Larose, 1958.

MURRAY, D. J., *The West Indies and the Development of Colonial Government, 1801–1834,* Oxford, Clarendon Press, 1965; New York, Oxford University Press, 1965.

NATH, DWARKA, *A History of Indians in British Guiana,* London, Nelson, 1950. 2nd rev. ed., London, published by the author, 30 Crowther Road, South Norwood, London, S.E.25, 1971.

OLIVIER, SYDNEY, *White Capital and Coloured Labour,* London, Independent Labour Party, 1910; Westport, Conn., Negro Universities Press, reprint of 1910 edition, n.d.

PARES, RICHARD, *Merchants and Planters,* Supplement 4 of *Economic History Review,* 1960.

——, *A West-India Fortune,* London, Longmans, 1950; Hamden, Conn., Archon Books, Shoe String Press, 1968.

PARRY, J. H., and SHERLOCK, PHILIP M., *A Short History of The West Indies,* London, Macmillan, 1956; 3rd rev. ed., 1971.

PARSONS, JAMES J., *San Andrés and Providencia: English-Speaking Islands in the Western Caribbean* (University of California Publications in Geography, Vol. 12, No. 1), Berkeley, University of California Press, 1956.

PATTERSON, H. ORLANDO, *The Sociology of Slavery,* London, MacGibbon and Kee, 1967; Rutherford, N.J., Fairleigh Dickinson University Press, 1970.

PITMAN, FRANK WESLEY, *The Development of the British West Indies, 1700–1763* [1917], Hamden, Conn., Archon Books, Shoe String Press, 1967.

RAGATZ, LOWELL JOSEPH, *The Fall of the Planter Class in the British Caribbean, 1763–1833: A Study in Social and*

Economic History [1928], New York, Octagon Books, 1963.

RAGATZ, LOWELL JOSEPH, comp., *A Guide for the Study of British Caribbean History, 1763–1834, Including the Abolition and Emancipation Movements,* Washington, D.C., Government Printing Office, 1932.

REVERT, EUGÈNE, *La Martinique: étude géographique,* Paris, Nouvelles Éditions Latines, 1949.

RUBIN, VERA, ed., *Social and Cultural Pluralism in the Caribbean,* Annals of the New York Academy of Sciences, Vol. 83, Article 5, New York, 1960.

SAUER, CARL ORTWIN, *The Early Spanish Main,* Berkeley, University of California Press, 1966.

SCHOMBURGK, ROBERT H., *The History of Barbados . . .* [1848] (Cass Library of West Indian Studies, No. 19), London, Frank Cass, 1971.

SCHWARTZ, BARTON M., ed., *Caste in Overseas Indian Communities,* San Francisco, Chandler, 1967.

SEWELL, WILLIAM GRANT, *The Ordeal of Free Labour in the West Indies* [1861], London, Frank Cass, 1968.

SMITH, M. G., *The Plural Society in the British West Indies,* Berkeley, University of California Press, 1965.

——, *Stratification in Grenada,* Berkeley, University of California Press, 1965.

STEDMAN, JOHN G., *Narrative, of a Five Years' Expedition, Against the Revolted Negroes of Surinam, in Guiana, on the Wild Coast of South America; from the year 1772, to 1777: Elucidating the History of That Country, and Describing Its Productions,* 2 vols., London, J. Johnson, 1806; Barre, Mass., Imprint Society, 1824 ed.

THOMAS, J. J., *Froudacity: West Indian Fables Explained* [1889], London, New Beacon Books, 1969.

TROLLOPE, ANTHONY, *The West Indies and the Spanish Main,* London, Chapman and Hall, 1860; Portland, Ore., International Scholarly Book Service, 1968.

WELLER, JUDITH ANN, *The East Indian Indenture in Trinidad* (Caribbean Monograph Series, No. 4), Río Piedras, Institute of Caribbean Studies, University of Puerto Rico, 1968.

West India Royal Commission Report (Moyne Report), Cmd. 6607, London, His Majesty's Stationery Office, 1945.

WEST, ROBERT COOPER, and AUGELLI, J. P., *Middle America: Its Lands and Peoples*, Englewood Cliffs, N.J., Prentice-Hall, 1966.

WILLIAMS, ERIC, *British Historians and the West Indies*, London, Andre Deutsch, 1964.

——, *Capitalism and Slavery*, Chapel Hill, University of North Carolina Press, 1944; New York, G. P. Putnam's, 1966.

——, *From Columbus to Castro: The History of the Caribbean, 1492–1969*, London, Andre Deutsch, 1970; New York, Harper and Row, 1971.

WOOD, DONALD, *Trinidad in Transition: The Years after Slavery*, London, Oxford University Press for the Institute of Race Relations, 1968.

WEST INDIAN PERIODICALS

Annales des Antilles. Société d'Histoire de la Martinique. Fort-de-France. Occasional.

Caribbean Review. Hato Rey, Puerto Rico. Quarterly.

Caribbean Studies. Institute of Caribbean Studies, University of Puerto Rico, Río Piedras, Puerto Rico. Quarterly.

Journal of the Barbados Museum and Historical Society. Bridgetown, Barbados. Irregular.

Journal of Caribbean History. Caribbean Universities Press, Barbados. About two per year.

Nieuwe West-Indische Gids. The Hague, Netherlands. Three per year.

Social and Economic Studies. University of the West Indies, Institute of Social and Economic Research. Kingston, Jamaica. Quarterly.

INDEX

Africa, xiii–xiv, 4–19 *passim,* 20, 21–45 *passim,* 96, 101, 153–54, 176, 178–79, 183, 277 (*see also* Africans [Afro-Americans, Afro-West Indians]); influences on social structure and society in the West Indies, 20, 21–45 *passim,* 74–75 ff., 176, 178–79, 183 (*see also* specific aspects, people, places); and slave trade and slavery in the West Indies, xiii–xiv, 4–19, 21 ff., 52, 53 ff.; socialization and personality of the slave in the West Indies and, 21–45

Africans (Afro-Americans, Afro-West Indians), xiii–xiv, 2, 4–19, 20, 21–45, 96, 101, 153–54, 176, 178–79, 183, 277 (*see also* specific islands, people, places); and cultural assimilation in a multiracial society (Creoles and East Indians in Trinidad), 277–85 *passim;* and cultural complexity in Trinidad, 286, 287–98; and cultural pluralism and nationalist politics in British Guiana, 300, 301–20; and

emancipation and free labor in the British West Indies, 136, 137–49; and emancipation and self-government, 150, 151–59, 160, 161–69; and the free colored in a slave society (Saint-Domingue), 94, 95–103; freed blacks and mulattos in Jamaica and, 74, 75–93; influence of Africa on, 20, 21–45 *passim,* 176, 178–79, 183 (*see also* specific aspects, people, places); and plural framework of Jamaican society, 174–93; and slavery and slave society in Jamaica, 20, 21–45; and slavery and slave society in Saint-Domingue, 4–19, 52, 53–72; and slavery and slave society in Surinam, 46, 47–51; and whites in a slave society (Saint-Domingue), 52, 53–72

Akan language, 30

Albanians, in Belgrade, 207

Allport, Gordon W., 43–44 n

America, Americans (U.S.). *See* United States of America (Americans)

ANCHOR BOOKS

AFRICAN AND AFRO-AMERICAN STUDIES

political science; psychology

Slaves, Free Men, Citizens
West Indian Perspective

Edited and Introduced by Lambros Comitas and David Lowenthal

West Indians see themselves as largely determined by a past that shapes their present circumstances and future hopes. Their history has produced an extraordinary social and cultural heterogeneity, notably a division into white, colored and black; and class and color still closely converge, despite legal sanctions against discrimination.

Slaves, Free Men, Citizens, together with *The Aftermath Of Sovereignty, Consequences of Class and Color* and *Work and Family Life*, each with the subtitle *West Indian Perspectives*, provide comprehensive information vital to understanding this section of the Third World.

Contributors

Slaves, Masters and Freedmen: C. L. R. James; Orlando Patterson; John G. Stedman; Médéric-Louis-Elie Moreau de Saint-Méry; Edward Long; Douglas Hall; William G. Sewell; James Anthony Froude; J. J. Thomas.

The Nature of the Social Order: M. G. Smith; David Lowenthal; Lloyd Braithwaite; Edith Kovats-Beaudoux; Daniel J. Crowley; Morton Klass; Leo A. Despres.

Cover Design by Rolf Bruderer.